INTERNATIONAL SALES LAW—CISG

IN A NUTSHELL®

by

FRANCO FERRARI
Professor of Law
Director, Center for Transnational Litigation,
Arbitration and Commercial Law
New York University School of Law

MARCO TORSELLO
Professor of Law
Verona University School of Law

Mat #41144034

Nutshell Series, In a Nutshell and the Nutshell Logo are trademarks registered in the U.S. Patent and Trademark Office.

© 2014 LEG, Inc. d/b/a West Academic

> 444 Cedar Street, Suite 700
> St. Paul, MN 55101
> 1-877-888-1330

West, West Academic Publishing, and West Academic are trademarks of West Publishing Corporation, used under license.

Printed in the United States of America

ISBN: 978-0-314-27530-1

PREFACE

The United Nations Convention on Contracts for the International Sale of Goods (hereinafter: "CISG") provides a set of uniform rules applicable to international contracts for the sale of goods. It is currently the law of international sales in 80 States, including most of the American, European and Asian States. It therefore seems correct to state, as commentators have done, that the CISG is the most relevant piece of legislation governing international commercial relationships.

The main goal pursued by the drafters of the CISG was to favor international trade by creating a "common bridge" between different jurisdictions. The basic assumption, as spelled out in the Preamble of the CISG, was that "the adoption of uniform rules which govern contracts for the international sale of goods and take into account the different social, economic and legal systems would contribute to the removal of legal barriers in international trade and promote the development of international trade." To the drafters of the CISG, the CISG's benefits stem from the considerable reduction of uncertainty and unpredictability as to the rules applicable to the transaction, brought about by the unification of law. In turn, the reduction of uncertainty and unpredictability reduces the costs and risks involved in any international transaction.

The success and relevance of the CISG, however, are not undisputed. Critics and sceptics raise doubts regarding the benefit of having a uniform law for international sales and often argue that the CISG provides rules which business operators and national courts are not familiar with. The novelty of the CISG's rules may thus increase the learning costs that business operators must bear, *i.e.*, the costs associated with having to become acquainted with the rules applicable to the transactions they are involved in. In fact, not only do operators have to be aware of the contents of domestic sales law, but they also need to become familiar with the rules laid out in the CISG. Furthermore, it is argued that since the CISG rules have to be applied by national courts, the CISG creates uncertainty rather than eliminating it, by reason of it being applied differently by the courts of different countries.

In these authors' view, there is some merit to the criticism levelled against the CISG. However, the analysis of both the characteristic features of the CISG and the existing case law applying its substantive rules support the conclusion that the CISG's application should be favored and promoted in the general interest of international trade.

With respect to the role that the CISG may play for business operators, it should be noted that the CISG's most salient features include the fact that it applies only to international sales and that it is dispositive in nature, meaning that the parties may exclude the CISG or derogate from most of its provisions. The combination of these two features is of great importance, in that it ensures that the existence of the CISG does not take anything away from the positive effects of the co–existence of a plurality of legislative sources of law, among which business operators are free to choose the rules that best suit their needs. Indeed, on the one hand, the fact that the CISG only applies to contracts for the international sale of goods implies that it does not displace domestic laws, which are still in place and applicable at least to domestic sales. On the other hand, the fact that the CISG is a dispositive piece of legislation implies that the parties are free to exclude the application of the CISG and to choose a different domestic sales law as the law applicable to their transaction. Therefore, the combination of the CISG's applicability only to international contracts coupled with the possibility to exclude its application makes it safe to assert that the CISG does not prevent a fruitful regulatory competition among legal systems, under which each jurisdiction has incentives to offer the most efficient rules for sales contracts. The CISG is one among many competitors: business operators are free to choose the rules applicable to their international sales transactions, with a range of options offered to them that includes, *inter alia*, the CISG.

Moreover, the CISG is beneficial to business operators willing to operate internationally as it reduces the transaction costs caused by the differences in the domestic laws of different legal systems. Indeed, to the extent that a business operator has strong enough a negotiating power to impose the choice of his domestic law, that business operator is clearly indifferent to the existence and the applicability of the CISG. He can continue to impose this choice of law by excluding the application of any alternative law, including the CISG. In practice, however, it is highly unlikely that many business operators will find themselves in the powerful condition just described. Business operators in the global market conclude a multitude of contracts, some of which are governed by their domestic law while other ones will be governed by foreign law. In practice, this may lead to one and the same operator finding himself subject to different domestic laws unknown to him, according to where he conducts business. Hence, on the assumption that the business operator needs to invest time and resources to acquire knowledge of the basic rules applicable to each transaction to which he is a party, it is apparent that the expansion of the business to multiple jurisdictions causes the need for resources to be multiplied by the number of jurisdictions involved. That being the case, it is indisputable that the application of the CISG may be beneficial, in that it reduces transaction costs. Indeed, in the model under consideration, to the extent that the CISG applies to all contracts with counterparties from foreign jurisdictions, it could be the only additional piece of legislation dealing with sales contracts that a business operator would be required to become familiar with, in addition to his own domestic.

There is, of course, at least one fundamental prerequisite that must be met in order for the model described above to work, namely that the uniform law be applied uniformly, i.e., that the uniformity aimed at be a uniformity in action and not only in the books. Indeed, in order to create uniformity, it is insufficient to create and enact uniform law instruments, such as the CISG, since these instruments can still be interpreted and, thus, applied differently by the courts of different jurisdictions. To reduce the risk of differing interpretations of one and the same text, that text must also be interpreted uniformly, since, as stated by Viscount Simonds on behalf of what was then the House of Lords in *Scruttons Ltd. b. Midland Silicones Ltd.* (1962 A.C. 446, 471), "it would be deplorable if the nations should, after protracted negotiations, reach agreement [. . .] and that their several courts should then disagree as to the meaning of what they appeared to agree upon."

The courts applying the CISG are thus urged to take an active role in fostering the uniform application of the CISG, in full compliance with the mandate laid out explicitly in Article 7(1) CISG. Pursuant to this provision, in interpreting the CISG regard is to be had to the CISG's "international character" and to the need to promote "uniformity in its application". Uniformity represents the ultimate goal of the CISG and its interpretation. This goal can only be reached if the interpreter frees himself of preconceived notions of his domestic law. While this is a prerequisite, it is not sufficient to reach the aforementioned goal. Having regard to the need to promote uniformity in the CISG's application also requires that courts of one contracting State to the

CISG have regard to what courts of other contracting States have done.

This book takes the aforementioned mandate into account and provides the reader with a handy tool for approaching the CISG's rules from a truly international and uniform perspective. It tries to analyze the international sales law as laid down by the CISG in a comprehensive and clear manner. And it does so without using the law of any specific legal system as the starting point, as evidenced by the case law cited, which is taken from very many jurisdictions. Where possible, reference to English translations of the cited case is provided.

FRANCO FERRARI

MARCO TORSELLO

24 March 2014

OUTLINE

TABLE OF CASES

References are to Pages

INTERNATIONAL SALES LAW—CISG

CHAPTER 1
INTRODUCTION

1. HISTORY, STRUCTURE AND NATURE OF THE CISG

The need to create internationally uniform rules for cases linked to more than one country designed to transcend national borders in order to maximize the utilization of resources and to create certainty was recognized as early as in the 1920s, when it was suggested by Ernst Rabel to start with the work of unifying the law of international sales of goods. Upon this suggestion, the International Institute for the Unification of Private Law, UNIDROIT, decided to undertake extensive studies in this field which led, in 1935, to the first draft of a uniform law on the international sale of goods. After World War II, which had interrupted the aforementioned efforts, work resumed with a conference at The Hague in 1951. Thereafter, other drafts followed, the last of which was discussed at the Diplomatic Conference held at The Hague in April 1964. The twenty–eight participating States approved two conventions, annexed to which were the Uniform Law on the International Sale of Goods (hereinafter: ULIS)[1] and

---

[1]   *See* Convention Relating to the Uniform Law of International Sale of Goods, July 1, 1964, with Annex, Uniform Law of International Sale of Goods, *reprinted in* 13 American Journal of Comparative Law 453 ff. (1964).

the Uniform Law on the Formation of Contracts for the International Sale of Goods (hereinafter: ULF).[2]

These laws were not as successful as expected; indeed, they came into force in only nine Countries. This led the United Nations Commission on International Trade Law, UNCITRAL, which was formed in 1966 with the task of promoting the progressive harmonization and unification of the law of international trade, to attempt the revision of the Hague Uniform Laws. When it became apparent, however, that a revision would not succeed without substantial modifications to the ULIS and ULF, a Working Group was tasked with drafting an entirely new text. Several drafts were proposed, the last of which, dating back to 1978, was the one upon which the General Assembly of the United Nations authorized the convening of a diplomatic conference, held from March 10 to April 11, 1980 in Vienna.[3] On that occasion, the United Nations Convention on Contracts for the International Sale of Goods (hereinafter: CISG) was approved. It came into force on January 1st, 1988,

---

[2]   *See* Convention Relating to the Uniform Law of the Formation of Contracts for the International Sale of Goods, July 1, 1964, with Annex, Uniform Law on the Formation of Contracts for the International Sale of Goods, *reprinted in* 13 American Journal of Comparative Law 472 ff. (1964).

[3]   The proceedings of the 1980 Diplomatic Conference as well as its results are *reprinted in* UNITED NATIONS CONFERENCE ON CONTRACTS FOR THE INTERNATIONAL SALE OF GOODS, OFFICIAL RECORDS: DOCUMENTS OF THE CONFERENCE AND SUMMARY RECORDS OF THE PLENARY MEETINGS AND OF THE MEETINGS OF THE MAIN COMMITTEES (Vienna, 10 March—11 April 1980) (United Nations ed., 1981).

and is today in force in the following countries: Albania; Argentina; Armenia, Australia; Austria; Bahrain, Belarus; Belgium; Benin; Bosnia and Herzegovina; Brazil; Bulgaria; Burundi; Canada; Chile; China (PRC); Colombia; Croatia; Cuba; Cyprus; Czech Republic; Denmark; Dominican Republic; Ecuador; Egypt; El Salvador; Estonia; Finland; France; Gabon; Georgia; Germany; Greece; Guinea; Honduras; Hungary; Iceland; Iraq; Israel; Italy; Japan; Republic of Korea; Kyrgyzstan; Latvia; Lebanon; Lesotho; Liberia; Lithuania; Luxembourg; Republic of Macedonia, Mauritania; Mexico; Republic of Moldova; Mongolia; Montenegro; Netherlands; New Zealand; Norway; Paraguay; Peru; Poland; Romania; Russian Federation; Saint Vincent and Grenadines; San Marino; Serbia; Singapore; Slovakia; Slovenia; Spain; Sweden; Switzerland; Syrian Arab Republic; Turkey; Uganda; Ukraine; United States; Uruguay; Uzbekistan; Bolivarian Republic of Venezuela, Zambia.

The CISG consists of four Parts. Although the majority of the CISG substantive rules are found in Parts II (Articles 14–24) and III (Articles 25–88), dedicated to the 'Formation of the Contract' and the 'Sale of Goods' respectively, Part I (Articles 1–13) on the 'Sphere of Application and General Provisions' also contains some substantive provisions, unlike Part IV, entitled 'Final Provisions' (Article 89–101). Article 8, for example, lays down rules of interpretation applicable to all contracts and statements subject to the CISG. Likewise, Article 11 lays down the rule of freedom from form requirements, which also is a substantive rule that, unless otherwise indicated in the CISG itself, applies to all statements and also governs the modification or termination of contracts governed by the CISG.

As for its nature, the CISG is a uniform substantive law convention, *i.e.*, a convention that sets forth a set of substantive (rather than private international law) rules created with the intention to be binding and applied in one and the same manner in more than one jurisdiction. More specifically, the CISG falls within the category of *limited*, rather than *unlimited,* uniform law conventions. Unlike an *unlimited* uniform law convention, which sets forth rules to govern both international and domestic situations,[4] the CISG, as a *limited* uniform law convention, applies solely to trans–border situations, in the sense of situations with connections to more than one country. Unlike unlimited uniform law conventions, the CISG does not *per se* impact domestic law. From a practical perspective, this means that the coming into force of the CISG in a given state does not displace that state's domestic law, which continues to govern all purely domestic legal matters, an advantage insofar as it allows a State to adopt a convention even where the convention's laws conflict with that

---

[4] Unlimited uniform law conventions are rather rare, although there are a few examples, such as the Convention providing a uniform law for bills of exchange and promissory notes of 7 June 1930 and the Convention providing a uniform law for checks of 19 March 1931.

State's domestic law. This is an advantage insofar as it allows a given State to enter into force a limited uniform law convention even where its rules contrast with that State's domestic law.

2. UNIFORM INTERPRETATION OF THE CISG

It is important to note that in order to create uniformity, it is insufficient to merely create and enact uniform law instruments, such as the CISG, since these instruments can still be interpreted and, thus, applied differently by judges from different countries. To reduce the risk of differing interpretations of one and the same text, that text must also be interpreted uniformly, since, as stated by Viscount Simonds on behalf of what was then the House of Lords in *Scruttons Ltd. v. Midland Silicones Ltd.*, "it would be deplorable if the nations should, after protracted negotiations, reach agreement [. . .] and that their several courts should then disagree as to the meaning of what they appeared to agree upon."[5]

The first step toward minimizing the danger of differing interpretations and, thus, diverging applications of uniform law, is to avoid recourse to the domestic legal background every interpreter necessarily has. One must avoid reading an international uniform law instrument through the lenses of domestic law, despite the fact that the

---

[5]   *Scruttons Ltd. v. Midland Silicones Ltd.*, 1962 A.C. 446, 471 (1961).

uniform law has become part of the domestic law. The drafters of the CISG, like the drafters of other uniform substantive law conventions, were very well aware of the need to go beyond domestic readings of the CISG, and said as much explicitly within the text: Article 7(1) states in relevant part that in interpreting the CISG "regard is to be had to its international character and to the need to promote uniformity in its application."[6]

On the one hand, such proscriptions against parochialism mean that, as a general matter,[7] one must interpret international uniform law "in an autonomous manner".[8] Interpretations in light of domestic law should be avoided, as difficult as this may be. Thus, in interpreting the CISG, one should generally not resort to the meanings one attaches to certain expressions within the ambit of a particular system.[9] Thus, even where the expressions employed in the CISG are literally the same as expressions that within a particular domestic legal system have a specific meaning—such as

---

[6]   *See, e.g.,* U.S. Court of Appeals [3rd Cir.], 21 July 2010 (*Forestal Guarani S.A. v. Daros International, Inc.*), available at http://cisgw3.law.pace.edu/cases/100721u1.html .

[7]   *See* Trib. Padova (Italy), 11 January 2005, available in English at http://cisgw3.law.pace.edu/cases/050111i3.html.

[8]   *See, e.g.,* High Court of New Zealand, 30 July 2010 (*RJ & AM Smallmon v. Transport Sales Limited and Grant Alan Miller*), available at http://cisgw3.law.pace.edu/cases/100730n6.html; Trib. Forlì (Italy), 16 February 2009, available in English at http://cisgw3.law.pace.edu/cases/090216i3.html.

[9]   *See* Polimeles Protodikio Athinon (Greece), docket n. 4505/2009 (no date indicated), available in English at http://cisgw3.law.pace.edu/cases/094505gr.html#ii2.

"avoidance", "reasonable", "good faith", etc.—they are independent and different from the latter,[10] since the expressions employed in uniform law conventions are generally intended to be neutral.[11] This interpretive approach appears to be accepted as a basic principle of international uniform law, arising out of the assumption, among others, that international uniform law does not wish to identify itself with any legal system, since it wants to conjugate with all. The drafters' choice of one expression rather than another should be seen, therefore, as the result of compromise, rather than an endorsement of a concept peculiar to one or another domestic legal regime.

At this point, it must be stressed, however, that not all expressions must be interpreted autonomously. Some expressions within the CISG do require a "domestic" interpretation—despite the negative effect this may have on the uniformity aimed at by the Convention's drafters. Unfortunately, the CISG itself does not identify these expressions, nor does it articulate the criteria to be used when deciding whether an expression is best interpreted autonomously or domestically, leaving the task to courts and commentators.

---

[10] *See* OLG München (Germany), 14 January 2009, available in English at http://cisgw3.law.pace.edu/cases/090114 g1.html; Supreme Court of Austria, 23 May 2005, available in English at http://cisgw3.law.pace.edu/cases/050523a3.html.

[11] *Contra see* U.S. Court of Appeals [8th Cir.], 14 February 2011 (*Dingxi Longhai Dairy, Ltd. v. Becwood Technology Group L.L.C.*), available at http://cisgw3.law.pace.edu/cases/110214u1. html.

One expression employed by the CISG that must be defined in light of a given domestic law is "private international law." As the CISG constitutes "merely" a substantive law convention and does not set forth any private international law rules, the reference to "private international law" found in Articles 1(1)(*b*) and 7(2) CISG is to be understood as a reference to a domestic concept of private international, specifically, that of the forum.

The concept of "private international law," however, is not the only one that requires a "domestic" interpretation. As will be shown later in more detail, the scope of the CISG is limited; it does not cover, among other issues, agency.[12] This, however, means that the concept of "party" cannot be interpreted autonomously, but rather in a "domestic" way. Thus, to give just one example, the decision of whether a principal or agent is party to a contract will turn on the applicable domestic law to be identified by means of the private international law rules of the forum.

Still, an autonomous interpretation of the CISG cannot by itself guarantee uniformity. To promote uniformity in the CISG's application, it is insufficient to consider the CISG an autonomous body of rules. In order to achieve the CISG's ultimate goal of uniformity, it is also necessary to consider practices in other jurisdictions. Decisions rendered by judicial bodies of other Contracting

---

[12]   *See*, *e.g.*, Trib. Vigevano (Italy), 12 July 2000, available in English at http://cisgw3.law.pace.edu/cases/000712i3.html.

States must be taken into account.[13] This does not mean that foreign case law binds the courts of a given country. Rather, foreign case law has merely persuasive value, and this is, in essence, also what Article 7(1) CISG demands when it provides that "*regard is to be had* [. . .] to the need to promote uniformity in its application." In other words, "[w]hat matters [. . .] is not a prejudicial effect of rulings by foreign courts or arbitration [. . .] tribunals and not that the decision taken by an organ, which by accident entrusted first to deal with a specific legal issue, is attached a particularly great importance; rather, the existing material in regard to relevant rulings has to be taken account of when giving the reasons for a decision."[14]

This view finds support not only in legal writing, but also in case law. The first court to confront the issue of what, if any, deference ought to be shown to foreign decisions was the Tribunale di Pavia in 1999. In arriving at a given substantive solution, the Court stated that, "this solution corresponds to that adopted by foreign case law [. . .] which, *although not binding*, is nevertheless to be taken

---

[13]   *See* Foreign Trade Court of Arbitration attached to the Serbian Chamber of Commerce, Arbitral Award of 28 January 2009, available in English at http://cisgw3.law.pace.edu/cases/090128sb.html.

[14]   Fritz Enderlein/Dietrich Maskow, International Sales Law 56 (1992).

into consideration as required by Article 7(1) of the CISG."[15]

More recently, in a famous decision of 2000, the Tribunale di Vigevano reached the same conclusion; it stated that "foreign case law, contrary to what a minority of authorities have argued, is not binding on this Tribunal. It must nevertheless be considered in order to assure and to promote the uniform application of the United Nations Convention, according to its Article 7(1)."[16] Italian courts are, however, not the only ones to have dealt with this methodological issue. In 2004, a United States District Court reached the same result. It stated that "[a]lthough foreign case law is not binding on this court, it is nonetheless instructive in deciding the issues presented here."[17] More recently, in 2006, a different United States District Court simply stated that "foreign decisions do not bind this Court,"[18] without at all addressing the issue of whether foreign decisions may be taken into account for their persuasive value.

---

[15] Trib. Pavia (Italy), 29 December 1999, available in English at http://cisgw3.law.pace.edu/cases/991229i3.html (emphasis added by the authors).

[16] Trib. Vigevano (Italy), 12 July 2000, available in English at http://cisgw3.law.pace.edu/cases/000712i3.html.

[17] U.S. District Court [N.D. Ill.], 21 May 2004 (*Chicago Prime Packers, Inc. v. Northam Food Trading Co., et al.*), available at http://cisgw3.law.pace.edu/cases/040521u1.html.

[18] U.S. District Court [S.D.N.Y.], 23 August 2006 (*TeeVee Tunes, Inc. et al. v. Gerhard Schubert GmbH*), available at http://cisgw3.law.pace.edu/cases/060823u1.html#ii1.

3.   INTERPRETIVE METHODS

The foregoing remarks all refer to the CISG's interpretive goals rather than its interpretive methods or criteria. This is unsurprising, since Article 7(1) CISG merely sets forth the CISG's interpretive goals against which all interpretation has to be measured rather than its interpretive methods or criteria.

As regards the interpretive methods and criteria, Article 7(1)'s mandate that regard be given to the CISG's international character and the need to promote uniformity in its application in the interpretation of the CISG should be understood as precluding recourse to domestic interpretive methods and criteria to solve interpretive problems. To which interpretive methods courts should resort *in concreto* is, however, not entirely clear since a uniform approach to the interpretation of uniform law has not yet been elaborated—though some convergence can be discerned. Nevertheless, it appears that some overarching methods of interpretation can be found.

One such method is that of literal *interpretation*. Pursuant to this method—which applies equally to the interpretation of other uniform law instruments—the starting point of any interpretation is the text of the CISG itself.[19] In

---

[19] *See*, *e.g.*, Supreme Court of Austria, 23 May 2005, available in English at http://cisgw3.law.pace.edu/cases/050523a3.html; U.S. District Court [E.D.N.Y.], 19 March 2005 (*Genpharm Inc. v. Pliva–Lachema A.S.*), available at http://cisgw3.law.pace.edu/cases/050319u1.html.

other words, the CISG, like any other treaty, is generally to be interpreted in accordance with its own terms and bound by the four corners of its text. This does not mean, however, that other methods of interpretation must be disregarded or cannot influence the interpretive result. An interpretation that contradicts the wording of the CISG can at times be justified, as in those instances where there exist very important reasons of justice, or when it is clear in light of other types of interpretation, such as the historical or contextual methods, that the result reached by means of the literal interpretation is untenable.

A literal interpretation of the CISG presents more problems than may appear at first glance, however. This is due, *inter alia,* to the fact that the CISG is in force in a single original in six equally authentic languages. On the one hand, this means that, theoretically, all six language versions have to be considered for interpretation purposes. This in itself may cause interpretive problems, since the various authentic language versions may conflict with each other. But there may be instances in which an interpretive problem can be due to reasons other than a conflict between the various language versions. To solve these problems one has to have recourse to the interpretive rules set forth in the 1969 Vienna Convention on the Law of Treaties [*hereinafter*: VCLT], and this is irrespective of whether the CISG provision to be interpreted is one of the "Final Provisions" contained in Part IV of the

CISG, to which some commentators suggest that application of the VCLT ought to be limited.

It is worth pointing out that the 1969 Vienna Convention on the Law of Treaties' rules on interpretation do not conflict with the rules set forth in Article 7(1) CISG. Thus, one may arrive at the same interpretive results under either set of rules. Still, the VCLT goes further, and deals with issues for which the CISG provides no solution. By way of example it may suffice to recall that Article 33 VCLT directly addresses problems arising in connection with a treaty being authenticated in two or more languages, while the CISG contains no solution whatsoever. Pursuant to Article 33 VCLT, and given that during both the drafting process leading up to the CISG and the Vienna Diplomatic Conference "English had been more or less the working language"[20], in case of doubts, more weight has to be given to the English version of the CISG.[21]

The fact that the CISG is in force in one single original authenticated in six different languages has not, however, prevented production of translations. However, these translations do not have the same standing as the various authentic language versions of the CISG. Rather, they serve solely as an aid to domestic interpreters and should be referred to with

---

[20] Official Records of the United Nations Conference on Contracts for the International Sale of Goods. Vienna, 10 March—11 April 1980, supra note 3, at 272.

[21] *See* Supreme Court of Switzerland, 13 November 2003, available in English at http://cisgw3.law.pace.edu/cases/031113s1.html.

caution, as errors and imprecisions that may be contained in these translations may lead to solutions that do not fully conform to the CISG.

Although the literal interpretation constitutes the starting point of any interpretation, interpretive efforts should stop there. This is due not only to the fact that there may well be instances where the literal interpretation may lead to more than one plausible interpretive result, but rather because any result of literal interpretation must be validated by other methods of interpretation, particularly, the historic interpretation and the contextual ones.

As regards historical interpretation, resort to which is advocated for the purpose of the interpretation of the CISG not only by commentators from Civil Law countries but also by those from Common Law countries (where courts and scholars have traditionally been reluctant to refer to *travaux préparatoires*), it requires that the legislative history of the provision to be interpreted be taken into account. As regards the CISG, this is not too difficult, since both the drafting process as well as the Diplomatic Conference are well documented. Moreover, many of the CISG's provisions can be traced back to the 1964 Hague Conventions, for which there exists abundant case law and commentary.

When interpreting the various CISG provisions, resort is also to be had to the contextual interpretation which requires that the interpreter also look into the context in which the provision to be interpreted is embedded. No provision should *a priori* be considered as standing alone. Furthermore, where there are provisions addressing issues related to those addressed in the provision to be interpreted, the interpretive solution derived from the contested provision should align with that derived from the other provisions addressing the same issue. In these authors' opinion, proper interpretation requires resort to the contextual interpretation in all cases, not only in those where recourse to other methods of interpretation presents no solution, such as when a literal interpretation leads to more than one plausible solution. Likewise, one must also deploy contextual interpretation in those instances where it appears that other interpretive methods *do* lead to a clear solution, since the results of a contextual interpretation may trump those of other methods of interpretation, including those of a literal interpretation. Thus, even in those cases where the literal meaning of a provision appears unequivocal, its language plain and explicit, interpreters may not stop there. Rather, they must always confirm that meaning in light of the larger context in which the provision is embedded. In other words, one must validate all interpretive results by means of a contextual interpretation.

As regards contextual interpretation, it is important to understand what the "context" against which a provision will be interpreted consists of. For the purpose of interpreting a provision of the CISG, "context" encompasses more than the CISG itself.

The argument that contextual interpretation does not allow one to take into account other uniform substantive law conventions is to be rejected, as is the view that other uniform substantive law conventions may only be taken into account when elaborated by the same intergovernmental organization or when in force in the same countries. Solutions reached, for instance, in interpreting the 1988 Unidroit Convention on International Factoring or the 1988 Unidroit Convention on International Financial Leasing should also be taken into account when interpreting the CISG, as these conventions are all based upon the same *ratio conventionis* and subject to the same interpretive principles. Moreover, only an inter–conventional interpretation, one that takes into account a broader context, can successfully lead to the creation of one uniform law that surpasses what would otherwise remain mere piece–meal unification. Of course, where uniform law conventions are based upon diverging legislative intentions, they cannot be resort to for the purpose of an inter–conventional interpretation.

4. GENERAL PRINCIPLES AND GAP–FILLING: GENERAL REMARKS

Although it has been suggested that the CISG constitutes a comprehensive code governing all international sales transactions and "exhaustively deals with all problems",[22] the CISG is neither a comprehensive code nor does it constitute an exhaustive body of rules. In other words, the CISG does not provide solutions for all the problems that can originate from an international sale. This can easily be gathered from the text of Articles 4 and 5 CISG, which expressly exclude some issues, to be identified at a later stage, from the CISG's scope of application. The CISG's limited scope of application gives rise to problems on how to deal with the CISG's incompleteness. It is to deal with this problem that Article 7(2) CISG provides that "[q]uestions concerning matters governed by this Convention which are not expressly settled in it are to be settled in conformity with the general principles on which it is based or, in the absence of such principles, in conformity with the law applicable by virtue of the rules of private international law."

Although Article 7(2) CISG addresses an issue different from the one addressed in Article 7(1) CISG, both provisions pursue a similar goal, namely, attempting to ensure the uniformity sought by the drafters of the CISG. To reach this goal, courts should, not only in the case of ambiguities or obscurities in the CISG's text, but also in the case of gaps, as much as possible refrain from resorting to domestic laws and try to find a solution within the CISG itself.

---

[22]   *See* Supreme Court of Switzerland, 19 February 2004, available at http://www.unilex.info/case.cfm?pid=1&do=case&id=979&step=FullText.

This approach, pursuant to which courts should try to solve issues from within the Convention, does, however, not apply indiscriminately. Specifically, it does not apply with respect to matters excluded from the CISG's scope of application, such as those contemplated in Arts. 4 and 5 CISG. These matters, sometimes labelled "external gaps", require a solution in conformity with the law applicable by virtue of the rules of private international law (or, where applicable, with other uniform substantive law conventions).[23] Matters that *are* governed by the CISG but not expressly settled in it—"internal gaps"—should instead be resolved in conformity first with the general principles on which the CISG is based;[24] and only absent such principles, in conformity with the law applicable by virtue of the rules of private international law or, where applicable, other uniform substantive law conventions. To fill internal gaps, the drafters of the CISG have, thus, advocated an approach that combines recourse to general principles with recourse (as *ultima ratio*) to the rules of private international law, a choice that demonstrates an awareness by the drafters that absolute independence from domestic law is unreachable.

At this point it appears appropriate to recall that to fill gaps, one can resort to various types of logical

---

[23]   *See* Trib. Padova (Italy), 31 March 2004, available in English at http://cisgw3.law.pace.edu/cases/040331i3.html.

[24]   *See, e.g.*, U.S. District Court [S.D.N.Y.], 20 August 2008 (*Hilaturas Miel, S.L. v. Republic of Iraq*), available at http://cisgw 3.law.pace.edu/cases/080820u1.html.

reasoning in order to find a solution within the CISG itself. Recourse to general principles constitutes merely one method of gap–filling. Therefore, one must wonder whether Article 7(2) CISG also covers other methods of legal reasoning, such as analogical application. These authors suggest not only that it does, but also that recourse to analogical application prevails over recourse to the general principles. However, when the matters settled in the CISG and the issue the internal gaps refers to are not so closely related that it would not be unjustified to adopt a different solution, one must resort to the general principles as contemplated in Article 7(2) CISG. This procedure differs from the analogical application in that it does not resolve the specific case solely by extending specific provisions dealing with analogous matters, but on the grounds of principles and rules which have a general character and therefore may be applied on a much wider scale.

5. GENERAL PRINCIPLES UNDERLYING THE CISG

As far as the general principles themselves are concerned, while there are some that can be identified more easily, since they are underlying one or more specific provisions, there are others the identification of which is more difficult. As for the former category, the most important principle pertaining to that category is that of party autonomy.[25] In effect, the wide autonomy parties enjoy under the CISG by virtue of Article 6 CISG confers dispositive nature to the CISG[26] and, thus, leads to the rules of the CISG merely being default rules. This allows one to state, among others, that where there is a conflict between the principle of party autonomy and any other general principle, the former always prevails.

Another one of the CISG's general principles is that of good faith.[27] Still, this principle is generally considered to be too vague to serve any practical purpose, which lead to the identification of general principles that can be traced back to that of good faith, but which have a narrower scope and may be of more use in practice. Among these general principles, are that of the prohibition of *venire contra factum proprium* as well as that of estoppel, and which can be derived from specific provisions of the CISG, such as Articles 16(2) and 29(2), and that pursuant to which parties are required to cooperate with each other, which means, *inter alia*, that

---

[25] *See* Polimeles Protodikio Athinon (Greece), docket No. 4505/2009 (no date indicated), available in English at http://cisgw3.law.pace.edu/cases/094505gr.html#ii2; Trib. Padova (Italy), 25 February 2004, available in English at http://cisgw3.law.pace.edu/cases/040225i3.html.

[26] *See* OG Kanton Bern (Switzerland), 19 May 2008, available at http://globalsaleslaw.com/content/api/cisg/urteile/1738.pdf.

[27] *See* OLG Celle (Germany), 24 July 2009, available in English at http://cisgw3.law.pace.edu/cases/090724g1.html; American Arbitration Association, Arbitral Award of 23 October 2007, available at http://cisgw3.law.pace.edu/cases/071023a5.html.

parties have to exchange information relevant for the performance of their respective obligations.

The aforementioned principles are not the only general principles which can be derived from one or more specific CISG provisions. The principle of informality (or freedom from form requirements, which can be derived from Article 11 CISG) also constitutes such a general principle[28], as does that of mitigation, set forth in Article 77 CISG;[29] that— underlying Article 9(2) CISG—pursuant to which the parties are bound, unless otherwise agreed, by a usage of which they knew or ought to have known and which in international trade is widely known to, and regularly observed by, parties to contracts of the type involved in the particular trade concerned[30]; that pursuant to which the creditor is entitled to interest on sums in arrears,[31] and this from the day of non–payment, irrespective of any notice of default;[32] that pursuant to which damages are limited to foreseeable ones, a principle that, as much as that of full compensation, can be derived from Article 74 CISG; the principle, laid down in Article 27 CISG, pursuant to which for the purpose

---

[28]   *See* Trib. Padova (Italy), 31 March 2004, available in English at http://cisgw3.law.pace.edu/cases/040331i3.html.

[29]   *See* Trib. Rimini (Italy), 26 November 2002, available in English at http://cisgw3.law.pace.edu/cases/021126i3.html.

[30]   *Id.*

[31]   Trib. Padova (Italy), 31 March 2004, available in English at http://cisgw3.law.pace.edu/cases/040331i3.html.

[32]   *See, e.g.*, HG Kanton Aargau (Switzerland), 26 November 2008, available at http://cisgw3.law.pace.edu/cases/081126s1. html.

of the effectiveness of a declaration or notice its dispatch is sufficient, unless otherwise stated in the CISG; the principle pursuant to which official holidays or non–business days are included in calculating a period of time which, however, has to be extended where the last day of the period falls on such holiday or non–business day; that pursuant to which the party at fault has to refund the amounts equal to its enrichment; that enshrined in Article 40 CISG pursuant to which "a grossly negligent unknowing buyer appears to be more protection–worthy than a seller acting fraudulently"[33], as well as the principle "*impossibilia nulla est obligatio*".

Apart from the foregoing general principles, which all can be traced back to specific provisions, there are other general principles which can be derived by looking at a wider, more comprehensive context. One such principle is that of "reasonableness".[34] Other principles of the kind at hand include: the principle pursuant to which the party acting in reliance upon a situation created by the opposing party is to be protected, a principle to be derived from Articles 16(2) and 29(2); the principle of *favor contractus*;[35] the principle pursuant to which the avoidance of the contract,

---

[33] OLG Köln (Germany), 21 May 1996, available in English at http://cisgw3.law.pace.edu/cases/980605s5.html.

[34] *See* OLG Koblenz (Germany), 24 February 2011, available at http://www.globalsaleslaw.org/content/api/cisg/urteile/2301.pdf.

[35] *See* Supreme Court of Switzerland, 28 October 1998, available in English at http://cisgw3.law.pace.edu/cases/981028s1.html.

where the contract is severable, solely affects the part of the contract the breach relates to; the principle pursuant to which "each party has to bear the costs of its obligation";[36] the principle, to be derived inter *alia* from Articles 58(1) and 71(1), pursuant to which a party is entitled to withhold its performance in case of the opposing party's breach of contract[37] as well as the principle pursuant to which performances have generally to be exchanged simultaneously.[38]

In these authors' opinion, there is no general principles underlying the CISG regarding the place of performance of monetary obligations,[39] nor is there a general principle pursuant to which the creditor's place of business controls all questions relating to payment, including the currency of the payment. On the contrary, as regards the allocation of the burden of proof, expressly dealt with for instance in Article 79(1) CISG, two general principles can be identified: that pursuant to which the party which wants to derive beneficial legal

---

[36] *See* KG Schaffhausen (Switzerland), 25 February 2002, available in English at http://cisgw3.law.pace.edu/cases/020225 s1.html.

[37] *See* Supreme Court of Poland, 11 May 2007, available in English at http://cisgw3.law.pace.edu/cases/070511p1.html; *contra* OLG Stuttgart (Germany), 20 December 2004, available in English at http://cisgw3.law.pace.edu/cases/041220g1.html.

[38] *See* Supreme Court of Austria, 30 November 2006, available in English at http://cisgw3.law.pace.edu/cases/061130 a3.html; Supreme Court of Austria, 8 November 2005, available in English at http://cisgw3.law.pace.edu/cases/051108a3.html.

[39] CA Paris (France), 14 January 1998, available in English at http://cisgw3.law.pace.edu/cases/980114f1.html.

consequences from a legal provision has to prove the existence of the factual prerequisites of the provision,[40] in other words, *ei incumbit probatio qui dicit, non qui negat*, and that according to which the party claiming an exception has to prove the factual prerequisites of that exception.[41]

---

[40]　*See* Trib. Cantonal du Valais (Switzerland), 28 January 2009, available in English at http://cisgw3.law.pace.edu/cases/090128s1.html; Supreme Court of Switzerland, 13 November 2003, available at http://cisgw3.law.pace.edu/cases/031113s1.html.

[41]　*See* Trib. Vigevano (Italy), 12 July 2000, available in English at http://cisgw3.law.pace.edu/cases/000712i3.html.

CHAPTER 2

CISG, PRIVATE INTERNATIONAL LAW, PARTY AUTONOMY, TRADE USAGES AND OTHER SOURCES OF LAW

1. UNIFORM LAW v. PRIVATE INTERNATIONAL LAW

Where the contract of sale is one that bears ties to more than one country, courts cannot simply resort to their domestic substantive law to solve substantive issues. Rather, they will need to determine which substantive rules to apply. It is often suggested that in order to identify the substantive rules applicable to an international contract, resort is to be had to rules of private international law of the forum, as these rules are specifically designed to solve the issue of what rules apply where a relationship has links to more than one country.

One has to wonder, however, whether this is the correct approach, as this approach does not at all take into account the coming into force of uniform substantive law rules, such as the rules set forth by the CISG, and their relationship with the private international law rules of the forum. In these authors' opinion, where uniform substantive law rules are in force in the forum State, resort to these rules has to be preferred over resort to private international law where the uniform substantive rules are *prima facie* applicable. In some countries, this approach can be justified on constitutional grounds, as some countries afford to international treaties (including those setting forth uniform substantive law) a higher standing in the hierarchy of sources of law than to purely domestic statutes (including those on private international law). Of course, this justification only works where the rules of private international law are themselves not originating from an international treaty.

There is a more general reason for resort to uniform substantive law rules to prevail over resort to private international law, namely the principle *"lex specialis derogat legi generali", pursuant to which the more specific rule overrides the more general one.* The CISG is more specific than private international law on several levels. On the one hand, the CISG is designed to be applicable to a more specific set of contracts than existing private international law rules: While the CISG merely applies to certain contracts for the sale of goods, provided that these meet specific—and rather restrictive— internationality requirements, private international law rules normally are devised to also apply to contracts other than just contracts for the sale of goods. But even where the sphere of application of the private international law rules is limited to contracts for the sale of goods, as is, for instance, that of the rules set forth in the 1955 Hague Convention on the Law Applicable to Contracts for the International Sale of Goods, the application of those rules is not limited to contracts that meet a specific internationality requirement.

Like other rules of private international law, which are supposed to apply whenever there is a conflict between different laws and, therefore, do not define internationality in one way or another, the rules laid down by the 1955 Hague Convention do not define internationality either, which makes them applicable to any kind of international contract for the sale of goods. The CISG, on the other hand, defines internationality in a very specific way (Article 1(1)), thus limiting its own sphere of application and making the CISG more specific.

Furthermore, the CISG is more specific in that it solves the substantive issues—meaning those issues that the parties ultimately want to see solved— "directly", thus avoiding the two steps required by resort to private international law, consisting in the identification of the applicable law and its application. From this it follows that where the CISG is in force, courts will have to first determine whether the CISG applies rather than resort to their rules of private international.[1]

2. PRIVATE INTERNATIONAL LAW UNDER THE CISG

In light of what has just been said, when faced with a dispute arising from a contract for the international sale of goods, courts of contracting States to the CISG will have to first determine

---

[1] For this reasoning, *see* Trib. Forlì (Italy), 16 February 2009, available in English at http://cisgw3.law.pace.edu/cases/090216i3.html; Trib. Vigevano (Italy), 12 July 2000, available in English at http://cisgw3.law.pace.edu/cases/000712i3.html.

whether the CISG applies. This, however, does not mean that resort to private international law has become superfluous with the coming into force of the CISG. It only means that resort to private international law has initially to give way to an analysis of the applicability of the CISG.

There are many instances in which resort to private international law is necessary for the purpose of solving a dispute arising from a contract for the international sale of goods and falling under the CISG. In effect, even a superficial reading of the CISG shows that the CISG itself does not eliminate resort to private international law, since the CISG itself refers on two occasions (namely in Articles 1(1)(b) and 7(2)) to private international law. Moreover, given the contexts in which reference to private international law is made, the importance of private international law for the CISG becomes evident. Article 1(1)(b), for instance, even lets the applicability of the CISG itself depend, where the CISG is not "directly" applicable due to the parties having their relevant place of business in different Contracting States to the CISG (Article 1(1)(a)), on a private international law analysis. Pursuant to Article 1(1)(b), the CISG "applies to contracts of sale of goods between parties whose places of business are in different States: [. . .] (b) when the rules of private international law lead to the application of the law of a Contracting State", thus making it unambiguously clear that private international law and uniform substantive (sales) law are ontologically intertwined rather than mutually exclusive.

The importance of private international law for contracts governed by the CISG also becomes evident if one bears in mind that the CISG, contrary to what a few commentators and courts have stated, does not constitute a "comprehensive code". As the CISG's scope of application is limited, resort to private international law is necessary to identify the law applicable to the issues not governed by the CISG—unless, of course, those issues are governed by other uniform substantive law conventions, such as the 1974 UNCITRAL Limitation Convention.

At this point, it is worth pointing out that the CISG does not define the concept of "private international law". One has to wonder whether this means that the concept at hand must, like most concepts used in the CISG, be interpreted by having regard to the CISG's "international character and the need to promote uniformity in its application", as mandated by Article 7(1). In other words, does that concept have to be interpreted without resorting to a given domestic law, or is that concept one of those that exceptionally have to be interpreted "domestically"? As pointed out both by commentators and courts, the concept at hand is not one of those that require the interpreters to go beyond their own legal background. Rather, the concept of "private international law" to which the CISG refers is that of the forum.[2] This means, *inter*

---

[2]   *See* Trib. Padova (Italy), 11 January 2005, available in English at http://cisgw3.law.pace.edu/cases/050111i3.html.

alia, that by choosing to start proceedings in one forum rather than another, the parties influence the private international law rules which the court seized will have to apply, which, in turn, has an impact not only on the law applicable to the issues not governed by the CISG, but also on the applicability of the CISG (where the CISG is not applicable pursuant to Article 1(1)(*a*)).

3. PARTY AUTONOMY AND SOURCES OF INTERNATIONAL SALES LAW OTHER THAN THE CISG

From what has just been said, it becomes evident that the CISG is not the only source of law for issues arising from contracts for the international sale of goods. This is acknowledged by the CISG itself, as can easily be derived from its Article 6, which allows the parties to "exclude the application of this Convention or, subject to Article 12, derogate from or vary the effect of any of its provisions". By providing for this possibility, which businesses apparently take advantage of rather often for fear of the unknown, the drafters of the CISG reaffirmed the principle that the primary source of the rules governing international sales contracts is party autonomy[3]. By stating that the CISG can be excluded, the drafters clearly acknowledged the CISG's dispositive nature[4] and the central role

---

[3]   *See* Trib. Rimini (Italy), 26 November 2002, available in English at http://cisgw3.law.pace.edu/cisg/wais/db/cases2/021126 i3.html.

[4]   For an express reference to the CISG's non–mandatory nature, *see* Shanghai High People's Court (China), 17 May 2007,

which party autonomy plays in international commerce and, particularly, in international sales[5].

As far as party autonomy is concerned, it must be pointed out that pursuant to Article 6 CISG it may take two different forms, relating, on the one hand, to the instance where the CISG's application is excluded in its entirety (or partially), and, on the other hand, to the instance where the parties derogate from—or modify the effects of—the CISG provisions on a substantive level. These two situations differ from each other in that, according to the CISG, the exclusion does not encounter any restrictions, whereas derogation does, since there are provisions that the parties are not allowed to derogate from.

The parties to a contract governed by the CISG are free to exclude the CISG as a whole or Parts of it. The issues that the exclusion of the CISG raises are different from that of the limits to party autonomy and mostly relate to how to exclude the CISG. Obviously, the exclusion can be express. One has to wonder, however, whether the CISG can also be excluded implicitly, given that the CISG, unlike

---

available in English at http://cisgw3.law.pace.edu/cases/070517 c1.html; Supreme Court of Italy, 19 June 2000, available in English at http://cisgw3.law.pace.edu/cases/000619i3.html; Supreme Court of Austria, 21 March 2000, available in English at http://cisgw3.law.pace.edu/cases/000321a3.html.

[5] *See* LG Stendal (Germany), 12 October 2000, available in English at http://cisgw3.law.pace.edu/cases/001012g1.html; Supreme Court of Germany, 4 December 1996, available in English at http://cisgw3.law.pace.edu/cases/961204g1.html.

the ULIS, does not include a provision expressly allowing the parties to implicitly exclude the Convention. In these authors' opinion, the lack of such a provision does not mean that under the CISG the exclusion always has to be agreed upon expressly, although some courts—mostly, albeit not exclusively,[6] from the United States—require that the exclusion be express.[7] Rather, it has a different meaning: To discourage courts from too easily inferring an "implied" exclusion or derogation.[8] Therefore, an implicit exclusion of the CISG is possible.[9] Of course, for the CISG to be implicitly

---

[6]   *See* OLG Linz (Austria), 8 August 2005, available in English at http://cisgw3.law.pace.edu/cases/050808a3.html; LG Landshut (Germany), 5 April 1995, available in English at http://cisgw3.law.pace.edu/cases/950405g1.html.

[7]   *See, e.g.,* U.S. District Court [N.J.], 7 October 2008 (*Forestal Guarani, S.A. v. Daros International, Inc.*), available at http://cisgw3.law.pace.edu/cases/081007u1.html; U.S. District Court [E.D. Mich.], 28 September 2007 (*Easom Automation Systems, Inc. v. Thyssenkrupp Fabco, Corp.*), available at http://cisgw3.law.pace.edu/cases/070928u1.html#iv; U.S. District Court [S.D.N.Y.], 19 July 2007 (*Cedar Petrochemicals, Inc. v. Dongbu Hannong Chemical Co., Ltd.*), available at http://cisgw3.law.pace.edu/cases/070719u1.html; U.S. District Court [Minn.], 31 January 2007 (*Travelers Property Casualty Company of America et al. v. Saint–Gobain Technical Fabrics Canada Limited*), available at http://cisgw3.law.pace.edu/cases/070131u1.html.

[8]   *See* Official Records of the United Nations Conference on Contracts for the International Sale of Goods. Vienna, 10 March—11 April 1980, *supra* note 3, at 17.

[9]   *See* Supreme Court of Austria, 2 April 2009, available in English at http://cisgw3.law.pace.edu/cases/090402a3.html; Trib. Forlì (Italy), 16 February 2009, available in English at http://cisgw3.law.pace.edu/cases/090216i3.html; Foreign Trade Court of Arbitration attached to the Serbian Chamber of Commerce, Arbitral Award of 28 January 2009, available in

excluded there must be clear indications that the parties really wanted such an exclusion;[10] that is to say, there must be a real—as opposed to theoretical, fictitious or hypothetical—agreement of parties.

This is not a mere theoretical problem, as evidenced by the variety of ways to implicitly exclude the CISG. A typical (and rather important) way of implicitly excluding the CISG is by way of the parties' choice of the applicable law. There is no doubt that such a choice must be considered as being an effective exclusion of the CISG, at least where the applicable law chosen by the parties is the law of a non–Contracting State.[11]

The choice of the law of a Contracting State poses greater problems. One of these problems relates to whether the CISG is applicable when the parties agree upon a national law, such as French, Swiss or

---

English at http://cisgw3.law.pace.edu/cases/090128sb.html; Polimeles Protodikio Athinon (Greece), docket No. 4505/2009 (no date indicated), available in English at http://cisgw3.law.pace. edu/cases/094505gr.html#ii2; Trib. Forlì (Italy), 11 December 2008, available in English at http://cisgw3.law.pace.edu/cases /081211i3.html.

[10]   See Supreme Court of France, 3 November 2009, available in English at http://cisgw3.law.pace.edu/cases/091103f1 .html; Supreme Court of Austria, 4 July 2007, available in English at http://cisgw3.law.pace.edu/cases/070704a3.html; U.S. Court of Appeals [5th Cir.], 11 June 2003 (*BP Oil International v. Empresa Estatal Petroleos de Ecuador*), available at http://cisgw3. law.pace.edu/cases/030611u1.html.

[11]   See, e.g., OLG Linz (Austria), 23 January 2006, available in English at http://cisgw3.law.pace.edu/cases/060123a3.html; Trib. Padova (Italy), 11 January 2005, available in English at http://cisgw3.law.pace.edu/cases/050111i3.html.

Italian law, as the law applicable to their contract. In these authors' opinion, the indication of the law of a Contracting State (or that of a State within a Federal State)[12] does not *per se* exclude the CISG's application.[13] Of course, when the purely domestic law of a Contracting State is chosen as the law applicable, the CISG will not apply.[14] Thus, where the parties choose to apply "the domestic German law"[15] or "the Swiss Law of Obligations"[16] to their contract, the CISG is implicitly excluded, as it is in

---

[12]   *See* U.S. District Court [Minn.], 31 January 2007 (*Travelers Property Casualty Company of America et al. v. Saint–Gobain Technical Fabrics Canada Limited*), available at http://cisgw3.law.pace.edu/cases/070131u1.html; U.S. District Court [M.D. Pennsylvania], 16 August 2005 (*American Mint LLC v. GOSoftware, Inc.*), available at http://cisgw3.law.pace.edu/cases/050816u1.html.

[13]   *See* Supreme Court, 2 April 2009, available in English at http://cisgw3.law.pace.edu/cases/090402a3.html; Polimeles Protodikio Athinon (Greece), docket n. 4505/2009 (no date indicated), available in English at http://cisgw3.law.pace.edu/cases/094505gr.html#ii2; U.S. District Court [E.D. Mich.], 28 September 2007 (*Easom Automation Systems, Inc. v. Thyssenkrupp Fabco, Corp.*), available at http://cisgw3.law.pace.edu/cases/070928u1.html; U.S. District Court [Minn.], 31 January 2007 (*Travelers Property Casualty Company of America et al. v. Saint–Gobain Technical Fabrics Canada Limited*), available at http://cisgw3.law.pace.edu/cases/070131u1.html.

[14]   *See* U.S. District Court [S.D.N.Y.], 29 May 2009 (*Doolim Corp. v. R Doll, LLC, et al.*), available at http://cisgw3.law.pace.edu/cases/090529u1.html; Supreme Court of Austria, 4 July 2007, available in English at http://cisgw3.law.pace.edu/cases/070704a3.html.

[15]   OLG Hamburg (Germany), 25 January 2008, available in English at http://cisgw3.law.pace.edu/cases/080125g1.html.

[16]   *See* AG Basel–Stadt (Switzerland), 22 August 2003, available in English at http://cisgw3.law.pace.edu/cases/030822s1.html.

those cases where the parties' choose to apply "the law of a contracting state insofar as it differs from the law of the national law of another Contracting State."[17]

The choice of the law of a State—whether Contracting or not—does not constitute the sole way to implicitly exclude the CISG's application. Indeed, in certain situations, the use of standard contract forms can also lead to the exclusion of the CISG's application, provided that these forms become part of the contract, and that (a) their content is so profoundly influenced by the rules and the concepts of a specific legal system that their use is incompatible with the CISG and implicitly manifests the parties' intention to have the contract governed by that legal system and (b) their use tends at the same time to exclude the application of the CISG as a whole. Where, on the contrary, standard contract forms are intended to merely regulate specific issues in contrast with the CISG, one must presume that only a derogation of some of the CISG provisions is intended.[18] Similarly, the reference in the contract to INCOTERMS does not exclude the CISG.[19]

---

[17]   See Supreme Court of Austria, 2 April 2009, available in English at http://cisgw3.law.pace.edu/cases/090402a3.html.

[18]   See Supreme Court of Germany, 4 December 1996, available in English at http://cisgw3.law.pace.edu/cases/961204g1.html.

[19]   See Supreme Court of Austria, 22 October 2001, available in English at http://cisgw3.law.pace.edu/cases/011022a3.html.

The choice of a given forum as well can lead to the exclusion of the CISG's application,[20] provided that two requirements are met: (a) one must be able to infer from the parties' choice their clear intention to have the domestic law of the State where the forum or arbitral tribunal is located govern their contract; and (b) the forum must not be located in a Contracting State. When these requirements are not met, the CISG applies.[21]

Quid iuris where the parties argue a case on the sole basis of a domestic law despite the fact that all of the CISG's criteria of applicability are met?

In these authors' opinion, the mere fact that the parties argue on the sole basis of a domestic law does not *per se* lead to the exclusion of the CISG. This is the view also held by most—albeit not all[22]— courts.[23] In this line of cases the CISG will be implicitly excluded if the parties are aware of the

---

[20]   *See* OLG Stuttgart (Germany), 31 March 2008, available in English at http://cisgw3.law.pace.edu/cases/080331g1.html; OLG Linz (Austria), 23 January 2006, available in English at http://cisgw3.law.pace.edu/cases/060123a3.html.

[21]   *See* Arbitral Tribunal of the Hamburg Chamber of Commerce, Arbitral Award of 29 December 1998, available in English at http://cisgw3.law.pace.edu/cases/981229g1.html.

[22]   *See* ICC Court of Arbitration, Arbitral Award n. 8453, available at http://www.unilex.info/case.cfm?pid=1&do=case&id=459&step=FullText.

[23]   *See* Trib. Padova (Italy), 25 February 2004, available in English at http://cisgw3.law.pace.edu/cisg/wais/db/cases2/040225 i3.html; LG Saarbrücken (Germany), 2 July 2002, available in English at http://cisgw3.law.pace.edu/cisg/wais/db/cases2/020702 g1.html; OLG Rostock (Germany), 10 October 2001, available in English at http://cisgw3.law.pace.edu/cisg/wais/db/cases2/011010 g1.html.

CISG's applicability,[24] or if the intent to exclude the CISG can otherwise be inferred with certainty. If the parties are not aware of the CISG's applicability and argue on the basis of a domestic law merely because they believe that this law is applicable, the judges will nevertheless have to apply the CISG. One Italian court stated this very clearly:

> The fact that during the preliminary legal proceedings in this case the parties based their arguments exclusively on Italian domestic law without any references to the CISG cannot be considered an implicit manifestation of an intent to exclude application of the Convention [. . .]. Reference in a party's brief to the non–uniform national law of a Contracting State—even though it is theoretically some evidence of an intent to choose the national law of that State—does not imply the automatic exclusion of the CISG. One has to assume that the parties wanted to exclude the application of the Convention only if it appears in an unequivocal way that they recognized its applicability and they nevertheless insisted on referring only to national, non–uniform law. In the present case, it does not appear from the parties' arguments that they realized that the CISG was the applicable law [. . .]; we cannot, therefore, conclude that they implicitly wanted to exclude

---

[24]   *See* OLG Linz (Austria), 23 January 2006, available in English at http://cisgw3.law.pace.edu/cases/060123a3.html.

the application of the Convention by choosing to refer exclusively to national Italian law.[25]

As mentioned earlier, the CISG's derogation poses problems that are partially different from those arising from the CISG's exclusion. In part, these differences relate to the limits to the parties' power to derogate from the CISG. Where, for instance, at least one of the parties to the contract governed by the CISG has its place of business in a State that has declared a reservation under Article 96 CISG, the parties may not derogate from or vary the effect of Article 12, on writing requirements. In those cases, according to Article 12, any provision that allows a contract of sale or its modification or termination by agreement or any offer, acceptance or other indication of intention to be made in any form other than in writing does not *per se* apply. This means, in other words, that in those instances, Article 12 leads to the principle of freedom from writing requirements set forth in Article 11 CISG not being applicable *per se*. What consequences this has on the applicable writing requirements is subject to dispute. According to one court, the sole fact that one party has its place of business in a State that declared an Article 96 reservation does not necessarily mean that the writing requirements of that State apply.[26] This view is to be preferred

---

[25]   Trib. Vigevano (Italy), 12 July 2000, available in English at http://cisgw3.law.pace.edu/cases/000712i3.html.

[26]   *See* RB Rotterdam (The Netherlands), 12 July 2001, available in English at http://cisgw3.law.pace.edu/cases/010712 n1.html.

over the alternative: that where one party has its relevant place of business in a State that declared an Article 96 reservation, the contract must necessarily be concluded or evidenced or modified in writing. Pursuant to the view advocated here, the law to be applied (whether a writing requirement must be met) will depend on the law to which the rules of private international of the forum lead. Thus, where the private international law of the forum leads to the law of a Contracting State that has declared an Article 96 reservation, that State's writing requirements will have to be applied. Where, however, the rules of private international law lead to the law of a Contracting State that has not declared an Article 96 reservation, the contract will not need to meet any writing requirement, a view also held in case law.[27]

It should be noted that although the Convention does not expressly mention it, Article 12 CISG is not the only provision that parties are not allowed to derogate from. In effect, the public international law provisions (*i.e.* Articles 80–101) cannot be derogated from either.[28] This is due to the fact that those provisions are addressed to Contracting States rather than private parties. Moreover, in a 2005 decision, the Tribunale di Padova not only confirmed that the parties cannot exclude the

---

[27]   *Id.*; Supreme Court of the Netherlands, 7 November 1997, available at http://www.unilex.info/case.cfm?pid=1&do=case&id=333&step=FullText.

[28]   *See* Trib. Padova (Italy), 11 January 2005, available in English at http://cisgw3.law.pace.edu/cases/050111i3.html.

CISG's final provisions, but also held that the parties cannot derogate from Article 28 either.[29] This view is correct, as Article 28 is not directed to the parties but rather to the courts of Contracting States.

It is worth pointing out that the distinction between exclusion and derogation is also important insofar as the rules to be applied in case of exclusion of the CISG are different from those to be applied in case the parties derogate from (or modify the effect of) the provisions of the CISG. Where the parties modify the effect of provisions of the CISG, the applicable rules will not have to be determined by means of a private international law approach, but rather by looking at the contract itself. On the contrary, where the parties exclude the CISG, the courts will have to resort to their rules of private international law to determine the applicable law (which, whenever it is the law of a contracting State, leads to the application of that State's domestic sales law rather than the CISG). Thus, where the parties do not choose the applicable law when excluding the CISG, the courts will have to determine the applicable law by means of objective connecting factors. Where, on the other hand, the parties choose the applicable law, courts will apply the law chosen, provided that the forum's private international law rules allow for a choice of law by the parties. Although most countries do, not all countries acknowledge a choice of law by the parties. This, of course, may be one of the reasons

---

[29] *Id.*

for opting for arbitral proceedings rather that proceedings in a given State court, as in arbitration choice of law is not only acknowledged generally, but to a much wider extent than in State court proceedings.

From what has been said in respect of Article 6, it becomes evident how many sources of law other the CISG can be relevant to solve disputes relating to international contracts for the sale of goods to which the CISG could be applicable.

4. CISG AND USAGE

Article 6 is not the only CISG provision that opens the door for other sources of law to apply to contracts for the international sale of goods subject to the CISG. Article 9 CISG is also relevant in this respect, as this dispositive provision expressly allows for sources other than the CISG to become applicable, namely rules "more highly tailored to the requirements of a particular industry"[30], when stating both that "[t]he parties are bound by any usage to which they have agreed and by any practices which they have established between themselves" (Article 9(1)) and that "[t]he parties are considered, unless otherwise agreed, to have impliedly made applicable to their contract or its formation a usage of which the parties knew or ought to have known and which in international trade is widely known to, and regularly observed by,

---

[30] Clayton Gillette, *Harmony and Stasis in Trade Usage for International Sales*, 39 VIRGINIA JOURNAL OF INTERNATIONAL LAW 707, 708 (1999).

parties to contracts of the type involved in the particular trade concerned" (Article 9(2)).

As far as Article 9(1) is concerned, it refers to two different sources, namely usages and practices established between the parties. The term "usage" is not defined in the CISG. This does not warrant recourse to domestic notions or definitions, however, as this would run counter to the *ratio conventionis*. As is the case with most of the terms used in the CISG, the concept of usage must in fact be autonomously interpreted—without resorting to particular domestic concepts or perceptions. Accordingly, usages within the meaning of the CISG include all those actions or modes of behavior (including omissions) that are generally and regularly observed in the course of business transactions in a specific area of trade or at a certain trade centre. It is not necessary, however, that the relevant commercial circles believe that the usages are binding.

In contrast to usages to which the parties are bound under Article 9(2), it is not necessary that usages under Article 9(1) be international. Local, regional or national usages may also be relevant under this provision. Furthermore, Article 9(1), as opposed to Article 9(2), does not require that the usages be "widely known". The fact that every rule agreed to by the parties supersedes those of the CISG has induced some authors to contend that an exact delimitation of usages is not relevant as far as Article 9(1) is concerned—although this is not true in respect of Article 9(2).

The issue of whether the usages agreed to by the parties are valid is not an issue governed by the CISG and, therefore, will depend on the national law applicable under rules of private international law of the forum—or, in the case of usages that are common to certain trade centres, such as seaports or stock exchanges, the law applicable in that location. If it is determined that these usages are applicable (and effectively agreed upon), they trump the provisions of the CISG. The same can be said for the "practices" which the parties have established between themselves, to which Article 9(1) CISG also refers, without, however, defining them. "Practices" within the meaning of Article 9(1) CISG are manners of conduct that are regularly observed by or have been established between the parties to a specific transaction, whichever the case may be, such as the prompt delivery of spare parts for sold machinery.[31] The individual practice between the parties, rather than the general practice, is thus decisive. This necessarily presupposes a business relationship characterized by a certain duration as well as the conclusion of a number of contracts. This is why it is no surprise that one court stated, for instance, that the conclusion of merely two contracts does not create such practices,[32] nor can such

---

[31]   ICC Court of Arbitration, Arbitral Award n. 8453, available at http://cisgw3.law.pace.edu/cases/978611i1.html.

[32]   *See* ZG Kanton Basel–Stadt (Switzerland), 3 December 1997, available in English at http://cisgw3.law.pace.edu/cases/971203s2.html; see also AG Duisburg (Germany), 13 April 2000, available in English at http://cisgw3.law.pace.edu/cases/000413 g1.html.

practices arise from one single delivery of goods between the parties.[33] Therefore, it seems surprising that the Supreme Court of Austria ruled it perfectly conceivable that a party's perceptions from preliminary discussions could be relevant as "practices" within the meaning of Article 9(1), even at the outset of the business relationship.[34]

The fact that parties are bound by those practices that have originated between them in the course of extended business relations is in keeping with the general principles of good faith underlying the CISG as well as the prohibition of *venire contra factum proprium*. Accordingly, for instance, a party cannot contend that the contract makes no specific requirements in respect of notification periods (with which the complaining party has not complied), if existing practices indicate the opposite. The parties may, of course, dispense with these practices by agreement.[35]

As mentioned, when an established practice exists between the parties, it trumps the provisions of the CISG; when, on the other hand, this practice contrasts with a usage agreed upon by the parties, it is that usage that prevails.

The usage agreed upon, referred to in Article 9(1), is not to be confused with the usage referred to in

---

[33]   *See* LG Zwickau (Germany), 19 March 1999, available in English at http://cisgw3.law.pace.edu/cases/990319g1.html.

[34]   Supreme Court of Austria, 6 February 1996, available in English at http://cisgw3.law.pace.edu/cases/960206a3.html.

[35]   *See* ICC Court of Arbitration, Arbitral Award n. 8817, available at http://cisgw3.law.pace.edu/cases/978817i1.html.

Article 9(2), according to which, absent any agreement to the contrary, the parties are bound by specific international trade usages that fulfil certain requirements. As a compromise to satisfy the concerns of several countries that feared the prevalence of usages unknown to them or, as the case may be, usages in the development of which they did not take part, the scope of application of the fictional agreement between the parties under Article 9(2), to be bound by certain usages, has been very narrowly circumscribed. These usages must be widely known and regularly observed in the particular international trade concerned. Moreover, the parties must have either known or ought to have known about the usages. If the aforementioned prerequisites are met, the usages are applicable[36] and take precedence over the provisions of the CISG.[37] However, in the event of a contradiction between, on the one hand, the usages agreed upon by the parties or the practices established between them and, on the other hand, the usages applicable pursuant to Article 9(2), the former take precedence. The same also applies to the relationship between the individual contract clauses and usages that are applicable via Article 9(2); the precedence of contractual clauses can clearly be derived from the

---

[36] *Contra* U.S. District Court [S.D.N.Y.], 10 May 2002 (*Geneva Pharmaceuticals v. Barr Laboratories*), available at http://cisgw3.law.pace.edu/cases/020510u1.html, according to which usages always apply, provided that the parties have not expressly excluded their application.

[37] *See* Supreme Court of Austria, 21 March 2000, available in English at http://cisgw3.law.pace.edu/cases/000321a3.html.

introductory language of Article 9(2). Should some of the usages applicable pursuant to Article 9(2) contradict each other, it may be assumed that the usages most closely related to the contractual relationship take precedence.

For usages to bind the parties pursuant to Article 9(2) they must be "widely known" in the relevant branch of international trade. This does not mean that all persons who are active in that particular branch of trade must know those usages, neither is it necessary that the usages be known throughout the world.

It is worth pointing out that the foregoing requirement does not preclude the application of usages which may be of mere local relevance, or valid only in certain places, such as usages at trade exhibitions or seaports. For such local usages to be valid under Article 9(2), however, it is necessary that international trade occur at these places and that the usages comply with all the requirements listed with regard to the degree of recognition and regular observance. In respect of this latter requirement, some commentators have suggested that it constitutes a "superfluous" prerequisite, since all usages that are widely known would be regularly observed. In these authors' opinion, this point of view cannot be shared, since it is most certainly possible that there are particular usages in certain countries that are also known in other countries, but not regularly observed there.

Pursuant to Article 9(2), the parties involved in a specific business transaction are bound only by usages if these usages are known to them at the time of conclusion of the contract, or if they ought to have been familiar with these usages. This requirement is often, but—and this is the point— not always met when usages are "widely known"; therefore, this requirement is not dispensable or redundant, as some commentators have suggested. One could in fact conceive of cases where usages were not known to the parties or where they ought not necessarily to have known about the usages, even though the usages are indeed "widely known".

In light of the foregoing, one can answer the question of whether INCOTERMS are binding upon the parties as usages by stating that they are, as they certainly meet the definition of "usage" under Article 9(1). Thus, if the parties agreed to their application, they are bound by them. INCOTERMS can, however, also be binding upon the parties under Article 9(2), provided that the prerequisites listed therein are met.

What has been said in respect of Article 9 CISG clearly shows that the rules governing an international contract for the sale of goods are not necessarily only those laid down by the CISG, even where the CISG itself applies. But it also shows that it is important to determine on what grounds one rule applies, as that rule's position in the hierarchy of sources of law for international sales contracts depends on those grounds.

5.   SUPRANATIONAL SETS OF RULES

It has already been pointed out that the CISG provides a set of rules for international sales of goods, which is not exhaustive, in that there are issues that the CISG intentionally does not govern (as those indicated in Articles 4 and 5 CISG) and other matters that are governed by the Convention, but—to use the language of Article 7(2)—"are not expressly settled in it". Therefore, it cannot surprise that the CISG is applied to contracts for the sale of goods concurrently with other sources of law. These sources include primarily domestic laws, which may apply to international contracts for the sale of goods by virtue of the private international law rules of the forum. Domestic laws may apply concurrently with the CISG, or they may constitute the sole sources of law where the CISG is not *per se* applicable, or where the parties have excluded its application pursuant to Article 6. However, other sources of rules may also apply concurrently with, or *in lieu* of the CISG, including sets of rules produced, not unlike the CISG itself, at the supranational level. In some instances, some other supranational uniform law conventions may apply concurrently with the CISG. This is the case, to give one example, when the sale of goods involves carriage and the contract of carriage is governed by one of the many supranational conventions in the field of transport law. It is also the case, to give another example, when the parties to the contract for the sale of goods create a security interest in the goods governed by the 2001 UNIDROIT Convention on Security Interest in Mobile Equipment[38]. Another relevant example relates to the frequent concurrent applicability of the CISG and the Convention on the Limitation Period in the International Sale of Goods[39]. In these and similar cases the rules of the CISG and those of the other supranational conventions apply concurrently to one and the same transaction, although in most cases it is rather clear how to make a distinction between issues governed by the CISG and issues governed by the concurrently applicable convention. In other words, although the need for coordination between the different instruments must be affirmed, it is a rather unlikely occurrence that there be an overlap and a conflict between the CISG and other supranational conventions. Still, if the conflict occurs, the solution is to be found in Article 90 CISG, which precludes the application of the CISG whenever another convention exists, "which has already been or may be entered into and which contains provisions concerning the matters governed by" the CISG.

The rule on conflict of conventions found in Article 90, however, only applies when another

---

[38]   *See* UNIDROIT Convention on International Interests in Mobile Equipment, signed in Cape Town on 16 November 2001, available with the Protocols applicable to different specific matters at http://unidroit.org/instruments/security–interests/cape –town–convention.

[39]   *See* the Convention on the Limitation Period in the International Sale of Goods, signed in New York on 14 June 1974 and currently in force in 29 States, available at http://www.uncit ral.org/uncitral/en/uncitral_texts/sale_goods/1974convention_lim itation_period.html.

"international agreement" is at stake. This means that the rule at hand only applies to instruments that have been adopted by States in the form of an international treaty or a convention. Conversely, the rule on conflict of conventions does not apply to the relationship between the CISG and other supranational sets of rules set forth in instruments that do not qualify as "international agreements". The foregoing does not mean that other supranational sets of rules cannot apply concurrently with, or *in lieu* of, the CISG. It merely means that the grounds for application of such other supranational sets of rules should be found elsewhere, and in particular in the binding force of trade usages under Article 9 CISG,[40] or in the parties' freedom of contract under Article 6 CISG.

With respect to the role of party autonomy, it is worth pointing out that there are several supranational sets of rules that may be incorporated into the parties' agreement by reference. The purpose served by these sets of rules is very important, in that they make it possible for the parties to reduce transaction costs by incorporating into the contract terms that are not unilaterally drafted by only one party, as is the case with the incorporation of one party's standard contract terms. These supranational sets of rules come in different formats, including sets of international trade terms, collections of principles, or, to some extent, legal guides, model contracts or model clauses, or other similar instruments.

---

[40]   *See supra* Section 4 of this Chapter.

Among the most relevant sets of supranational set of trade terms dealing with international contracts for the sale of goods are the INCOTERMS of the International Chamber of Commerce (I.C.C.), whose latest publication was released in 2010.[41] The introduction to the publication explains that "[t]he INCOTERMS rules explain a set of three–letter trade terms reflecting business–to–business practice in contracts for the sale of goods. The INCOTERMS rules describe mainly the tasks, costs and risks involved in the delivery of goods from sellers to buyer." Therefore, parties to a contract of sale willing to incorporate the rules referred to by a specific INCOTERM may incorporate those rules simply by including in their agreement the three–letter acronym that indicates the chosen INCOTERM (*e.g.*, "CIF" for "Cost, Insurance and Freight Paid To" the named port of destination).

Among the supranational sets of principles and rules that the parties may incorporate into their agreement by reference are the UNIDROIT Principles of International Commercial Contracts, the third edition of which was published in 2010.[42] The UNIDROIT Principles set forth principles and rules dealing with many aspects of international commercial contracts including, but not limited to, international contracts of sale. They purport to represent a restatement of international commercial

---

[41]   International Chamber of Commerce, *INCOTERMS® 2010*, ICC Publication No. 715E (2010).

[42]   *See* UNIDROIT Principles of International Commercial Contracts, available at www.unilex.info.

usages in this field. However, as the UNIDROIT Principles, unlike international conventions, are not intended to be adopted at national level, the issue of the legal grounds of their applicability is somewhat controversial. In fact, in light of the primacy of parties' freedom of contract, it is undisputed that they can be applied if the parties choose to incorporate the Principles into their agreement.[43] However, the Preamble to the Principles suggests that they may also be applied on other occasions, including the instances when the parties have agreed that their contract "be governed by general principles of law, the *lex mercatoria* and the like". Moreover, the Preamble posits that the Principles may be used "to interpret or supplement international uniform law instruments,"[44] a statement that cannot be fully shared in light of the gap–filling rule laid out in Article 7(2) CISG.[45]

The adoption of the UNIDROIT Principles at the international level has been paralleled by a similar production of principles and rules applicable to international contracts at the European level. Several academic–driven projects have surfaced in Europe over the last decades, including the Principles of European Contract Law ("PECL"), published by the "Lando Commission." The goal of

---

[43]   *Accord*, Trib. Padova (Italy), 11 January 2005, available in English at http://cisgw3.law.pace.edu/cases/050111i3.html.

[44]   For a court decision applying the UNIDROIT Principles to interpret or supplement the CISG, see Supreme Court of Belgium, 19 June 2009, available in English at http://cisgw3. law. pace.edu/cases/090619b1.html.

[45]   *See supra* Chapter 2, Section 4.

the PECL was to serve at the European level a purpose similar to that served by the UNIDROIT Principles at the global level. In short, the PECL were intended to promote some degree of harmonization of the law of contract in Europe. However, at the European level, the endeavour has not been very successful, notwithstanding the active role taken by some EU institutions,[46] and the extensive work carried out by several study groups on projects aiming at the harmonization of European contract law. At last, on October 11th, 2011, a Proposal was issued for a Regulation providing an optional instrument setting forth a Common European Sales Law ("CESL"),[47] supposed to apply only to supranational, intra–European contracts for the sale of goods, to the extent that the parties chose the CESL as the set of rules governing the contract. Although at present it is still unclear how likely it is that the Proposal will be adopted, it is nonetheless possible to report that a large debate has taken place, on the occasion of which the CESL has been heavily criticized. But criticism has been levelled more against the sphere and the optional nature of the instrument than against the CESL's substantive provisions, the quality of which is not seriously disputed. It should be pointed out, however, that if adopted, the Proposal would cause

---

[46]   *See, e.g.,* EU COMMISSION, *Green Paper on policy option for progress towards a European Contract Law for Consumers and Businesses,* COM[2010] 348 final.

[47]   *See* Proposal for a Regulation of the European Parliament and of the Council on a Common European Sales Law, 11 October 2011, COM[2010] 635 final.

serious difficulties of coordination between the CESL and the CISG.

Among the other sets of supranational rules possibly applicable to international contracts of sale are legal guides. Legal guides are not specifically intended to provide rules directly applicable to contracts, but rather to provide informative tools to better understand how a specific transaction works. At times, however, the understanding of a specific transaction as provided by a legal guide can in itself have an impact on the conduct of the parties. Also, legal guides may contain recommendations or guidelines, which may be referred to by the parties as rules of conduct to abide by. Legal guides worth mentioning here by way of example include the Guide to International Master Franchise Arrangements,[48] and the Legal Guide on Drawing Up International Contracts for the Construction of Industrial Work.[49]

A purpose similar to that of other supranational sets of rules is also served by model contracts and model clauses. The similarity lies in that model contract and model clauses, too, are intended to reduce transaction costs by providing pre–drafted agreements or individual clauses, which the parties

---

[48]   *See* UNIDROIT, Guide to International Master Franchise Arrangements (2nd ed., 2007), available at http://www.unidroit.org/instruments/franchising/guide/second–edition–2007.

[49]   United Nations Legal Guide on Drawing Up International Contracts for the Construction of Industrial Work, adopted by UNCITRAL on 14 August 1987, available at http://www.uncitral.org/uncitral/en/uncitral_texts/procurement_infrastructure/1988Guide.html.

may simply "cut and paste" into their agreement. Several institutions and associations, including in particular many sector–specific ones, offer model contracts to the parties involved in the business sector in which the drafting institution or association operate. A more general (*i.e.*, non–sector–specific) model for international contracts of sale has been drafted by the International Chamber of Commerce. Moreover, that institution has also drafted some relevant model clauses, which parties to a contract of sale can include into their agreement by reference, or by reproducing the model clause in the agreement. These clauses include the ICC Force Majeure Clause 2003 and the ICC Hardship Clause 2003.[50] Another example— albeit not a very successful one in practice—of model clauses drafted by an international institution and available to parties to an international contract of sale is the UNCITRAL Model Uniform Rules on Contract Clauses for an Agreed Sum Due upon Failure of Performance. These Uniform Rules were aimed at providing uniform legal solutions dealing with the controversial issue of liquidated damages and penalty clauses in international commercial contracts.

---

[50]   *See* Force Majeure Clause 2003 and Hardship Clause 2003, ICC Publication No. 650 (2003).

CHAPTER 3

INTERNATIONAL SPHERE OF APPLICATION AND APPLICABILITY *STRICTO SENSU*

1. THE CISG'S INTERNATIONAL SPHERE OF APPLICATION

As mentioned in the earlier Chapter, the CISG does not have to be the only set of rules to apply to a contract for the international sale of goods. Where it is applicable, however, it constitutes the default set of rules, which is why it is necessary to examine what requirements have to be met for the CISG to apply.

One such requirement is an internationality requirement. This is in line with the situation under the CISG's predecessors, the 1964 Hague Conventions relating to a Uniform Law on the International Sale of Goods (hereinafter: ULIS) and a Uniform Law on the Formation of Contracts for the International Sale of Goods (hereinafter: ULF) respectively. In effect, at first sight, the most important common feature of the various instruments appears to be their international sphere of application, since they all apply solely to sales contracts deemed to be "international", a choice which has been criticized by some authors on the grounds that nowadays the differences which one time existed between transnational sales and sales of the same goods within one legal system have no reason to exist. Despite that apparent commonality, the spheres of application of the aforementioned instruments are, however, fundamentally different. This is due, among others, to the very different criteria adopted by these Conventions in order to determine the internationality of a sales contract as well as to their relation with further applicability requirements. Indeed, under both the ULIS and the ULF only those sales contracts are international that present two elements of internationality: a subjective *and* an objective one. This means that under the ULIS and the ULF, unlike under the CISG, the criteria employed to determine the internationality of a contract do not only relate to the parties (subjective internationality requirement), but they also relate to specific aspects of the contractual relationship (objective internationality requirement). As far as the first element is concerned, the 1964 Hague Conventions required the parties' place of business (or, absent a place of business, their residence) to be located in different States (citizenship is irrelevant for the determination of the internationality). As for the second element, the objective one, Article 1(1) ULIS requires that either the acts constituting offer and acceptance were effected in different States, or that the goods were sold during international transport or were to be transported internationally, or that the act of offer and acceptance were made in a State other than the State of the place of delivery.

Whenever the two internationality requirements, the subjective and the objective one, were met, the

Hague Conventions were applicable. Unlike the CISG, the Hague Conventions did not require a specific link with a Contracting State's territory or its law to be applicable. This approach generates much criticism as it led to the so–called *erga omnes* approach. According to this approach, the provisions of the 1964 Hague Conventions had to be applied whenever the contract was considered international according to the aforementioned definition (requiring that the contract be international both from a subjective and an objective point of view), and apparently even in those cases where the contractual relationships developed outside the territory of Contracting States, and independently of the application of private international law rules (resort to which Article 2 ULIS expressly excluded for the purpose of determining the applicability of the Conventions). To most Contracting States, this approach, also defined as "universal" or "universalist", appeared to be excessive. This is why all the Contracting States—except Israel—declared reservations with the intention of limiting the applicability of the 1964 Hague Conventions.

The aforementioned tendency to restrict the 1964 Hague Conventions' applicability by declaring reservations along with the aforementioned criticism undoubtedly influenced the drafters of the CISG who decided not only against the adoption of the objective criterion of internationality but also— and more importantly—against the *erga omnes* approach. The rejection of the *erga omnes* approach has led to a clear distinction between the CISG's internationality requirements and its applicability requirements *stricto sensu*, a distinction unknown under the 1964 Hague Conventions.

As regards the CISG's internationality requirement—the burden of proof relating to the existence of which lies, according to both commentators and courts,[1] on the party asserting the applicability of the CISG—the sole criterion on the basis of which to determine the internationality of a sales contract corresponds to the subjective internationality requirement of the 1964 Hague Conventions. Thus, under the CISG, the internationality of a contract depends solely on the parties having their places of business (or habitual residences) in different States.[2]

Still, due to the CISG's drafters' rejection of the *erga omnes approach*, under the CISG, the internationality of a sales contract alone does not lead to the CISG's applicability.[3] Furthermore, it cannot be argued—as some commentators do—that the different States in which the parties must have their places of business in order for a sales contract to be international under CISG must also be

---

[1]   *See* Trib. Vigevano (Italy), 12 July 2000, available in English at http://cisgw3.law.pace.edu/cases/000712i3.html.

[2]   *See* Polimeles Protodikio Athinon (Greece), docket No. 4505/2009 (no date indicated), available in English at http://cisgw3.law.pace.edu/cases/094505gr.html#ii2; Trib. Padova (Italy), 25 February 2004, available in English at http://cisgw3. law.pace.edu/cases/040225i3.html.

[3]   *See, e.g.*, Trib. Rimini (Italy), 26 November 2002, available in English at http://cisgw3.law.pace.edu/cases/021126 i3.html.

Contracting States,[4] this being a criterion of applicability *stricto sensu* of the CISG, rather than one of internationality, as will be pointed out in more detail later.[5]

From what has been said thus far in respect to the CISG's criterion of internationality, it also follows that where the "subjective international prerequisite" is missing, for example, where the parties have their relevant places of business (or habitual residence) in different legal units of one and the same Contracting State, the CISG will not be applicable *per se*, even if the contract's performance involves different States. This view was also adopted by a German court in 1991:[6] the court refused to apply the CISG to a case where a German buyer had acquired tickets from a German seller for the 1990 Soccer World Cup final to be handed over in Rome, on the grounds that the contract was not an international one.

On the other hand, the CISG can be applicable even in cases where the goods do not cross any border and where the parties have the same citizenship,[7] as long as the contract can be

---

[4] *See* LG Hamburg (Germany), 26 September 1990, available in English at http://cisgw3.law.pace.edu/cases/900926 g1.html.

[5] *See infra* this Chapter, Sections 3 and 4.

[6] Compare OLG Köln (Germany), 27 November 1991, available at http://cisgw3.law.pace.edu/cases/911127g1.html.

[7] For court decisions referring to the fact that the citizenship of the parties does not have any impact on the internationality of the contract, *see* OLG Graz (Austria), 29 July 2004, available in English at http://cisgw3.law.pace.edu/cases/

considered, from a subjective point of view, an international one—that is to say, as long as the parties have—at the time of conclusion of the contract—their places of business in different States.

2. THE "PLACE OF BUSINESS" UNDER CISG

In light of the fact that by virtue of Article 1(1) CISG the internationality of a sales contract governed by the CISG (and, thus, the applicability of the CISG itself) depends solely on the location of the parties' places of business—at the time of the conclusion of the contract[8]—the importance of the definition of "place of business" becomes evident, which is why the concept of "place of business" will be examined in greater detail below.

A closer look at this concept is necessary, because—unfortunately—the concept is not defined in the CISG, as it was not defined in the CISG's predecessors.[9] This is apparently due to the lack of a uniform definition acceptable to all the delegates to

---

040729a3.html; Supreme Court of Germany, 31 October 2001, available in English at http://cisgw3.law.pace.edu/cases/011031g1 .html.

[8] *See* Trib. Forlì (Italy), 11 December 2008, available in English at http://cisgw3.law.pace.edu/cases/081211i3.html; Trib. Padova (Italy), 11 January 2005, available at http://www.unilex. info/case.cfm?pid=1&do=case&id=1005&step=FullText.

[9] *See* Trib. Cantonal du Valais (Switzerland), 23 May 2006, available in English at http://cisgw3.law.pace.edu/cases/060523 s1.html.

the Vienna Diplomatic Conference, where the most disparate definitions were suggested. The Argentinian and Belgian delegates, for example, suggested that the place of business should be defined as a stable place where the entire (or part of) the contract is performed and which has an autonomous power to conduct the bargaining and to conclude the contract. In contrast, the Norwegian delegation, even though it agreed upon the stability requirement, stated that there could be a place of business even without power to conclude the contract, as long as there was power to bargain.

Although no agreement was reached on the occasion of the Vienna Diplomatic Conference on a definition of "place of business", in these authors' view, it is possible to come up with an autonomous definition of the said concept, although one should never forget that whether a "place of business" exists is an issue to be decided on a case–by–case basis rather than in an abstract way.

Still, as a general rule it can be asserted that there is a place of business only where there is a stable business organization, or as stated by the Supreme Court of Germany (albeit in relation to the 1964 Hague Conventions), where "the center of the business activity directed to the participation in commerce" is located,[10] that links the contracting

---

[10] Supreme Court of Germany, 2 June 1982, NEUE JURISTISCHE WOCHENSCHRIFT 2730, 2731 (1982).

party to the State where the business is actually[11] conducted, provided that that party has autonomous or independent power.[12]

Given what has just been said, it should come as no surprise that commentators and courts alike have defined the "place of business" under the CISG as "the place where commercial activities are carried out and that [is] characterized by a certain duration, stability as well as a certain autonomy."[13]

As regards autonomous power as an element characterizing the concept at hand, it is evidenced by the fact that an arbitral award considered a contract concluded between a Chinese seller and an Austrian buyer as being international, despite the fact that the buyer had conducted the negotiations partially through its liaison office located in China;[14] as also pointed out by a more recent Supreme Court of France decision,[15] a liaison office

---

[11]   For this requirement, *see* AG Duisburg (Germany), 13 April 2000, available in English at http://cisgw3.law.pace.edu/cases/000413g1.html.

[12]   *See* Supreme Court of Austria, 10 November 1994, available in English at http://cisgw3.law.pace.edu/cases/941110 a3.html.

[13]   OLG Hamm (Germany), 2 April 2009, available at http://www.globalsaleslaw.com/content/api/cisg/urteile/1978.pdf; Trib. Forlì (Italy), 11 December 2008, available in English at http://cisgw3.law.pace.edu/cases/081211i3.html.

[14]   *See* ICC Court of Arbitration, Arbitral Award n. 7531, available in English at http://cisgw3.law.pace.edu/cases/947531i1. html.

[15]   *See* Supreme Court of France, 4 January 1995, available in English at http://cisgw3.law.pace.edu/cases/950104f1.html.

must not be considered a "place of business", because it does not have the autonomy required.

From the other element characterizing the concept *de quo*, *i.e.*, the stability requirement, it follows that places of temporary sojourn cannot be considered "places of business". This is why one cannot consider conference centers of exhibitions or hotels or rented offices at exhibitions[16] as being "places of business" under the CISG.

Although in practice the concept of "place of business" will probably not cause too many problems, the exact determination of the relevant place of business does, at least in those cases where a party to the contract has more than one place of business.

Neither the ULIS nor the ULF answered the question of which among several places of business of one and the same party was to be considered the relevant one. This is why a dispute arose among legal scholars as to what criteria had to be used in order to solve the problem. While several commentators favored the view pursuant to which the relevant place of business was the principal place of business, others suggested that the solution had to depend on a determination of which place of business had the closest relationship with the contract.

---

[16]   *See* Trib. Cantonal du Valais (Switzerland), 23 May 2006, available in English at http://cisgw3.law.pace.edu/cases/060523s1 .html.

The dispute was finally solved in 1982 by the Supreme Court of Germany,[17] which stated that the preferred solution was the latter one and that "one must not share [. . .] the point of view according to which the decisive place of business is always the principal one."[18]

Under the CISG, this dispute does not arise at all, since the CISG expressly provides for a solution to the aforementioned issue. According to this solution, laid down in Article 10(a) CISG, the place of business relevant to the determination of the internationality of a sales contract is the one having the closest relationship with the contract.[19] The CISG has, in other words, expressly rejected the so—called "theory of the principal place of business" in favor of the "closest connection theory".[20]

However, while Article 10(a) prevents a dispute as to which theory should apply ("principal place of business theory" or "closest relationship theory"), it does not solve all of the problems. *Quid iuris* where the contract is concluded at one place of business

---

[17]   *See* Supreme Court of Germany, 2 June 1982, NEUE JURISTISCHE WOCHENSCHRIFT 2730, 2731 (1982).

[18]   *Id*.

[19]   *See* U.S. District Court [N.D. Cal.], 2 November 2005 (*McDowell Valley Vineyards, Inc. v. Sabaté USA Inc. et al.*), available at http://cisgw3.law.pace.edu/cases/051102u1.html#iii.

[20]   *Contra* U.S. District Court [E.D. Kentucky], 18 March 2008, (*Sky Cast, Inc. v. Global Direct Distribution, LLC.*), available   at   http://cisgw3.law.pace.edu/cases/080318u1.html, stating that the CISG applies to contracts between "parties whose principal places of business are in different nations if those nations are signatories to the treaty".

and has to be executed at another one? Of course, where the parties have agreed upon which place of business must be considered as being relevant, the problem will not arise, since that agreement is to be taken into account in determining the relevant place of business. Where, however, there is no agreement concerning the relevant place of business, Article 10(a) CISG creates a new problem, namely, how to determine the "closest relationship with the contract and its execution." In order to facilitate this task, Article 10(a) CISG expressly refers to some elements to be used. However, these elements have not been employed often by courts,[21] although some courts might have had reason to do so.[22]

According to Article 10 CISG, one must take into account all the (objective) circumstances known to or contemplated by the parties at any time before (or contemporaneous to) the conclusion of the contract. Consequently, one is not allowed to take into consideration the circumstances which become apparent only after the contract is concluded. At times, however, the circumstances are insufficient to unequivocally determine the relevant place of

---

[21] For a reference in case law to the provision at hand, *see* Superior Court of Massachusetts, 28 February 2005 (*Vision Systems, Inc. v. EMC Corporation*), available at http://cisgw3.law. pace.edu/cisg/wais/db/cases2/050228u1.html.

[22] In U.S. District Court [S.D.N.Y.], 14 April 1992 (*Filanto S.p.A. vs. Chilewich International Corp.*), available at http://cisg w3.law.pace.edu/cisg/wais/db/cases2/920414u1.html, the court did not address the issue of which of several places of business was the "relevant" one, although the buyer had places of business both in the United States and England.

business. Ambiguity may arise, for instance, if one place of business is more closely connected with the formation of the contract and a second place of business is more closely linked to a performance of one party's contractual obligations. In this line of cases it is here suggested that the international character of a sales contract should be determined by resorting to the places of business involved in the conclusion of the contract, since these places of business will always be known to both parties. However, where both parties know that the contract is performed at a place of business different than the one involved in the conclusion of the contract, the text of Article 10(*a*) CISG suggests that the relevant place of business is the one where the performance takes place.

However, since the parties do not always have a place of business, Article 10(*b*) CISG provides that in (such rare) cases one must resort to the parties' habitual residence in order to determine whether a sales contract is international, that is, one has to look at the real place of sojourn for a long period of time.

For the applicability of the CISG it is, however, not sufficient that the parties have their places of business in different States, *i.e.*, that the sales contract is an international one. Even though it is not required that the parties be conscious of the applicability or existence of the CISG,[23] its Article

---

[23] *Contra* U.S. District Court [S.D. Fla.] 22 November 2002 (*Impuls I.D. Internacional, S. L., Impuls I.D. Systems, Inc., and*

1(2) requires that the internationality be apparent to both parties, *i.e.*, that the contract does not appear to be a merely domestic one. In order to determine whether this prerequisite of apparent internationality of the contract exists, the following objective elements, exhaustively listed in Article 1(2) CISG itself, must be taken into account: the contract itself, and the dealings between, or the information disclosed by, the parties before or at the conclusion of the contract. Although this "apparent internationality" requirement undoubtedly limits the sphere of application of the CISG, it is important, since it protects the reliance upon the domestic setting of a sales transaction. From what has been said thus far, it follows, for instance, that the CISG is not applicable "[. . .] where the parties appeared to have their place of business in the same State but one of the parties was acting as the agent for an undisclosed foreign principal."[24]

As far as the burden of proof is concerned, it is on the party invoking the impossibility of recognizing the international character of the sales contract (and, thus, the inapplicability of the CISG).[25]

PSIAR, SA., v. Psion–Teklogix Inc.), available at http://cisgw3. law.pace.edu/cisg/wais/db/cases2/021122u1.html.

[24]   Official Records of the United Nations Conference on Contracts for the International Sale of Goods. Vienna, 10 March—11 April 1980, *supra* note 3, at 15.

[25]   *See* Trib. Vigevano (Italy), 12 July 2000, available in English at http://cisgw3.law.pace.edu/cases/000712i3.html.

3.   THE CISG'S DIRECT APPLICATION PURSUANT TO ARTICLE 1(1)(*a*)

As pointed out by both commentators and courts,[26] for the CISG to be applicable—as part of the law of the forum—[27]it is insufficient that the sales contract is an international one, unlike under the CISG's predecessors, which had adopted the "universalist" approach referred to earlier.[28] This can be derived from Article 1(1) CISG which lists two alternative applicability requirements. The existence of either one is sufficient for the CISG to be applicable, provided, of course, that all the other requirements, such as the internationality one, are met.

According to the criterion set forth in Article 1(1)(*a*), the CISG is "directly"[29] or "autonomously"[30] applicable when the parties have their places of business in different *Contracting States*, regardless

---

[26]   *See, e.g.*, Trib. Forlì (Italy), 11 December 2008, available in English at http://cisgw3.law.pace.edu/cases/081211i3.html; Trib. Padova (Italy), 25 February 2004, available in English at http://cisgw3.law.pace.edu/cases/040225i3.html.

[27]   *See* Federal Court of Australia, Australia, 28 September 2010 (*Castel Electronics Pty. Ltd. v. Toshiba Singapore Pte. Ltd.*), available at http://www.austlii.edu.au/au/cases/cth/FCA/2010/1028.html: "The Convention is not to be treated as a foreign law which requires proof as a fact".

[28]   *See supra* this Chapter, Section 1.

[29]   Supreme Court of Switzerland, 11 July 2000, available in English at http://cisgw3.law.pace.edu/cases/000711s1.html.

[30]   Trib. Vigevano (Italy), 12 July 2000, available in English at http://cisgw3.law.pace.edu/cases/000712i3.html; Supreme Court of Austria, 20 March 1997, available in English at http://cisgw3.law.pace.edu/cases/970320a3.html.

of whether the parties are aware of the fact that the States where their places of business are located are Contracting States. Thus, whenever this requirement is met and the forum is located in a Contracting State to the CISG and the parties have not excluded the CISG, the CISG is applicable, irrespective of the law applicable by virtue of the rules of private international law.[31] Where, however, the parties have their places of business in different Contracting States, but the forum is located in a non–Contracting State and its rules of private international law lead to the application of either the law of the forum or the law of a non–Contracting State, the CISG will not be applicable *per se*.

From what has just been said one can easily gather that shortly after the CISG's coming into force, when the number of Contracting States was still rather small, the aforementioned criterion of applicability *stricto sensu* rarely led to the CISG's application. Today, however, as there are eighty Contracting States already, this criterion is the one which most often leads to the CISG's application.

Unlike the criterion of indirect applicability, which will be discussed later, the criterion of "direct" applicability causes generally no problems. Problems may, however, arise in respect of whether a State is considered a Contracting State or not (as

---

[31]   *See* Supreme Court of Italy, 20 September 2004, available in English at http://cisgw3.law.pace.edu/cases/040920i3.html; Supreme Court of Austria, 10 September 1998, available at http://cisgw3.law.pace.edu/cases/980910a3.html.

is the case with Hong Kong, which, despite some views to the contrary, should not be considered a Contracting State).[32] It is commonly understood that all States can be deemed Contracting States once they have either ratified, approved, accepted or acceded to the CISG, and once a specific period of time—fixed by the CISG itself—has elapsed. However, as far as the applicability of Part II (Formation of Contracts) of the Convention is concerned, it presupposes that a State is a Contracting one before the offer is made. Thus, the offer has to be made once the CISG has come into force in the Contracting States concerned, as also pointed out by the Supreme Court of Italy,[33] when it had to decide a dispute which had arisen between an Italian seller and a German buyer in relation to a contract for the sale of fruit concluded prior to the CISG's entry into force in Italy in 1988. Similarly, a U.S. court expressly stated that the CISG's applicability by virtue of Article 1(1)(*a*) CISG was

---

[32]   For decisions stating that Hong Kong is not a Contracting State to the CISG, *see* U.S. District Court [N.D. Ga.], 17 December 2009 (*Innotex Precision Limited v. Horei Image Products, Inc., et al.*), available at http://cisgw3.law.pace.edu/cases/091217u1.html; Federal Court of Australia, South Australia District Registry, 24 October 2008 (*Hannaford v. Australian Farmlink Pty. Ltd.*), available at http://cisgw3.law.pace.edu/cases/081024a2.html; Supreme Court of Austria, 17 December 2003, available in English at http://cisgw3.law.pace.edu/cases/031217a3.html; *contra* U.S. District Court [N.D. Ill.], 3 September 2008 (*CNA Int'l, Inc. v. Guangdong Kelon Electronical Holdings et al.*), available at http://cisgw3.law.pace.edu/cases/080903u1.html.

[33]   Supreme Court of Italy, 24 October 1988, English abstract available at http://cisgw3.law.pace.edu/cases/881024i3.html.

excluded, since one of the parties' place of business was located in a State that "was not a signatory to the CISG at the time 'when the proposal for concluding the contract' was formulated."[34]

For the applicability of Part III of the Convention (Rights and Obligations of Buyer and Seller), it is sufficient, pursuant to Article 100(2) CISG, that the CISG came into force either in the Contracting States referred to in Article 1(1)(*a*) or in the Contracting State referred to in Article 1(1)(*b*) at a date not later than that of the conclusion of the contract.

As regards the concept of "Contracting State", it must further be pointed out that under the CISG Contracting States may declare a limited number of expressly listed reservations, some of which have an impact on the status of Contracting State.

In this respect, the first reservation to be mentioned is that which the Contracting States may declare pursuant to Article 92, a provision introduced upon the insistence of the Scandinavian countries which wanted to make sure that some of their domestic provisions would not be superseded by those of the CISG. According to this provision, a State may declare that it will not be bound by Part II or by Part III of the CISG, dealing with the "formation of contract" and "the rights and

---

[34]   U.S. District Court [S.D. Fla.], 22 November 2002 (*Impuls I.D. Internacional, S. L., Impuls I.D. Systems, Inc., and PSIAR, SA., v. Psion–Teklogix Inc.*), available at http://cisgw3. law.pace.edu/cisg/wais/db/cases2/021122u1.html.

obligations of the parties" respectively. The effect of this reservation is set forth in Article 92 CISG itself: a party that has its relevant place of business in a State that has made an Article 92 reservation is to be considered as having its place of business in a non–Contracting State for the purposes of the Part excluded. Thus, where one party has its place of business in such a State, the CISG can never be applicable by virtue of Article 1(1)(*a*) CISG in its entirety. Article 1(1)(*a*) will merely lead to the application of the Part(s) by which both States in which the parties have their places of business are bound. This does not necessarily mean that the Part to which the reservation relates does not apply; rather, that Part's applicability will depend, as will be shown later, on whether the rules of private international law of the forum lead to the law of a Contracting State that did not make such a declaration. If they do, the Part excluded will apply by virtue of Article 1(1)(*b*).

In one case, a German court[35] had to decide whether the CISG was applicable to a contract for the sale of 3000 tons of nickel–copper electrolyte cathodes between a German buyer and a Finnish seller. The court held that the CISG was applicable to the rights and obligations of the parties by virtue of Article 1(1)(*a*), but that the issue of the contract's formation could not be governed by Part II (Formation of Contracts) of the CISG, at least not by virtue of Article 1(1)(*a*), since Finland had declared

---

[35]   *See* OLG München (Germany), 8 March 1995, available in English at http://cisgw3.law.pace.edu/cases/950308g1.html.

an Article 92 reservation and therefore could not be considered a Contracting State in respect to that Part. Nevertheless, the court held that by virtue of Article 1(1)(b) the CISG had to govern the formation as well, since the German private international law rules made German law applicable to that issue.[36]

It should be noted that according to both commentators and courts,[37] the foregoing solution applies not only if a dispute is brought before the courts of a Contracting State that did not declare an Article 92 reservation, but also where the forum is located in a State that did declare such a reservation.

Where, on the contrary, the private international law rules lead to the law of a Contracting State that declared the Article 92 reservation, there can be no doubt that that State's domestic law will apply, as pointed out, among others, by a German court in 1995.[38] The German court had to decide whether a dispute between a Danish seller and a German buyer should be solved by resorting to the rules of the CISG. The court held that since both Germany and Denmark were Contracting States at the moment of the conclusion of the contract, the CISG

---

[36] *Contra*, without any valid reason, LG Bielefeld (Germany), 12 December 2003, available in English at http://cisgw3.law.pace.edu/cases/031212g1.html.

[37] *See* Østre Landsret (Denmark), 23 April 1998, English abstract available at http://cisgw3.law.pace.edu/cases/980423d1.html.

[38] Compare OLG Rostock (Germany), 27 July 1995, available in English at http://cisgw3.law.pace.edu/cases/950727g1.html.

applied by virtue of Article 1(1)(*a*), except in so far as the formation of the contract was concerned. Since Denmark had made an Article 92 reservation by virtue of which it is not bound by Part II of the CISG, it cannot "be considered a Contracting State within paragraph (1) of Article 1 of [the] Convention." The German court therefore correctly resorted to its private international law rules and applied Danish domestic non–uniform law to the formation of the contract.

A reasoning similar to the one just referred to applies in those cases where at least one of the parties to the contract has its place of business in a territorial unit of a Contracting State, where the Contracting State made a declaration pursuant to which the CISG does not extend to that territorial unit. In this line of cases, by virtue of Article 93(3) the CISG cannot apply "directly", *i.e.*, pursuant to Article 1(1)(*a*), because the party that has its place in that territorial unit is considered as having its place of business in a non–Contracting State. Consequently, where the forum is located in a Contracting State, the CISG can only be applicable, if at all, by virtue of Article 1(1)(*b*), provided that the rules of private international law lead to the law of a Contracting State that did not declare an Article 93 reservation.

Although a declaration made pursuant to Article 94 also triggers the need for a private international law analysis, it does so for different reasons, as an Article 94 reservation does not have the effects of either an Article 92 or an Article 93 reservation. A

State declaring an Article 94 reservation will not be considered a non–Contracting State (not even for part of the CISG). The purpose of this reservation is to make the CISG inapplicable to contractual relationships between parties that have their places of business in countries that have a sales law that is largely uniform in order to allow regional unification efforts to prevail over the CISG. Consequently, where both parties have their places of business in Contracting States that made an Article 94 declaration, the CISG will not apply, thus making it necessary to resort to the private international law rules of the forum to determine the applicable law. If the applicable law is that of a Contracting State that declared an Article 94 reservation, there is no doubt that the CISG will not apply where the forum is also located in a Contracting State that made an Article 94 declaration. Where, however, the forum is located in a Contracting State that has not made such a declaration, in these authors' opinion, the CISG will apply.

4.   THE CISG'S "INDIRECT" APPLICATION AND THE ARTICLE 95 RESERVATION

From what has been said hitherto, it is apparent that the CISG's applicability is not necessarily excluded where the parties do not have their places of business in different Contracting States. In effect, pursuant to what has been defined as a "classical solution", provided for by Article 1(1)(*b*) CISG, the CISG can be applicable where one or even both parties do not have their relevant place of business in Contracting States, provided that the rules of private international law lead to the application of the law of a Contracting State, as expressly stated by Article 1(1)(*b*).

For the understanding of how this provision operates and, thus, when it can lead to the application of the CISG, it is paramount to first determine what is meant by "private international law", a concept which the CISG itself does not define. One has to wonder whether this means that this concept, like most other concepts used in the CISG, has to be interpreted by having regard to the CISG's "international character and the need to promote uniformity in its application", *i.e.*, "autonomously", or whether this concept is one of those that exceptionally have to be interpreted "domestically"?

The importance of the answer to this question becomes evident if one considers the differences that exist between the rules of private international law of different countries. Whilst, for instance, the parties' freedom to choose the law applicable to their contract has long been accepted in many countries, in some countries a similar choice does not necessarily produce any effect. Although this may appear to be the most significant difference, it is certainly not the only one. As far as private international law rules relating to contracts are concerned, many countries have, as have many international conventions, rejected the doctrine of *renvoi*; nevertheless, there are a few countries which still accept that doctrine.

The question, of course, is whether these differences are really relevant. Obviously, such differences would be irrelevant if the concept at hand were to be interpreted autonomously. In these authors' opinion, however, the concept at hand is one of the concepts which have to be construed in light of domestic law.[39] And this is why it is not surprising that in some Contracting States, which require courts to acknowledge party autonomy as a connecting factor, the CISG has been applied by virtue of a choice of law in cases where it was not applicable by virtue of Article 1(1)(*a*).[40]

Overall, one must conclude that where the CISG makes reference to "private international law", it refers to a domestic concept of "private international law". More particularly, the CISG refers to the private international law of the forum.[41]

In practice this means, for instance, that where the forum is located in a Contracting State in which the relevant rules of private international law of sales contracts are those set forth by the EEC

---

[39]   *Accord* Trib. Padova (Italy), 25 February 2004, available in English at http://cisgw3.law.pace.edu/cases/040225i3.html.

[40]   *See*, *e.g.*, Supreme Court of France, 17 December 1996, available in English at http://cisgw3.law.pace.edu/cases/961217 f1.html; OLG Köln (Germany), 22 February 1994, available in English at http://cisgw3.law.pace.edu/cases/940222g1.html.

[41]   *See* Trib. Padova (Italy), 25 February 2004, available in English at http://cisgw3.law.pace.edu/cases/040225i3.html; Trib. Rimini (Italy), 26 November 2002, available in English at http://cisgw3.law.pace.edu/cases/021126i3.html.

Convention on the Law Applicable to Contractual Obligations,[42] as in many European countries, the CISG will generally be applicable when the law either chosen by the parties or, absent choice of law, that having the closest connection with the contract, is the law of a Contracting State.

As far as party autonomy under the Rome Convention is concerned, and the same holds true for the Rome I Regulation[43] that took the place of the Rome Convention as regards contracts concluded after 17 December 2009, it does not raise insurmountable problems, it being a concept widely acknowledged throughout European private international law codifications long before even the coming into force of the foregoing European instruments. This is why its application to international sales contracts does not cause too many difficulties, as evidenced by the fact that many courts have already relied upon the parties' designation of the applicable law to make the CISG applicable by virtue of Article 1(1)(*b*).[44]

Absent choice of law, the Rome Convention makes applicable the law of the country with which the

---

[42]   EEC Convention on the Law Applicable to Contractual Obligations, *reprinted in* 19 INTERNATIONAL LEGAL MATERIALS 1492 (1980).

[43]   *See* Regulation (EC) No 593/2008 of the European Parliament and of the Council of 17 June 2008 on the law applicable to contractual obligations (Rome I).

[44]   *See* Supreme Court of Germany, 11 May 2010, available at http://www.globalsaleslaw.com/content/api/cisg/urteile/2125.pdf; Supreme Court of France, 17 December 1996, available in English at http://cisgw3.law.pace.edu/cases/961217f1.html.

contract is most closely connected.[45] And since it is presumed that the contract is most closely connected with the country where the party who is to effect the contract's characteristic performance has its place of business—and since the monetary obligation is generally not the characteristic one,[46]—the law applicable to international sales contracts is generally (*i.e.* where the presumption is not rebutted)[47] the law of the seller, since it is the seller who has to execute the characteristic performance consisting of the transfer of ownership and the delivery of the goods.[48] As regards the Rome I Regulation, the result is basically the same, since its Article 4(1)(*a*) states that "a contract for the sale of goods shall be governed by the law of the country where the seller has his habitual residence."

It must be noted that despite the coming into force of the Rome Convention and the Rome I Regulation, these instruments are not necessarily the instruments to be resorted to in the States in

---

[45]   *See* RB Amsterdam (The Netherlands), 5 October 1994, NEDERLANDS INTERNATIONAAL PRIVAATRECHT 195 (1995); LG Düsseldorf (Germany), 25 August 1994, available in English at http://cisgw3.law.pace.edu/cases/940825g1.html.

[46]   *See* OLG Koblenz (Germany), 16 January 1992, available at http://www.unilex.info/case.cfm?pid=1&do=case&id=30&step=FullText.

[47]   For a case in which the presumption was rebutted and the law of the buyer was applied rather than the law of the seller, *see* LG Kassel (Germany), 22 June 1995, available at http://www.cisg–online.ch/cisg/urteile/370.htm.

[48]   *See, e.g.*, LG Berlin (Germany), 24 March 1998, available in English at http://cisgw3.law.pace.edu/cases/980324g1.html; LG München (Germany), 6 May 1997, available at http://cisgw3.law.pace.edu/cases/970506g1.html.

which they came into force to determine the law applicable to contracts for the international sale of goods. In other words, despite the Rome Convention's or the Rome I Regulation's coming into force in the forum State, the courts may well have to apply a different set of private international law rules. Indeed, since Article 21 of the Rome Convention (not unlike Article 25 of the Rome I Regulation) states that it "shall not prejudice the application of international conventions to which a Contracting State is, or becomes, a party", other rules may have to be resorted to in order to determine the law applicable to contracts for the international sale of goods. This is true, for instance, in those States in which the Rome Convention (for contracts concluded prior to 18 December 2009) and the Rome I Regulation (for contracts concluded on or after 18 December 2009) as well as the 1955 Hague Convention on the Law Applicable to International Sales of Goods apply,[49] such as in France and Italy. In those States, one must resort to the rules of the Hague Convention rather than those of the Rome Convention (or the Rome I Regulation, for that matter), as correctly pointed out by many courts.[50]

---

[49]   For the official text (in French only) of the 1955 Hague Convention on the Law Applicable to International Sales of Goods, *see* http://www.hcch.net/f/conventions/text03f.html.

[50]   *See* Trib. Padova (Italy), 31 March 2004, available in English at http://cisgw3.law.pace.edu/cases/040331i3.html; Trib. Padova (Italy), 25 February 2004, available in English at http://cisgw3.law.pace.edu/cases/040225i3.html.

For completeness, it should be mentioned that as far as party autonomy is concerned, the application of the 1955 Hague Convention rather than the application of the Rome Convention or the Rome I Regulation does not lead to diverging results, as Article 2 of 1955 Hague Convention also obliges judges to acknowledge the choice of law made by the parties. Thus, where the parties choose the law of a Contracting State, Article 2 will lead to the application of the CISG under the 1955 Hague Convention as well.[51]

Absent choice of law, under the 1955 Hague Convention courts have to apply the law of the seller[52] (independently of whether the contract is more closely connected with the law of a different State), except in cases where the seller receives the order in the buyer's country, in which case the law of the buyer governs.[53]

From all of the foregoing, it should be apparent that Article 1(1)(*b*) CISG (which some commentators consider to be superfluous and open to criticism) extends the CISG's sphere of application which

---

[51]   *See* RB Koophandel Oudenaarde (Belgium), 10 July 2001, available at http://www.law.kuleuven.ac.be/ipr/eng/cases/2001–07–10.html.

[52]   *See* RB Koophandel Hasselt (Belgium), 9 October 1996, available at http://www.law.kuleuven.ac.be/int/tradelaw/WK/1996–10–09.htm; CA Grenoble (France), 26 April 1995, available in English at http://cisgw3.law.pace.edu/cases/950426f2.html; Pretore della Giurisdizione Locarno–Campagna (Switzerland), 27 April 1992, available in English at http://cisgw3.law.pace.edu/cases/920427s1.html.

[53]   *See* Supreme Court of France, 26 June 2001, available at http://www.cisg–france.org/decisions/2606012v.htm.

otherwise would have been too restrictive, but without going as far as its predecessors, the 1964 Hague Conventions. Furthermore, the CISG's approach has another advantage: it coordinates the rules of the CISG with those of private international law, a coordination which had not been provided for by the 1964 Hague Conventions, which expressly stated that "the rules of private international law shall be excluded for the purpose of the application of the present Law."

As mentioned earlier, the CISG's "indirect" application has been criticized, mainly by former Socialist Countries as well as the United States. As a consequence of such criticism, the drafters of the CISG introduced Article 95 CISG, which gives the Contracting States the option not to enforce Article 1(1)(*b*), thus limiting the applicability of the CISG, where the CISG does not apply by virtue of Article 1(1)(*a*) upon which the Article 95 reservation does not have any impact.[54]

Unfortunately, however, there is no agreement on the extent to which the Article 95 reservation narrows down the CISG's applicability. According to

---

[54] For the CISG's applicability by virtue of its Article 1(1)(*a*) in the courts of States declaring an Article 95 reservation, *see, e.g.,* U.S.: District Court [W.D Penn.], 10 September 2013 (*Roser Technologies, Inc. v. Carl Schreiber GmbH*), 2013 WL 4852314; U.S. District Court [Md.], 8 February 2011 (*CSS Antenna, Inc. v. Amphenol–Tuchel Electronics, GmbH*), available at http://cisg w3.law.pace.edu/cases/110208u1.html; U.S. District Court [S.D.N.Y.], 18 January 2011 (*Hanwha Corporation v. Cedar Petrochemicals, Inc.*), available at http://cisgw3.law.pace.edu/cases/110118u1.html.

a decision rendered by the United States District Court for the Western District of Washington, at Seattle, in *Prime Start Ltd. v. Maher Forest Products Ltd. et al.*,[55] as well as one rendered by the United States District Court for the Southern District of Florida,[56] in the courts of Contracting States that declared an Article 95 reservation "the *only* circumstance in which the CISG could apply is if all the parties to the contract were from Contracting States [. . .] even if a traditional choice–of–law analysis leads to the application of the law of the United States (or one of its states) or any other signatory State."[57]

In these authors' opinion, this statement is at least partially incorrect; nevertheless, in the case just referred to, the District Court for the Western District of Washington reached the correct conclusion when it found that the CISG did not apply to a contract for the international sale of Western Red Cedar siding concluded between a seller who had its place of business in the British Virgin Islands and a buyer who had its place of business in the United States. The reasons for this

---

[55]   *See* U.S. District Court [W.D. Wash.], 17 July 2006 (*Prime Start Ltd. v. Maher Forest Products Ltd. et al.*), available at http://cisgw3.law.pace.edu/cases/060717u1.html.

[56]   *See* U.S. District Court [S.D. Fla.], 22 November 2002 (*Impuls I.D. Internacional, S. L., Impuls I.D. Systems, Inc., and PSIAR, SA., v. Psion–Teklogix Inc.*), available at http://cisgw3. law.pace.edu/cisg/wais/db/cases2/021122u1.html.

[57]   U.S. District Court [W.D. Wash.], 17 July 2006 (*Prime Start Ltd. v. Maher Forest Products Ltd. et al.*), available at http://cisgw3.law.pace.edu/cases/060717u1.html.

will become apparent as the impact of the Article 95 reservation is analyzed.

In these authors' opinion, several lines of cases must be distinguished.

(A) The first line of cases covers instances similar to the one dealt with by the District Court for the Western District of Washington, *i.e.* those cases where *the forum is located in a reservatory State* the rules of private international law of which lead to the applicability of the law of a Contracting State (independently from whether this State declared a reservation or not). Not unlike the District Court, some commentators argue that the CISG cannot apply at all in those instances, since the courts of Contracting reservatory States are bound to apply the CISG only where both parties have their places of business in Contracting States. It is certainly true that in this line of cases the courts of reservatory States cannot apply the CISG by virtue of Article 1(1)(*b*), as correctly pointed out also in *Prime Start*. Nevertheless, it is here suggested that even the courts of a reservatory State should apply the CISG in the aforementioned line of cases—not by virtue of Article 1(1)(*b*), of course—but as part of the law of the Contracting State to which the conflict of law rules lead. There is, however, a limit: if it is true, as it has been suggested, that the rationale behind the possibility of the Article 95 reservation is to promote the application of domestic law, it must be concluded that in cases where the forum is located in a Contracting reservatory State the private international law rules of which lead to the law of the forum, the CISG is inapplicable. This is also the reason why it can be stated that the District Court for the Western District of Washington reached the correct result when it excluded the applicability of the CISG, since the applicable rules of private international law led to the law of the United States, *i.e.* the reservatory forum State's own law.

(B) There is a dispute in another line of cases as well, namely where *the forum is located in a Contracting non–reservatory State* the rules of private international law of which lead to the applicability of the law of a Contracting State that has declared an Article 95 reservation. According to some commentators, the CISG should not be applicable in this line of cases, because, it is argued, the judges from the reservatory State would themselves not apply the CISG. In these authors' opinion, the preferable view, however, seems to be the contrary, not only because generally a reservation of the kind at hand made by one State cannot bind another State, unless, obviously, the forum State adheres to the comity doctrine, but also because, from the point of view of the Contracting (forum) State, all the prerequisites for the applicability of the CISG set forth in Article 1(1)(*b*) are met. In these authors' opinion, this view is to be preferred despite some German commentators' opinions to the contrary, who prefer to apply domestic law rather than the CISG in cases where the rules of private international law lead to the law of a reservatory State. In this case, the German commentators' views are not necessarily decisive in guiding the interpreter, due to the fact that in Germany the courts do not have the possibility of deciding differently, a statute having been passed in Germany according to which German courts are bound to apply the domestic sales law of the reservatory State rather than the CISG when their rules of private international law lead to the law of a Contracting reservatory State.

(C) There is disagreement also in respect of those cases where *the forum is located in a non–Contracting State* the rules of private international law of which lead to the law of a Contracting State that declared an Article 95 reservation. Despite some statements according to which the CISG should not apply at all, it is suggested here that the CISG should be applied in this line of cases as well. Obviously, in these cases the application cannot be based upon Article 1(1)(*b*); rather, it must be based upon the CISG being part of the applicable (foreign) law. One should, in other words, adopt the same solution employed in those cases where the rules of private international law of the non–Contracting State lead to the applicability of the law of a Contracting State that did not declare a reservation. In this line of cases, the courts have to apply the CISG for the very same reasons, *i.e.*, not by virtue of Article 1(1)(*b*), as wrongly stated by various courts,[58] by which they are not bound, but rather by

---

[58]   *See, e.g.*, RB Amsterdam (The Netherlands), 7 December 1995, NEDERLANDS INTERNATIONAAL PRIVAATRECHT 196 (1995); RB Koophandel Hasselt (Belgium), 18 October 1995, available at http://www.law.kuleuven.ac.be/ipr/eng/cases/1995–10–18.html.

virtue of the CISG being part of the applicable foreign law. This view is not only held by commentators, but it has already found judicial application in many instances.[59]

To summarize: in these authors' opinion, the Article 95 reservation has an impact on the application of the CISG solely in those cases where the forum is located in a reservatory State the private international law rules of which lead to the forum State's own law. In this line of cases, the CISG cannot be applied, as this would violate the rationale behind the Article 95 reservation.

5.   THE APPLICATION OF THE CISG BY ARBITRAL TRIBUNALS

In order for the CISG to be applicable in the courts of Contracting States, either the requirements set forth in its Article 1(1)(*a*) or those laid down in Article 1(1)(*b*) must be met. In order for it to be applicable in the courts of non–Contracting States, the rules of private international law must lead to the law of a Contracting State (reservatory or not). These principles have also been adopted by arbitral tribunals. Indeed, there are several arbitral awards which apply the CISG on the grounds that both parties have their places of business in

---

[59]   *See, e.g.*, RB Koophandel Kortrijk (Belgium), 16 December 1996, available at http://www.unilex.info/case.cfm?pid=1&do=case&id=340&step=FullText; RB Koophandel Hasselt (Belgium), 9 October 1996, available at http://www.unilex.info/case.cfm?pid=1&do=case&id=264&step=FullText; OLG Koblenz (Germany), 27 September 1991, available in English at http://cisgw3.law.pace.edu/cases/910927g1.html.

different Contracting States.[60] There are also many arbitral awards which make the CISG applicable because the rules of private international law resorted to by the arbitrators lead to the law of a Contracting State.[61] From this it follows that arbitration tribunals do generally apply the CISG as if they were courts located in Contracting States.

It is worth mentioning, however, that some arbitral tribunals have applied the CISG even where the contract fell outside the CISG's stated sphere of application. In one case, an ICC Arbitral Tribunal[62] applied the CISG to a series of contracts concluded in 1979, on the grounds that "[t]here is no better source to determine the prevailing trade usages than the terms of the United Nations Convention on the International Sale of Goods of 11 April 1980 [. . .]. This is so even though neither the [country of the Buyer] nor the [country of the Seller] are parties to that Convention." In another case, the Iran–United States Claims Tribunal[63] applied the

---

[60]   *See, e.g.,* ICC Court of Arbitration, Arbitral Award n. 9887, available at http://www.unilex.info/case.cfm?pid=1&do= case&id=469&step=FullText.

[61]   *See, e.g.,* ICC Court of Arbitration, Arbitral Award n. 9978, available at http://www.unilex.info/case.cfm?pid=1&do= case&id=471&step=FullText;   Schiedsgericht   der Handelskammer Hamburg (Germany), Award of 21 March 1996, available in English at http://cisgw3.law.pace.edu/cases/960321 g1.html.

[62]   *See* ICC Court of Arbitration, Arbitral Award n. 5713, available at http://www.unilex.info/case.cfm?pid=1&do=case&id= 16&step=FullText.

[63]   *See* Iran–United States Claim Tribunal, Arbitral Award n. 370 (*Watkins–Johnson Co. 7 Watkins Johnson Ltd. vs. The Islamic Republic of Iran & Bank Saderat Iran*), available at

CISG as part of the so–called "lex mercatoria" or as relevant trade usages to a contract concluded, again, before the drafting of the CISG. This line of cases, which opens the door to the applicability of the CISG even to cases not falling under its scope, has been criticized for several reasons. It has been said, for instance, that the CISG's provisions do not necessarily reflect uniform commercial practices, but are rather the result of a careful political compromise. Most importantly, however, the application of the CISG to contracts concluded before its coming into force violates a principle which appears to be recognized by most developed legal systems according to which, absent an agreement among the parties, the law in force at the moment a contract is concluded governs the contract even if that law is modified. Therefore, one can only hope that the arbitral tribunals, not unlike State courts, hold, as a few recent arbitral awards have actually done, that the CISG be inapplicable to operative facts that occurred before the CISG's coming into force in the countries involved.

---

http://www.unilex.info/case.cfm?pid=1&do=case&id=38&step=FullText.

CHAPTER 4

SUBSTANTIVE SPHERE OF APPLICATION AND ISSUES GOVERNED BY THE CISG

1. CONTRACTS FOR THE SALE OF GOODS

For a contract to be governed by the CISG, it is not sufficient that the contract meets the requirements discussed in the foregoing chapters; the contract must also fall within the CISG's substantive sphere of application *i.e.*, it must be a contract for the sale of goods (or any other type of contract governed by the CISG). The first question to be dealt with, therefore, is what constitutes a "sale". In this respect, it must be noted that the CISG does not define the sales contract. According to some commentators, this lack of definition is due to the fact that there are no relevant differences amongst the definitions of a sales contract in the various legal systems. However, this lack of an express definition does not make it impossible to—autonomously—define sales contract for purposes of the CISG. A definition of "sales contract" can be inferred from Articles 30 and 53, the provisions laying down the obligations of the parties to a sales contract governed by the CISG. Thus, independently from the civil or commercial character of the parties or of the contract itself (Article 1(3)), the sales contract can—and has been—defined as the contract "pursuant to which one party—the seller—is bound to deliver the goods and transfer the property in the goods sold and the other party—the buyer—is obliged to pay the price and accept the goods."[1] Thus, it cannot surprise that one court held that the essence of the sales contract lies in goods being exchanged for money.[2]

The sales contract as defined above is not the only contract governed by the CISG. *Contracts modifying an international sales contract* also fall under the CISG's sphere of application, since they directly affect the rights and obligations of the parties to the international sales contract. Similarly, the agreement to conclude a contract for the international sale of goods subject to the CISG can also be governed by the CISG. *Contracts for the delivery of goods by installments* are also governed by the CISG.[3]

With regards to *distribution agreements*, the preferable view is that distribution agreements are not covered by the CISG, basically because these types of agreements "rather focus on the concept of distribution, the fixing of global commitments to delivery and acceptance or other framework

---

[1]   Trib. Forlì (Italy), 16 February 2009, available in English at http://cisgw3.law.pace.edu/cases/090216i3.html; Trib. Cantonal du Valais (Switzerland), 28 January 2009, available in English at http://cisgw3.law.pace.edu/cases/090128s1.html;   Trib.   Forlì (Italy), 11 December 2008, available in English at http://cisgw3. law.pace.edu/cases/081211i3.html.

[2]   KG Zug (Switzerland), 21 October 1999, available in English at http://cisgw3.law.pace.edu/cases/991021s1.html.

[3]   *See* CA Colmar (France), 12 June 2001, available in English at http://cisgw3.law.pace.edu/cases/010612f1.html.

conditions"[4] and not on the transfer of title in the goods as well as their delivery. That is also why franchise agreements are considered to fall outside the CISG's substantive sphere of application.[5] It is worth pointing out, however, that the single contracts concluded in performance of a distribution agreements fall under the CISG's sphere of application. Like distribution agreements, *barter transactions* and *leasing contracts* (not even where they contain a purchase option) are not governed by the CISG.

The CISG governs only international sales contracts (or other international contracts which the CISG compares to sales contracts) concerning "goods", a concept which the CISG does not expressly define, despite its importance. This, however, does not allow one to resort to domestic definitions. The concept of "goods" is as much an "autonomous" concept as that of "sale".[6]

As far as the concept of "goods" under the CISG is concerned, it essentially corresponds to that of the 1964 Hague Conventions. Thus, "goods" under the CISG are only goods that, at the time of delivery,[7]

---

[4]   OG Kanton Luzern (Switzerland), 8 January 1997, available in English at http://cisgw3.law.pace.edu/cases/970108 s1.html.

[5]   *See* Supreme Court of Germany, 23 July 1997, available in English at http://cisgw3.law.pace.edu/cases/970723g2.html.

[6]   *See* Trib. Padova (Italy), 25 February 2004, available in English at http://cisgw3.law.pace.edu/cases/040225i3.html.

[7]   *See, e.g.*, Trib. Forlì (Italy), 16 February 2009, available in English at http://cisgw3.law.pace.edu/cases/090216i3.html.

are "moveable and tangible",[8] including, for example, live stock, plants, art objects, as well as chemical substances needed for the production of pharmaceuticals. Whether the goods are solid or not is as irrelevant as whether they are used or new goods.[9]

From what has just been said it follows that the sale of immovable property, or that of intangible goods, such as industrial property rights, a membership interest in a limited liability company[10] or receiveables, does not constitute a sale of "goods" under the CISG. By virtue of the aforementioned definition of "goods", the sale of "know–how" as well is to be excluded from the CISG's sphere of application.

Whereas computer hardware clearly falls under the CISG's concept of "goods",[11] it is not clear whether the CISG's understanding of "goods" also encompasses computer software and, if so, to what extent. In these authors' opinion, the sale of

---

[8]   *See* Trib. Forlì (Italy), 11 December 2008, available in English at http://cisgw3.law.pace.edu/cases/081211i3.html; Trib. Padova (Italy), 11 January 2005, available at http://www.unilex.info/case.cfm?pid=1&do=case&id=1005&step=FullText.

[9]   *See* Trib. Forlì (Italy), 16 February 2009, available in English at http://cisgw3.law.pace.edu/cases/090216i3.html.

[10]   *See* Court of Arbitration attached to the Hungarian Chamber of Commerce and Industry, 20 December 1993, English abstract available at http://cisgw3.law.pace.edu/cases/931220h1.html.

[11]   *See* LG München (Germany), 29 May 1995, available in English at http://cisgw3.law.pace.edu/cases/950529g1.html.

software that is being made available by means of a tangible support may be subject to the CISG.[12]

2.   MIXED CONTRACTS

Even though the sales contract as defined above still constitutes the "commercial contract par excellence", it has undergone a change, at least in respect of business–to–business relationships. This change is due to the fact that modern trade not only calls for ready–made goods, but also for goods to be manufactured, and therefore by extension, for the "sale" of labor and services. The tendency to also consider as sales contracts those contracts "which require further activities besides the traditional exchange of goods with money" goes back many years. That is why it is unsurprising that the drafters of the CISG extended its applicability to the point that it governs (within certain limits) also contracts which under some domestic laws are considered to be work contracts: Article 3(1) CISG deals with the CISG's applicability to contracts for the supply of goods to be manufactured or produced, whereas Article 3(2) CISG deals with contracts that include the supply of labor or other services amongst the "seller's obligations". Thus, the CISG contains some provisions which "confront the scholar with contractual schemes which have uncertain functional characteristics" and "which

---

[12]   *See* Supreme Court of Austria, 21 June 2005, available at http://www.unilex.info/case.cfm?pid=1&do=case&id=1047&step =FullText; RB Arnhem (The Nethertlands), 28 June 2006, available in English at http://cisgw3.law.pace.edu/cases/060628 n1.html.

therefore raise the problem of whether such contracts fall under its sphere of application." This is true, above all, in those cases where the seller is liable not only for the transfer of title and the delivery of the goods, but also for providing labor or services. It is also true for those cases where the buyer has to supply part of the materials needed for the production of the goods.

Among the contracts falling under the latter category are those contemplated the contracts for the supply of goods to be manufactured or produced. By analogizing these contracts to the more "classical" contracts for the sale of goods, it is made clear that the sale of goods to be manufactured or produced is as much subject to the CISG as the sale of ready–made goods and that domestic peculiarities are irrelevant for the purposes of determining whether the CISG applies to the international sale of made–to–order goods. This is why, for instance, the *Werklieferungsvertrag* (known in German speaking legal systems) can as much be subject to the CISG as the French *louage d'ouvrage*.

Under Article 3(1) CISG, contracts for the supply of goods to be manufactured or produced are governed by the Convention if they are to be considered "sales": in practice, this is the case "unless the party who orders the goods undertakes to supply a substantial part of the materials necessary for such manufacture or production." As for the determination of the concept of "substantial part", it is suggested that one should not only use a quantitative criterion, but also a qualitative one.

This view is justified on two grounds. First, the French language counterpart of the "substantial part' requirement reads "partie essentielle", thus stressing the importance of the "essence"—and, therefore, the quality and the function—of the materials as well.[13] Second, the wording used, "substantial part", is different from that used in Article 3(2) which speaks of "preponderant part", a concept undoubtedly referring to a mere quantitative approach. Consequently, the materials to be provided by the buyer may constitute a substantial part of the goods sold even where their value represents less than 50% of the value of the goods.

Irrespective of what has just been said, design specifications or any other indications provided by the seller should not be relevant in deciding whether a contract is excluded from the CISG pursuant to Article 3(1), because design specifications or any other indications do not constitute "material necessary for the manufacture or production" of the goods.

The applicability of the CISG extends not only to contracts for the sale of made–to–order goods. Article 3(2) CISG extends it also to contracts pursuant to which the seller undertakes to supply labor or other services alongside the obligations to deliver the goods, transfer the property and hand over the documents, as long as the supply of labor or

---

[13]   *See* OLG München (Germany), 3 December 1999, available in English at http://cisgw3.law.pace.edu/cases/991203 g1.html.

services does not constitute the "preponderant part" of the seller's obligation.

The relevant basis on which to decide whether the CISG is applicable to contracts for the supply of goods and labor or services is the "preponderance" of the seller's obligations regarding the supply of services or labor. This criterion seems to mainly be a quantitative one, and requires a comparison between the economic value of the obligations regarding the supply of labor and services, on the one hand, and the economic value of the obligations regarding the delivery of the goods, on the other hand, as if two separate contracts had been made.[14] Thus, where the economic value of the obligation regarding the supply of labor or services is "preponderant", *i.e.*, where it amounts to—even a little—more than 50%, the CISG is inapplicable. It must be noted, however, that some courts stated that, since a clear calculation would not always be possible, other circumstances such as those surrounding the conclusion of the contract as well as the purpose of the contract should also be taken into account in evaluating whether the obligation to supply labor or services is preponderant.[15] As for the burden of proof, to be allocated on the basis of the general principle underlying the CISG referred to earlier,[16] it is upon the party claiming that the

---

[14]   *See* HG Kanton Zug (Switzerland), 14 December 2009, available at http://globalsaleslaw.com/content/api/cisg/urteile/20 26.pdf.

[15]   *See* LG Mainz (Germany), 26 November 1998, available in English at http://cisgw3.law.pace.edu/cases/981126g1.html.

[16]   *See supra* Chapter 1, Section 5.

CISG does not apply due to the preponderance of the service obligations to prove the preponderance of such obligations.[17]

A more articulated way to look at mixed contracts in light of Article 3(2) CISG requires a distinction to be made between *separate* and *unified contracts*, and leads to the application of the "preponderance" test only in the event that the transaction constitutes one single contract. This view in turn requires one to determine how to decide whether the transaction is unified or severable. Although the Secretariat's Commentary suggests that this question be decided on the basis of the applicable domestic law,[18] most commentators suggest that the issue of the unitary or severable nature of the transaction be dealt with on the basis of the Convention itself. This solution seems more in line with the mandate set forth in Article 7(1) CISG to promote the CISG's uniform application. This said, it must be pointed out that the parties' intention should in any event be taken as the guiding element to assess whether the contract is one or severable.

Article 3(2) CISG is thus deemed to provide guidance only in the event of a (single) mixed contract. In this line of cases, it is generally

---

[17]   *See* OLG Oldenburg (Germany), 20 December 2007, available in English at http://cisgw3.law.pace.edu/cases/071220 g1.html.

[18]   *See* OFFICIAL RECORDS OF THE UNITED NATIONS CONFERENCE ON CONTRACTS FOR THE INTERNATIONAL SALE OF GOODS. VIENNA, 10 MARCH—11 APRIL 1980, *supra* note 3, at 16–17 (1981).

assumed that the unitary contract at hand should not be subject to a sort of contractual *dépeçage*. Rather, the contract is to be treated as a single entity, and a single set of rules should apply to the entire unitary contract. This statement, which reflects an approach common to many jurisdictions, is not entirely satisfactory with respect to the CISG, because it does not take into due consideration the non–exhaustive character of the CISG, with which the rule under Article 3 CISG has to be coordinated. In particular, the non–exhaustive character of the CISG entails that a contract governed by the CISG may well be subject to the application of other sources of law with respect to issues which are beyond the CISG's scope.[19]

If the CISG were an exhaustive piece of legislation, the statement that a contract is governed by the CISG would imply the exclusion of all concurrent sources. Conversely, given the non–exhaustive character of the CISG, the application of the CISG under Article 3 merely implies that the CISG is applicable to the contract at hand insofar as the CISG contains rules dealing with the several contractual aspects relevant in a given case. However, when issues are at stake that are not governed by the CISG, the CISG itself instructs the interpreter to apply to the contract a different set of sources of law, either supranational (whenever a different instrument exists that deals with the issue not covered by the CISG), or domestic (whenever the CISG's external gap is to be filled by resorting to the

---

[19]   *See supra* Chapter 1, Section 4 and Chapter 4, Section 4.

domestic law applicable by virtue of the private international law rules of the forum).

What has just been said leads one to suggest a different reading of Article 3(2) CISG, dealing with mixed contracts. It is safe to assert (and in line with the traditional reading of the provision) that Article 3(2) CISG has a negative (exclusionary) implication, in that it prevents the application of the CISG when the "preponderant" part of the supplier's obligations is constituted by the supply of "labour or other services". The provision in question, however, cannot be deemed to also have a positive implication, in that the preponderance of the supply of goods does not prevent—given the non–exhaustive character of the Convention—the severability of the contract and the concurrent application of different sources of law to the several obligations undertaken under the unitary contract. In short, the non–exhaustive character of the CISG makes the contractual *dépeçage* possible and, often, necessary. By and large, nothing in Article 3 CISG (nor in any other CISG provision) prevents the concurrent application of the CISG to part of the contract (the part providing for sale–type rights and obligations), and of a different set of rules to another part of the same contract (the part relating to non–sale–type right and obligations).

3. ARTICLE 2 EXCLUSIONS FROM THE CISG'S SUBSTANTIVE SPHERE OF APPLICATION

For the applicability of the CISG it is not sufficient that the aforementioned applicability requirements set forth in Articles 1 and 3 are met. The CISG's sphere of application is restricted by several provisions, among others, Article 2 CISG. Article 2 excludes a number of exhaustively listed categories of contracts from the CISG's sphere of application, thus laying down negative applicability requirements in so far as it requires courts to determine that the contracts in dispute are not of the kind excluded.[20] These exclusions can be divided into three categories, relating to the purpose of the acquisition of the goods (Article 2(*a*)), the type of sales contract (Article 2(*b*) and (*c*)), and the kind of goods sold (Article 2(*d*), (*e*) and (*f*)).

As regards the first category, it excludes the sale of goods bought for personal, family or household use from the CISG's sphere of application. This exclusion, which leads *de facto* to a limitation of the CISG's sphere of application to commercial contracts, can be justified on the grounds that the draftsmen intended to avoid a conflict between CISG and domestic rules aimed at consumer protection, although such a conflict cannot always

---

[20]   *See* U.S. District Court [S.D.N.Y.], 29 May 2009 (*Doolim Corp. v. R Doll, LLC, et al.*), available at http://cisgw3.law.pace.edu/cases/090529u1.html; OLG München (Germany), 14 January 2009, available in English at http://cisgw3.law.pace.edu/cases/090114g1.html.

be avoided, since domestic law defines "consumer sales" differently than the CISG, which is why there can be some overlap.[21]

As for the prerequisites, a sales contract must meet for it to be excluded by virtue of Article 2(*a*) from the CISG's sphere of application, the sole criterion to be taken into account is the intention with which the goods are bought.[22] From the text of Article 2(*a*), one can thus gather that the goods must be bought exclusively for a non–commercial or non–professional purpose for the contract not to be governed by the CISG. The fact that the goods are consumer goods is generally speaking irrelevant for the purposes of the Article 2(*a*) exclusion. As for the aforementioned purpose, only the purpose at the time of purchase is relevant.[23] It follows that it is irrelevant that the buyer's use of the goods purchased is different from the one intended at the time of the conclusion of the contract. Consequently, the CISG will not apply where the goods are bought for an intended personal use, even though the buyer later changes its mind and uses them for commercial purposes.

Pursuant to Article 2(*a*), it is also important that the "consumer" purpose of the purchase be known,

---

[21]   Supreme Court of Germany, 31 October 2001, available in English at http://cisgw3.law.pace.edu/cases/011031g1.html.

[22]   *See* LG Saarbrücken (Germany), 25 November 2002, available in English at http://cisgw3.law.pace.edu/cases/021125 g1.html.

[23]   *See* Supreme Court of Germany, 31 October 2001, available in English at http://cisgw3.law.pace.edu/cases/011031 g1.html.

or ought to have been known,[24] to the seller at the time of the conclusion of the contract. To determine whether the "personal use" purpose was at least recognizable, one can turn to the goods' being or not generally destined for personal use, as in the case of the purchase of clothing, food or a caravan.[25] On the other hand, the purchase of several items of the same type of goods, even where they are generally destined for personal use, might lead to the opposite presumption, that is, that they are bought for a purpose other than personal use. There are indicia that do not relate to the nature of the goods, but to the "buyer". Where, for instance, the buyer concludes a contract providing a business address as the one to which the goods must be delivered, then the buyer's intent to use the goods for non–commercial purposes is certainly not recognizable. The same is true where the buyer concludes a sales contract using the letterhead of a business, or where the buyer uses a business office during the bargaining process.

As already pointed out, the Article 2 exclusions are not only based upon the purpose behind the acquisition of the goods or upon the type of sales contract (such as the auction sales or the sales on execution or otherwise by authority of law mentioned in Article 2(c)), but also on the kind of

---

[24]   *See* OLG Stuttgart (Germany), 31 March 2008, available in English at http://cisgw3.law.pace.edu/cases/080331g1.html.

[25]   Compare RB Arnhem (The Netherlands), 27 May 1993, available at http://www.unilex.info/case.cfm?pid=1&do=case&id=72&step=FullText.

goods sold (Article 2(*d*), (*e*) and (*f*)). Article 2(*d*) excludes the sales of stocks, shares, investment securities, negotiable instruments, and money from the CISG's sphere of application in order to avoid a conflict between CISG rules and domestic rules, which in this area are often mandatory. The negotiable instruments referred to in Article 2(*d*) include bills of exchange, checks, as well as other instruments calling for the payment of money. The sales of documents controlling the delivery of goods, such as warehouse receipts and bills of lading, are, on the contrary, governed by the CISG, since the real subject of those sales are the goods, rather than the documents. As regards the exclusion of the sale of money, it refers to the sale of money that is legal tender in any country. The sale of "money" which is no longer in use can be governed by the CISG. The same goes for the sale of shares that merely have artistic or historic value.

Article 2 also excludes the sale of electricity, ships,[26] vessels, hovercraft and aircraft[27] from the CISG's sphere of application, irrespective of whether they are subject to a registration requirement. From

---

[26] *See* Tribunal of International Commercial Arbitration at the Russian Federation Chamber of Commerce and Industry, Arbitral Award n. 236/1997, available in English at http://cisgw3. law.pace.edu/cases/980406r1.html; Yugoslav Chamber of Economy Arbitration Proceeding 15 April 1999, Arbitral Award n. T–23/97, available in English at http://cisgw3.law.pace.edu/cases/990415y1.html.

[27] *See* Tribunal of International Commercial Arbitration at the Russian Federation Chamber of Commerce and Industry, Arbitral Award n. 255/1996, available in English at http://cisgw3. law.pace.edu/cisg/wais/db/cases2/970902r1.html.

this one can derive that even the sale of smaller vessels can fall within the scope of the Article 2(*e*) exclusion. But this does not mean that all purchases of small watercraft are excluded from the CISG's substantive sphere of application. It only means that the exclusion must be based upon a criterion different from the size of the watercraft, such as the functional characteristics of the watercraft. Consequently, the sale of watercraft which does not have the function that ships or vessels have, *i.e.*, the sale of watercraft which is not permanently destined for the transport of goods or persons, does not fall within the exclusion *de quo* (independently from the size of the watercraft). This is why the sale of row boats or sailing boats can be governed by the CISG.

4.   ISSUES GOVERNED BY THE CISG

Even though the CISG may apply to a given contract, it may not settle a specific matter, as the matter may fall outside the CISG's scope of application. This is due to the fact that the CISG does not constitute an "exhaustive body of rules", contrary to what has been stated by one court.[28] Like any other substantive uniform law convention, the CISG only deals with certain matters, thus making resort to sources of law other than the CISG necessary.

For the purpose of determining the CISG's scope of application, the most relevant provision is Article

---

[28]   *See* Supreme Court of Switzerland, 19 February 2004, available at http://www.unilex.info/case.cfm?pid=1&do=case&id=979&step=FullText.

4, since it identifies both the matters that the CISG is concerned with ("this Convention *governs only* the formation of the contract of sale and the rights and obligations of the seller and the buyer arising from such a contract"), and some of the matters that are excluded from its scope ("In particular, except as otherwise expressly provided in this Convention, it is not concerned with: (a) the validity of the contract or of any of its provisions or of any usage; (b) the effect which the contract may have on the property in the goods sold").

As far as the first part of the provision is concerned, it is worth pointing out that despite the wording, the matters listed are not the only ones that the CISG is concerned with. For example, Article 8 sets forth rules relating to the interpretation of any statement or conduct of a party, thus addressing an issue that does not relate to any of the matters listed in Article 4. Similarly, the issue dealt with in Article 29 (modification of contracts) also cannot be classified as one of the matters listed in Article 4.

It must also be stressed that not all issues relating to those listed in Article 4 as governed by the CISG actually fall within the scope of the Convention. As far as formation of contract is concerned, for instance, the CISG merely governs the mechanism leading to the conclusion of a contract, in other words, it is concerned solely with the objective requirements for conclusion of a contract. The issue of whether a contract is validly formed, however, is subject to the applicable national rules, as can easily be derived from Article 4(*a*), except for those issues for which the Convention provides exhaustive rules (such as Article 11, laying down the principle of freedom from form requirements). Thus, issues such as capacity to contract, and the consequences of mistake, duress and fraud, are left to applicable domestic law. Where, however, one party errs with respect to the qualities of the goods to be delivered or the solvency of the other party, the rules of the applicable law give way to those of the Convention, since the Convention exhaustively deals with those issues.

As far as the reference to "the rights and obligations of the seller and the buyer arising from [an international sales] contract" is concerned, it must be pointed out that it leads to third party rights not falling within the CISG's scope. "Rights and obligations of the seller and the buyer" are basically those arising between the parties.

As mentioned, Article 4 not only lists some of the matters that the CISG is concerned with, but it also contains a non–exhaustive list of matters it is not concerned with (Article 4(*a*) and (*b*)), except where the CISG otherwise expressly deals with the issue. These matters are the validity of the contract or of any of its provisions or of any usage, as well as the effect the contract may have on the property in the goods sold. In practice this means that where a dispute concerns a matter listed either in Article 4(*a*) or Article 4(*b*) and, therefore, apparently, excluded from the CISG's scope of application, one has to first examine whether the CISG provides a solution to the specific problem. When an issue arises with respect to validity, for instance, one has to first look into whether the specific validity issue in dispute is expressly dealt with by the CISG, as is the formal validity, for instance, before resorting to a sources of law other than the CISG.

As regards the validity exclusion just referred to, it is not limited to the validity of the contract or of its individual provisions, such as a retention of title clause inserted into the contract. It also encompasses the validity of usages. This validity issue must be distinguished from the questions of how usages are to be defined, under which circumstances they are binding on the parties, and what their relationship is to the substantive rules set forth in the CISG. These issues are dealt with in Article 9 CISG.

Article 4 is not the only provision relevant for determining the CISG's scope of application. Article 5 is also relevant. Pursuant to this provision, the CISG is not concerned with liability for death or personal injury caused by the goods to any person. As this provision has been interpreted as covering both injury to the buyer or other persons participating at least indirectly in the contract and also injury to non–participating third parties, the buyer's claims for pecuniary loss resulting from a claim made against the buyer by its own customer for personal injury caused by the goods is also excluded from the CISG's scope of application.

Whereas liability for personal injury is excluded from the CISG's scope, liability for damage caused to property is not. This, of course, may cause a conflict between contractual claims based on the CISG and tort claims based on domestic law. The issue is whether the damaged party can also bring a tort claim or whether the CISG pre–empts that possibility, even though the CISG is not concerned with tort law. In these authors' opinion, the view that the CISG is exclusively applicable in these property damage situations, *i.e.*, that the CISG necessarily prevails also over domestic tort law, is to be rejected. The reason for this can be summarized as follows: If the goods are defective and cause bodily injury, resort to a source of law other than the CISG is necessary in light of Article 5. But even if only property damages were caused, one is outside the principal domain of interests created by contracts and protected by contractual remedies, and would have entered the field of genuinely extra–contractual remedies. Therefore, a tort action for property damages caused by defective and non–conforming goods should not be barred by an omission to give notice within reasonable time under Article 39 CISG.

Articles 4 and 5 expressly list by way of example only a few matters with which the CISG is not concerned. There are many other matters that fall outside the CISG's scope of application. Such matters include the validity of a choice of forum clause, the validity of a penalty clause, the validity of a settlement agreement, agency, the assignment of receivables, the assignment of a contract, the applicable statute of limitations, the issue of jurisdiction, the assumption of debts, the acknowledgement of debts, the effects of the contract on third parties, the issue of joint liability, as well as set–off and the determination of the currency of payments.

5.   VALIDITY AND ITS RELATIONSHIP WITH DOMESTIC REMEDIES

As pointed out earlier, the CISG is not concerned with "the validity of the contract or of any of its provisions or of any usage from the CISG's scope of application", "except as otherwise expressly provided in [the] Convention [itself]" (Article 4 CISG). Still, given the importance of that exclusion from the CISG's scope of application and its impact on the possibility to resort to certain remedies available under the applicable law, in particular rescission for mistake, duress or fraud, a closer look seems appropriate.

In these authors' opinion, simply stating, as some commentators do, that mistake, duress and fraud are matters not at all governed by the CISG, on the sole grounds that Article 4 expressly identifies the "only" matters the CISG governs and that mistake like fraud and duress are not expressly referred to, is far too simplistic and, ultimately, untenable. As mentioned in the previous section, despite the wording of Article 4 the matters listed *are not the only ones* the CISG is concerned with.

From what has been said it results that the introductory wording of Article 4 CISG is not really useful for the purpose of assessing whether, and, if so, to what extent there is interaction between the CISG and domestic contractual remedies, such as rescission for mistake, *i.e.*, to what extent there is preemption or concurrence of CISG and domestic contractual remedies.

In these authors' opinion, the relationship between domestic contractual remedies and defences, such as mistake, fraud and duress, and CISG remedies has to be solved on the basis of a different part of Article 4, namely that part which lays down the so–called "validity exception", according to which "except as otherwise expressly provided in this Convention, it is not concerned with: (a) the validity of the contract" (Article 4(*a*)). This does not mean, however, that these commentators all share the same view as to how the validity–exception impacts on said relationship, since they disagree as to the interpretation of the term "validity". The interaction of CISG remedies and domestic contractual remedies and defences (*i.e.*, the issue of the preemption or concurrence of CISG and domestic contractual remedies and defences) appears to hinge, in other words, on the interpretation of the term "validity", the importance of which becomes evident if one considers how different the definitions are that can be found in the various legal systems.

Some commentators, however, seem not to recognize this and very simplistically (and without any justification) equate mistake and fraud and duress with some kind of "invalidity" and, therefore, exclude mistake and duress and fraud from the CISG's scope of application.

Most commentators, however, approach the issue as one relating (to a great extent) to the interpretation of the term "validity", and wonder whether that term has to be interpreted autonomously or in a more parochial way. Some scholars argue that since the CISG specifically excludes "validity" from its scope of application, the concept of "validity" is a purely domestic concept. For them, this means that whether a party can rescind the contract for mistake is not determined by the CISG, but rather by the applicable domestic law. The better view is, however, to the contrary. There is no reason, nor is there an indication in the legislative history, that the term "validity" is not to be interpreted "autonomously", like most other CISG concepts.[29] Most recently, an attempt at defining the concept (autonomously) has been made by the U.S. District Court for the Southern District of New York, in *Geneva Pharmaceuticals Tech. Corp. v. Barr Labs., Inc.*[30] On that occasion, the Court has defined as a validity issue "any issue by which the domestic law would render the contract void, voidable, or unenforceable."

---

[29]   *See supra* Chapter 1, Section 2.

[30]   U.S. District Court [S.D.N.Y.], 10 May 2002 (*Geneva Pharmaceuticals Tech. Corp. v. Barr Labs., Inc.*), available at http://cisgw3.law.pace.edu/cisg/wais/db/cases2/020510u1.html.

It must be doubted, however, whether resorting to the aforementioned definition (or to any other one, for that matter) is by itself sufficient to solve the issue as to whether domestic contractual remedies can coexist with the CISG or whether the latter preempts any such remedy or defence. In these authors' opinion, to solve this dilemma, one must rather rely on that part of Article 4 that provides for the exception to the validity–exception, *i.e.*, on the part where it is stated that "except as otherwise expressly provided in this Convention", the CISG is not concerned with validity. Pursuant to this wording, even where a dispute concerns a matter that can be qualified as one of "validity" (in an autonomous sense) the CISG cannot simply be disregarded in favor of domestic law remedies. Rather, as briefly mentioned in the previous section, one has to first examine whether the CISG provides an "express" solution to the specific problem to be dealt with. At first sight, this approach seems to favor the view of those authors that claim that the CISG is not concerned with domestic remedies, such as rescission for mistake, fraud and duress, since nowhere does the CISG "expressly" refer to the fact that its governs these issues. The lack of any "express" reference, however, is not at all conclusive, since "except as otherwise expressly provided in this Convention" does not mean that a solution must be expressly provided for. For resort to domestic law, what is required is that no solution to a given problem can be derived from the CISG.

This view is corroborated by the way the CISG deals with form requirements: When stating that "[a] contract of sale need not be concluded in or evidenced by writing and is not subject to any other requirement as to form", Article 11 CISG does not "expressly" provide that contrary to Article 4(*a*) it deals with an issue that can be analogized to a validity issue;[31] nevertheless, there is no doubt at all that Article 11 supersedes domestic rules which make validity conditional on the observance of form requirements.

In light of the foregoing, the following rule can be established to deal with the preemption or coexistence of the CISG and domestic contractual remedies and defences: where, in relation to a specific set of facts, the CISG provides solutions that are exhaustive and functionally equivalent to the otherwise applicable domestic remedies, the CISG preempts recourse to those domestic remedies, independently from any domestic labeling of the specific issue to be dealt with (as one of validity, non–performance, etc.).

In practice, this means that once a court has decided that an issue is one of "validity" as autonomously defined under the CISG and, therefore, (potentially) excluded from the CISG's scope of application on the grounds of Article 4, the court will have to identify the applicable domestic law to a specific contract and determine whether

---

[31]   *See* Trib. Padova (Italy), 31 March 2004, available in English at http://cisgw3.law.pace.edu/cisg/wais/db/cases2/040331 i3.html.

domestic remedies or defences are available to the parties in the specific case. The courts then have to look into whether the CISG makes available solutions that are functionally equivalent to the remedies and defences they have identified as being available to the parties under the applicable domestic law. If the CISG does so, its rules will preempt the corresponding domestic remedies and defences; where no functionally equivalent solutions are available under the CISG, it is the domestic law that determines what remedies and defences the parties can rely on *in concreto*.

In light of the foregoing, it cannot surprise that commentators hold that the issue of capacity to contract is left to the applicable domestic law. Furthermore, nor can it surprise that proponents of this reading of Article 4 favor the view that the CISG is not concerned with cases of aggravated defect of intention, such as fraud and duress, since the CISG does not at all provide rules that, from a functional point of view, are comparable to those that in domestic law fall under the heading of fraud and duress.

As far as mistake is concerned, the solution to the preemption/coexistence dilemma is more complex, as there are too many types of mistake to be able to provide a one–for–all–solution.

Where the mistake relates to the characteristics of the goods, and the applicable law does not itself preempt recourse to rescission by obliging the mistaken party to resort to domestic remedies for non–conformity, as does German law for instance, the CISG preempts resort to domestic (rescission) law. This is because the CISG provides a set of rules that exhaustively deals with the consequences of such a mistake, namely Articles 35 and 45 *et seq.*, on non–conformity and remedies for breach of contract by the seller respectively, the circumvention of which has to be prevented.[32] Similarly, domestic rules governing mistake regarding the characteristics of the opposing party, such as the seller's ability to perform and the buyer's creditworthiness, are preempted,[33] since Article 71 CISG sets forth a rule regarding the consequences of the one party's potential inability to perform that arises after the conclusion of the contract, and, thus, excludes resort to domestic remedies addressing the situation that—after the conclusion of the contract—serious doubts arise as to that party's ability to perform the obligations undertaken.

In some countries, in case of a mistake as to the existence of the goods at the time the contract is concluded (*i.e.*, in case of initial impossibility), the contract is considered void. In other countries, the issue is not treated as one of validity, but rather as one of non–performance and excuse. The same can be said for the CISG, which leads to the CISG preempting domestic law in respect of this type of

---

[32]   *See* Supreme Court of Austria, 13 April 2000, available in English at http://cisgw3.law.pace.edu/cases/000413a3.html.

[33]   *See* Supreme Court of Austria, 12 February 1998, available in English at http://cisgw3.law.pace.edu/cisg/wais/db/cases2/980212a3.html.

mistake as well. Also, where a mistake "in the transmission of the communication" has been made, the mistaken party cannot rely on domestic rules governing the rescission for that mistake, since Article 27 exhaustively addresses the consequences of this kind of mistake, thus preempting domestic law.

There are other types of mistake, however, for which the CISG does not provide functionally equivalent solutions. This is true, for instance, in respect of a mistake concerning the identity of the opposing party. It is therefore on the basis of domestic law that courts will have to decide whether one may rescind the contract for this kind of mistake. Similarly, the CISG does not provide rules that serve the same function as domestic rules on rescission for mistake regarding the identity of the goods.[34]

The issue of preemption or concurrence of CISG and domestic remedies does not only arise in respect of domestic remedies based on contract law, but also where they are based on tort law, since what constitutes a breach of contract (delivery of non–conforming goods) under the CISG may at the same time constitute a tort under domestic law.

The starting point for any discussion of the issue at hand is Article 5, which, as mentioned on an earlier occasion, states that the CISG "does not

---

[34]   *See* Supreme Court of Switzerland, 11 December 2000, available in English at http://cisgw3.law.pace.edu/cisg/wais/db/cases2/001211s1.html.

apply to the liability of the seller for death or
personal injury caused by the goods to any person".
This does not mean that the seller is not liable for
death or personal injury caused by the goods, but
rather that a domestic liability regime applies, to be
identified by means of the private international law
rules of the forum. This is true as regards the
liability for death or personal injury "to any person",
including the buyer's claims for pecuniary loss
resulting from a claim against the buyer for
personal injury caused by the goods the buyer sold
in a sub–sale.

Whereas liability for death and personal injury is
expressly excluded from the CISG's scope, provided
that the death or personal injury is "caused by the
goods", liability for damage caused to property is not
at all excluded from its scope.[35] This, of course, may
cause the preemption/concurrence dilemma referred
to earlier. Where the damaged party does not want
to or cannot claim damages on the grounds of the
CISG, it may want to resort to the applicable tort
law; the issue is whether that party is entitled to do
so.

In these authors' opinion, the view according to
which the CISG is exclusively applicable, that it
basically preempts all domestic tort law, is to be
rejected. The justification for this can be found in
the functional equivalence approach referred to
earlier: According to that approach, which is based

---

[35]   *See* HG Kanton Zürich (Switzerland), 26 April 1995,
available at http://www.unilex.info/case.cfm?pid=1&do=case&id=
166&step=FullText.

on a positive reading of Article 4 and applies not merely to "validity" issues, the CISG preempts possibly concurring domestic law solely where it provides a comprehensive solution to a specific problem that is functionally equivalent to that found in domestic law. As far as the preemption/concurrence dilemma at hand is concerned, this means that the CISG cannot preempt all domestic tort law, as tort law is based on different policy considerations and serves functions different from those of contract law and, thus, those of the rules of the CISG. Whereas contract law and, thus, the CISG as well protect "what [a party] is entitled to expect under the contract"[36], *i.e.*, contractual interests the shape and extent of which depend on the parties' agreement, tort law protects a much wider and more fundamental range of interests, and independently so from any contractual relationship between the parties. This does not mean, however, that where such a contractual relationship exists, the protection of those fundamental interests is not due. A party to a contract can expect that the other party uses the same care in protecting its fundamental interests as that party does in protecting that of persons with which that party does not entertain any contractual relationship. Ultimately, this means that "[t]here is no difficulty in regarding the imposition of a duty of care in tort as independent of any contractual liability, and [of] the CISG, [that] was designed only

---

[36]   Article 25 CISG.

to deal with the contractual side"[37], and not with tort law.[38]

Thus, to the extent that the protected interests overlap (as in the case where the goods bought are damaged), the CISG applies exclusively and trumps domestic law. Where there is no overlap, resort to domestic tort law is not excluded *a priori*; rather, the concurrent application of domestic tort law will depend on the answer to be found in the applicable law to the question of whether such a *cumul* is excluded, as in French law, or whether that kind of *Anspruchskonkurrenz* is admitted, as in German law.

---

[37]   Joseph Lookofsky, *In Dubio Pro Conventione? Some Thoughts about Opt–Outs, Computer Programs and Preemption under the 1980 Vienna Sales Convention (CISG)*, 13 DUKE JOURNAL OF COMPARATIVE AND INTERNATIONAL LAW 263, 286 (2003).

[38]   *See* U.S. District Court [S.D.N.Y.], 10 May 2002 (*Geneva Pharmaceuticals Tech. Corp. v. Barr Labs., Inc.*), available at http://cisgw3.law.pace.edu/cases/020510u1.html#svib;   U.S. District Court [E.D. Penn.], 29 August 2000 (*Viva Vino Import Corporation v. Farnese Vini S.r.l.*), available at http://www.cisg.law.pace.edu/cisg/wais/db/cases2/000829u1.html.

CHAPTER 5

FORM, FORMATION OF CONTRACT AND PRE–CONTRACTUAL LIABILITY

1.   FORM

Any discussion on form requirements has to necessarily start with Article 11 CISG, which sets forth the principle of freedom from form requirements. Thus, a contract governed by the CISG does generally not need to be concluded in writing.[1] This means that a contract can also be concluded orally[2] as well as through the conduct of the parties.[3] Furthermore, Article 11 also overrides domestic rules that require a contract to be signed for it to bind the parties.

As far as the scope of the aforementioned freedom from form requirements is concerned, from a substantive point, Article 11 CISG merely refers to the conclusion of contracts, thus expressly making that principle applicable only to the statements that

---

[1]   *See* Supreme Court of Austria 9 March 2000, available at http://www.cisg.at/6_31199z.htm; Oregon Court of Appeals, 12 April 1995 (*GPL Treatment v. Louisiana–Pacific*), available at http://www.cisg.law.pace.edu/cisg/wais/db/cases2/950412u1.html.

[2]   *See* U.S. Court of Appeals [11th Cir.], 29 June 1998 (*MCC–Marble Ceramic Center, Inc. v. Ceramica Nuova D'Agostino, S.p.A.*), available at http://www.cisg.law.pace.edu/cisg/wais/db/cases2/980629u1.html.

[3]   *See* Hof Beroep Gent (Belgium), 17 May 2002, available at http://www.law.kuleuven.ac.be/int/tradelaw/WK/2002–05–17.htm; OLG München (Germany), 8 March 1995, available in English at http://cisgw3.law.pace.edu/cases/950308g1.html.

are relevant in the formation process (such as offer, withdrawal, revocation, acceptance, etc.). Still, the principle of freedom from form requirements generally applies to all statements made by the parties, as long as they are governed by the CISG. In respect of statements that relate to the termination or modification of a contract governed under the CISG this can be evinced from Article 29 CISG, which presupposes the principle set forth in Article 11 CISG and extends it to also cover these statements. Consequently, a written contract can be modified orally, provided that the written contract does not contain a provision requiring any modification or termination by agreement to be in writing.[4] In the light of what has just been said, it cannot surprise that an implied termination of the contract has been held possible.[5]

In respect of those statements to which neither Article 11 nor Article 29 CISG apply directly, the freedom from form requirements is to be evinced from the general principle upon which the CISG is based, which can be derived from Articles 11 and 29 CISG, pursuant to which the parties are free to make any statement in any form, be it in writing or orally or in any other form. Of course, this general principle can solely be resorted to where the statements relate to issues dealt with in the CISG.

---

[4]   *See* ICC Court of Arbitration, Arbitral Award n. 9117, available at http://www.unilex.info/case.cfm?pid=1&do=case&id=399&step=FullText.

[5]   *See* Supreme Court of Austria, 29 June 1999, available in English at http://cisgw3.law.pace.edu/cases/990629a3.html.

Therefore, it is up to the applicable domestic law to decide what form requirements have to be met for a choice of forum clause or an agreement restricting competition to be valid, as those matters fall outside the CISG's scope of application.

According to Article 11 CISG, the contract not only does not have to be concluded in writing, it also "is not subject to any other requirement as to form". The CISG does, however, not provide a definition of what amounts to a "requirement as to form". The CISG merely contains a (dispositive) provision, Article 13, which compares telegrams and telexes to writings. This does not compare to a definition of "writing", but rather an interpretive rule that is supposed to make sure that telegrams and telexes are considered "writings". Although the provision only refers to telegrams and telexes, other means of communication also meet the "writing" requirements, as the list of means of communication it refers to is not exhaustive. Thus, it is possible to state that a telefax also constitutes a "writing".[6] Similarly, communications transmitted electronically are also to be considered "writings".

As mentioned, Article 13 merely provides a rule of interpretation in respect of "writing"; it does not define "requirements as to form" referred to in Article 11. This does not mean that one should resort to domestic law to define that concept. "Requirements as to form" is a term to be defined—

---

[6]   *See* Supreme Court of Austria, 2 July 1993, available at http://www.unilex.info/case.cfm?pid=1&do=case&id=165&step= FullText.

as most other terms used in the CISG— "autonomously", not in the light of any domestic law. Therefore it cannot surprise that the expression at hand has been defined extensively, so as to include all requirements that "make validity conditional on the observance of requirements as to form and which therefore render contracts invalid, void, or voidable (but possible curable) where those requirements have not been observed."

It must be pointed out that Article 11 does not only set forth the principle of freedom from form requirements for substantive purposes, but also for evidentiary ones. By doing so, the drafters wanted to make sure that the parties are freed from having to comply with domestic requirements as to the means to be used in proving the existence of a contract governed by the CISG. Consequently, domestic rules requiring a contract to be evidenced in writing in order for it to be enforceable are superseded, which is why it is generally correct to state, as did several courts, that "the contract can be proven with any means",[7] among others, through witnesses.

As far as the evidence presented by the parties is concerned, the CISG does not deal with its probative value; in other words, the CISG does not establish a hierarchy of the probative value of different types of

---

[7] *See* RB Koophandel Hasselt (Belgium), 22 May 2002, available at http://www.law.kuleuven.ac.be/int/tradelaw/WK/ 2002–05–22.htm; OLG München (Germany), 8 March 1995, available in English at http://cisgw3.law.pace.edu/cases/950308g1 .html.

evidence. Thus it is up to the judges to determine—within the limits set by the procedural rules of the forum—how to evaluate that evidence. Consequently, a judge may well attribute more weight to a written document than to oral testimony.[8]

According to Article 12 CISG, the principle of freedom from form requirements does not *per se* apply where one party has its relevant place of business in a State that made an Article 96 declaration. The effects of an Article 96 declaration will depend on the law applicable by virtue of rule of private international law of the forum. This means that the form requirements of the State having declared an Article 96 reservation do not necessarily apply. The legislative history appears to corroborate this view, since during the Vienna Diplomatic Conference a proposal was rejected pursuant to which the form requirements of the State that had made an Article 96 reservation had to be applied. Thus, where rules of private international law lead to the law of a State that made an Article 96 reservation, the form requirements of that State will have to be complied with; where, on the other hand, the law applicable is that of a Contracting State that did not make an Article 96 reservation, the

---

[8]   *See* RB Koophandel Hasselt (Belgium), 22 May 2002, available at http://www.law.kuleuven.ac.be/int/tradelaw/WK/2002–05–22.htm.

principle of freedom from form requirements applies.[9]

2. GENERAL ISSUE RELATING TO THE CISG'S RULES ON FORMATION OF CONTRACT

Unlike other uniform substantive law conventions, the CISG does not only address issues specific to the type of contract it governs, namely that for the international sale of goods, but it also addresses matters of a more general nature. One such matter is that of the "Formation of the Contract", to which Part II of the CISG is dedicated (Articles 14–24). It is worth mentioning from the outset that although the provisions of Part II govern all contractual agreements covered by the CISG, including an agreement to terminate, modify, or supplement an already existing contract, it only governs the external mechanism through which to reach an agreement,[10] and it does so "by following the conventional mechanism of offer and corresponding acceptance."[11] Therefore, except for form requirements, substantive validity requirements are not governed by the CISG, and must be determined according to the applicable domestic law—to be identified on the basis of the

---

[9]   *See* RB Rotterdam (The Netherlands), 12 July 2001, available in English at http://cisgw3.law.pace.edu/cases/010712 n1.html.

[10]   *See* Supreme Court of Austria, 6 February 1996, available in English at http://cisgw3.law.pace.edu/cases/960206a3.html.

[11]   LG Zwickau (Germany), 19 March 1999, available at http://www.globalsaleslaw.org/content/api/cisg/urteile/519.htm.

rules of private international law of the forum. Thus, domestic law is applicable to some issues relevant for determining whether a contract has been validly concluded. This is true, for instance, as regards the legal capacity of a person and the capacity to contract, as well as questions concerning defects of intent, such as duress, fraud and mistake (except for issues relating to mistake as to the quality of goods and to mistake as to the other party's capacity to perform or the other party's solvency, which are all governed by the CISG), and questions concerning the power of representation in the case of a contract concluded by an agent. Although the CISG's rules on formation of contract are based, as mentioned, on the conventional scheme of contract conclusion through offer and acceptance, "other forms of getting to an agreement [are] not excluded [by the CISG]."[12] Hence, parties "can get to a contract even if offer and acceptance are not clearly distinguishable",[13] provided there is agreement between the parties as to the *essentialia negotii.*

As to the reach of the CISG's rules on formation, it extends to the question of whether standard contract terms are incorporated into a contract. To determine whether standard contract terms are part of the offer and, therefore, are part of the contract, special regard must be given to Article 8. Hence,

---

[12]   OLG München (Germany), 8 March 1995, available in English at http://cisgw3.law.pace.edu/cases/950208g1.html.

[13]   Hof Beroep Gent (Belgium), 15 May 2002, available in English at http://cisgw3.law.pace.edu/cases/020515b1.html.

where the offeree knew or could not have been unaware of the fact that it was the offeror's intent that the standard contract terms be part of the offer, these terms have to be considered an integral part of the offer (Article 8(1).[14] Even absent the aforementioned requirements, the standard contract terms must be considered an integral part of the offer if "a reasonable person of the same kind" as the offeree "in the same circumstances" (Article 8(2)) would have understood that the terms were supposed to be part of the offer. Pursuant to Article 8(3), in determining the understanding a reasonable person of the same kind as the offeree would have had, due consideration is to be given to all relevant circumstances of the case including the negotiations, any practices which the parties have established between themselves, usages and any subsequent conduct of the parties.[15] "An effective incorporation of standard contract terms therefore requires above all that the addressee of the offer could become aware of offeror's intent to incorporate his standard contract terms into the contract. Furthermore, the [CISG] requires [. . .] from the user of standard contract terms that he send their text to the addressee or make them available in another way."[16] In contrast, domestic law is applicable to the question of whether standard contract terms that

---

[14]   Supreme Court of Germany, 31 October 2001, available in English at http://cisgw3.law.pace.edu/cases/011031g1.html.

[15]   *See* Supreme Court of Austria, 31 August 2005, available in English at http://cisgw3.law.pace.edu/cases/050831a3.html.

[16]   Supreme Court of Germany, 31 October 2001, available in English at http://cisgw3.law.pace.edu/cases/011031g1.html.

have been incorporated into a contract are valid, provided that this issue is not to be decided on the sole basis of form requirements being met.

The issue of whether the failure to object to a commercial letter of confirmation also constitutes an issue of contract formation and, therefore, is generally subject to Part II CISG. Since, however, pursuant to Article 9(2) CISG there are instances in which usage prevails over the (default) rules of the CISG, including those contained in Part II, rules concerning the failure to object to a commercial letter of confirmation other than those set forth in the CISG may be relevant, provided that these rules can be considered "usages" in the sense of Article 9(2) CISG. This requires, as mentioned previously,[17] that both contractual parties must have their relevant place of business in a geographical area that subscribes to that particular usage (or must maintain commercial operations in that area on a regular basis), that the usage be one that is widely known in international trade, and is regularly observed by parties to contracts of the type involved in the particular trade concerned.[18]

Since the provisions found in Part II are by nature dispositive, the parties can (explicitly or implicitly) agree to exclude them or derogate from them. This agreement may be subject to rules other than those contained in Part II of the CISG. This is

---

[17]   *See supra* Chapter 2, Section 4.

[18]   *See* OLG Frankfurt (Germany), 5 July 1995, available in English at http://cisgw3.law.pace.edu/cases/950705g1.html.

the case, for instance, where the parties agree upon the exclusion in a framework agreement concluded prior to the conclusion of the sales contract itself. What, however, if the offeror attempts to exclude the CISG unilaterally by inserting a clause to that effect into the offer relating to the sales contract? In this line of cases, the rules of Part II of the CISG apply, which means that the question of whether there is an offer that includes that clause is to be answered on the basis of the CISG, just as much as the question of whether a reply by the offeree constitutes an acceptance. If the offeree issues a statement mirroring the offer, an agreement as to the CISG's exclusion is reached. If the offeree does not agree to the CISG's exclusion, by virtue of Article 19 no such agreement is reached and the CISG applies. The same is true if it is the offeree who wants to exclude the CISG, as the offeree's reply containing an exclusion clause not contained in the offer would necessarily be a reply which materially alters the terms of the offer; as such, this would, by virtue of Article 19(2), constitute a counter–offer, with the effect of not being able to be considered an acceptance and, therefore, to exclude the CISG.

3.   OFFER

As mentioned in the earlier chapter, the CISG's rules on formation are based on the mechanism of offer and acceptance. As regards the offer, it is Article 14 that identifies the substantive requirements that a proposal has to meet to amount to an offer. One such requirement is that the statement be addressed to one or more specific persons. A statement is considered to be addressed to a group of specific persons not only where it addresses each member by name, but also where the party making the proposal has a clear idea of the persons addressed. This is why, for instance, sending a prospectus, a catalogue, or a price list is not making an offer. The same is true with respect to advertisements in newspapers, on the radio or on television, as well as statements addressed to an indefinite group of persons via the Internet, for instance by sending out a high number of emails. If, however, the offeror manifests his intention to be bound unambiguously, even a proposal addressed to a larger audience may amount to an offer. This is the case, for instance, where the proposal contains a "while stocks last" clause, or any clause that makes it clear that the availability of goods is limited. The existence of the intent to be bound must also be assumed where the proposal addressed *ad incertas personas* contains the following wording: "This advertisement constitutes an offer" and "These goods will be sold to the first person who presents cash or an appropriate banker's account."

Furthermore, in order for a proposal to constitute an offer under the CISG it has to be so definite that the sole acceptance of the proposal leads to the conclusion of the contract or that "in case of acceptance it can constitute the basis for a decision."[19] Pursuant to Article 14(1), this requirement is met, if the goods are (expressly or implicitly) indicated and if the quantity and the price are expressly or implicitly fixed, or if provision is made for their determination. Consequently, a contract is concluded if a proposal meeting these requirements is accepted, irrespective of whether the parties reached an agreement on additional issues, since what is crucial is "that the parties have agreed to the essential minimum content the parties wanted to agree to."[20]

For a proposal to be an offer, it must also indicate the offeror's intent to be bound in case of an acceptance of the proposal.[21] Whether the intention to be bound exists is generally to be assessed on a case–by–case basis; still, some assumptions can be made. Thus, for instance, it is possible to assume that the more a proposal complies with the specificity requirement also set forth in Article 14 (concerning, for instance, the goods, quantity and price) the more probable it is that the intention to be bound exists. Article 14(2) itself establishes the rule that intent to be bound generally does not exist where the proposal is addressed to an indefinite group of persons. However, even a proposal addressed to one or more specific persons can fail to manifest an intention to be bound. It is to be

---

[19]   *See* OLG Frankfurt (Germany), 4 March 1994, available in English at http://cisgw3.law.pace.edu/cases/940304g1.html.

[20]   LG München (Germany), 8 February 1995, available in English at http://cisgw3.law.pace.edu/cases/950208g4.html.

[21]   *See* Supreme Court of Austria, 18 June 1997, available in English at http://cisgw3.law.pace.edu/cases/970618a3.html.

assumed, for instance, that such intent is lacking where the proposal contains expressions such as "without obligation", "non–binding", or other expressions to the same effect. A proposal containing the reservation "subject to contract" lacks the necessary intention to be bound. A letter of intent, which normally contains all the other elements referred to in Article 14 and is usually addressed to a specific person, generally also lacks the intention to be bound. The same is true for a "memorandum of understanding". On the other hand, it must be assumed that the intention to be bound exists where goods are being sent to a party with indication of the purchase price.

The issue of whether a proposal meets the aforementioned requirements is subject to Article 8 (on interpretation). In light of this provision, where the offeree did not know or could not have been unaware of the offeror's intent, the proposal is to be interpreted "according to the offeror's intent that was recognizable to the addressee."[22] "In doing so, pursuant to Article 8 CISG due consideration is to be given to the negotiations, any practices which the parties have established between themselves, usages and any subsequent conduct of the parties."[23] Furthermore, where a proposal remains ambiguous despite an interpretation in light of Article 8, no acceptable offer exists. If the proposal is composed in a language unknown to the

---

[22] Supreme Court of Austria, 6 February 1996, available in English at http://cisgw3.law.pace.edu/cases/960206a3.html.

[23] *Id.*

addressee or in a language that a reasonable person of the same kind as the addressee would not know, the proposal cannot be considered an offer; this is provided that a different result cannot be reached on the grounds of practices established between the parties, any usage that is binding upon the parties on the basis of Article 9, or from an agreement they have reached on the occasion, for instance, of a framework agreement.

It is worth noting that the offer not only has to meet all Article 14 requirements, but also any validity requirements of the applicable law, determined on the basis of the private international law of the forum, such as requirements concerning legal capacity, the absence of certain kinds of mistake, duress, etc. In principle, form requirements do not have to be fulfilled in order for a proposal to be able to be considered an offer under the CISG. Thus, oral declarations, as well as silence and implied conduct, such as the handing over of goods, may amount to an offer (provided that the requirements mentioned earlier are met). The choice of the communication medium (telephone, telex, facsimile, e–mail, etc.) is also subject to the offeror's discretion. The offeror can indicate in its offer that the acceptance has to take a particular form. An offer providing that silence will be treated as acceptance is, however, not binding upon the offeree.

It is worth pointing out that if it results from an agreement of the parties (*e.g.* a framework agreement), the practices established between them, the usages (as referred to in Article 9) that the proposal has to contain additional elements in order to be considered an offer, an "acceptance" relating solely to the aforementioned essential elements will not lead to the conclusion of the contract.

Pursuant to Article 15 CISG, an offer becomes effective only when it reaches the addressee. Consequently, an offer that does not reach the addressee is ineffective and cannot, therefore, be accepted (even if the addressee learns of the contents of the offer in a different manner). An offer "reaches" the addressee when it is made orally to him or delivered by other means to him personally, to his place of business or mailing address, or if he does not have a place of business or mailing address, to his habitual residence. In other words, when considering the question of when the offer might become effective (such as at the time of declaration, time of dispatch, time of receipt by the offeree, time of knowledge by the offeree), the drafters of the CISG decided in favor of the point in time that best spreads the risk of non–receipt and incorrect transmission of the offer between the persons concerned, *i.e.*, the offeror and the offeree. The offeror bears the risk of transmission until the time of delivery, which entails that the offer becomes effective as it was delivered and not as it was declared. On the contrary, the addressee bears the risk (loss, destruction, late knowledge, etc.) after delivery has occurred.

The time when an offer reaches its addressee does not only determine when the aforementioned risk to the offeror passes, but also when the offer can be accepted. Thus, it determines the beginning of the time period within which the offer can be accepted and also the point after which a revocable offer can be revoked. But the moment when the offer reaches the offeree also determines the moment until which an offer—even an irrevocable one—can be withdrawn—by way of a statement aiming at the offer *in itinere* (or part of it) from becoming effective, as long as that statement reaches the offeree before or at the same time as the offer that it aims to withdraw.

Once the offer reaches the offeree without having been withdrawn, it produces its effects. This does not necessarily mean that the offeror cannot change his mind after that moment. In effect, since under the CISG an offer is generally revocable, the offeror may prevent the offeree from being able to accept the offer by means of a revocation, which constitutes one of the main grounds for termination of an offer—another one being the rejection of the offer by the offeree (Article 17). In order for a revocation to be effective different preconditions must be met. As regards its contents, the revocation must be designed in a way to allow a "reasonable person of the same kind" as the offeree "in the same circumstances" (Article 8(2)) to understand that it refers to the offer and is intended to prevent it from becoming accepted by the offeree. Furthermore, like the withdrawal, the revocation must reach its addressee to become effective, which means that it is not necessary that the offeree gain knowledge of the revocation.

The offeror's right to revoke the offer is, however, not unlimited. Unsurprisingly, the conclusion of the contract curtails the offeror's right to revoke the offer. Pursuant to Article 16(2), the right to revoke an offer also ends when the offeree dispatches an acceptance. Thus, a revocation that reaches the offeree after the offeree has dispatched an acceptance is ineffective, irrespective of whether the lateness is due to the offeror or not.

It is worth pointing out that not all offers are necessarily revocable. An offer may itself indicate that it is irrevocable. Thus, where the offeror makes an offer irrevocable (by using, for instance, words such as "fix" or "irrevocable"), a revocation will remain ineffective and the offeree can accept the offer despite that revocation. The irrevocability of an offer does not necessarily need to be stated explicitly. Pursuant to Article 16(2)(*a*), the irrevocability of an offer can also be indicated "otherwise", as long as the offeror's intention to render the offer irrevocable is real. According to the foregoing provision, this appears to be the case where the offer states a fixed time for acceptance. In these authors' view, however, fixing a time for acceptance does not necessarily compare to rendering an offer irrevocable. Rather, it merely creates a rebuttable presumption of irrevocability of the offer. This means, for instance, that where it is shown that fixing a time for acceptance is merely intended to let the offer lapse after that time, an offer cannot be considered irrevocable.

Article 16(2) also lists another instance where an offer cannot be revoked: where it was reasonable for the offeree to rely on the irrevocability of the offer and the offeree acted in reliance on the offer. As for the first prerequisite, it is met where the offeree could assume, in light of the specific circumstances, that the offeror felt irrevocably bound to the offer; this assumption is "reasonable" only where a "reasonable person of the same kind" as the offeree would, "in the same circumstances", reach the same conclusion. Furthermore, the offeree also has to have acted (or omitted to do so) in reliance on the irrevocability of the offer. It can be said that the offeree has done so, for instance, where production is started, material is obtained or new personnel is employed. For the purposes of the issue at hand it may also be relevant that the offeree has rejected other offers.

4. ACCEPTANCE

As mentioned on several occasions already, the CISG's rules on formation of contract are based upon the traditional approach of contract conclusion via offer and acceptance. This makes it necessary to focus on the acceptance, after having focused on the offer in the previous part.

As for the acceptance, it is defined in Article 18 as a "statement made by or other conduct of the offeree indicating assent to an offer". This is, however, but a rudimentary definition of acceptance. With the help of other provisions, a more precise definition can be elaborated. Article 19, for instance, makes it clear that although for a reply to an offer to amount to an acceptance and, thus, lead to the conclusion of the contract, it generally must fully correspond to the offer, a reply that purports to be an acceptance may lead to the conclusion of the contract even though it differs from the offer. This compares to an exception to the so–called "mirror–image–rule". This exception is, however, limited in scope, as a reply that purports to be an acceptance can only lead to the conclusion of the contract to the extent that the points on which the reply differs from the offer do not materially alter the offer.

In light of the foregoing and other provisions to be found in Part II, the acceptance can be defined as a reply by the offeree, generally free form any form requirements, indicating assent to the offer, whether through a statement or by conduct, that: must be made with the intention to be bound, must—as a general matter—reach the offeror to be effective, and this within a given time frame, and, from a substantive point of view, must not contain additional or different terms that materially alter the terms of the offer.

As regards the offeree's intention to be bound, it allows one to distinguish the acceptance from other kinds of statements addressed by the offeree to offeror and that are more interlocutory in nature. The issue of whether a statement by the offeree amounts to an acceptance or merely constitutes, for example, a confirmation of receipt of the offer, a request for clarification, or any other statement which will not lead to the conclusion of a contract, must be determined through interpretation based on the rules of interpretation set forth in Article 8.[24]

In principle, the acceptance is not subject to any form requirement, which leads, *inter alia*, to the acceptance not necessarily having to have the same form as the offer. Where, however, one of the parties has its place of business in a contracting State that declared an Article 96 reservation, a contract for the international sale of goods—and, thus, the acceptance as well—may be subject to form requirements. Also, where the offeror requires that the acceptance take a particular form, which the offeror as the "master of the offer" is certainly entitled to do, an acceptance taking a form other than the one imposed by the offeror does not lead to the conclusion of the contract, as it merely amounts to a counter–offer.

As regards the language of the acceptance, it must be pointed out that if the acceptor uses a language different from the one used by the offeror, the acceptor's reply does not amount to an acceptance, unless the language used is that of the offeror, the language used during the negotiations, or a language the use of which was authorized in the offer.

---

[24]   *See* OLG Frankfurt (Germany), 30 August 2000, available in English at http://cisgw3.law.pace.edu/cases/000830g1.html.

As one can gather from the definition of acceptance, acceptance does not necessarily have to occur by means of an express declaration; a given conduct can also amount to acceptance and, thus, lead to the conclusion of the contract. However, "[s]ilence or inactivity does not in itself amount to acceptance" (Article 8(1) CISG).

Although it has to be determined on the basis of a case–by–case approach whether a given conduct amounts to acceptance, there are certain types of conduct that generally indicate assent to the offer. This is true, for instance, for the shipment of the goods the offeror offered to buy. The same is true with respect to the payment of the purchase price.[25] Further examples of conduct that generally amounts to acceptance are: the opening of a letter of credit for the purchase price,[26] the dispatch of an invoice or the signature thereof by the buyer,[27] the cashing of a cheque sent with the offer, the

---

[25] *See* U.S. District Court [W.D. Wash.], 13 April 2006 (*Barbara Berry, S.A. de C.V. v. Ken M. Spooner Farms, Inc.*), available at http://cisgw3.law.pace.edu/cases/060413u1.html: payment of the purchase price and opening of the packaging constitute an acceptance; HG Kanton St. Gallen (Switzerland), 29 April 2004, available at http://cisgw3.law.pace.edu/cases/041202 s1.html: payment of the sums requested in the offer compares to an acceptance.

[26] *See* U.S. District Court [N.D. Ill.], 7 December 1999 (*Magellan International Corp. v. Salzgitter Handel GmbH*), available at http://cisgw3.law.pace.edu/cases/991207u1.html.

[27] *See* Cámara Nacional de Apelaciones en lo Comercial de Buenos Aires (Argentina), 14 October 1993, abstract available in English at http://cisgw3.law.pace.edu/cases/931014a1.html.

processing of the goods by the buyer,[28] the entering into transactions to make the production of the goods possible and the commencing of production.

One must wonder about the relationship that exists between the possibility to conclude a contract through conduct indicating assent (Article 18(2)) and the basic necessity that the acceptance reach the offeror provided for in Article 18(1). Article 18 itself deals with that relationship by providing in para. 3 for an exception (for certain conduct indicating assent) to the principle that acceptance must reach the offeror for it to lead to contract conclusion. Accordingly, receipt is not necessary in those cases in which the acceptor is, as an exception, not required to give notice to the offeror of the conduct indicating assent. "Thus, conduct indicating assent generally amounts to acceptance only in those cases where notice thereof reaches the offeror in a way that allows the offeror to gain knowledge of that notice."

As can be derived from the aforementioned definition of acceptance, as a general matter, a declaration of acceptance must reach the offeror for it to become effective. This requirement generally applies also to conduct indicating assent. From this it follows that such conduct only becomes effective— and leads to the conclusion of the contract—when a notice (of any kind) of said conduct reaches the

---

[28]   *See* OLG Saarbrücken (Germany), 13 January 1993, available at http://cisgw3.law.pace.edu/cases/930113g1.html.

offeror in a manner that allows the offeror to gain knowledge of that notice.

From the foregoing requirement it follows, among other things, that the acceptance "travels" at the risk of the acceptor. This in turn means that the acceptor is bound by the acceptance as it is received by the offeror, subject to the acceptor's possibility to avoid the contract on the basis of the applicable domestic law.

From Article 18(3) it can be derived that, by way of an exception, conduct indicating assent may be effective and, thus, lead to the conclusion of the contract, even if the offeror is in no position to become aware of such conduct. This requires, however, that the acceptor is authorized to not notify the offeror of the performance of acts indicating assent. Such authorization, which can either relate to a specific act indicating assent or be framed in more general terms, can originate from a waiver on the part of the offeror of the need for a notice, from an agreement between the parties, from practices established between the parties, or from usages that are binding upon the parties pursuant to Article 9. As "master of the offer", the offeror is certainly entitled to waive the need for a notice informing him of the performance of acts indicating assent to reach him and, thus, anticipate that the moment in time at which the contract is concluded will be the time the act indicating assent is performed.

An indication of assent that does not need to reach the offeror becomes effective as soon as it occurs. A notice to the offeror of the assent being given is not necessary for the acceptance to be effective.

For an acceptance to lead to the conclusion to the contract, it must become effective within a given timeframe, so as to limit the time period within which the addressee of the offer can speculate at the cost of the offeror.

The time period for acceptance can be fixed by the offeror, either expressly or implicitly. The offeror's discretion regarding the length of the time period for acceptance is limitless. It is therefore irrelevant whether the time for acceptance fixed by the offeror would otherwise be considered "unreasonable".

Where no time has been fixed by the offeror for acceptance, the acceptance must reach the offeror within a reasonable time (but for oral offers, which must be accepted immediately). In determining that "reasonable time", Article 18(2) expressly requires that due account be "taken of the circumstances of the transaction." These circumstances can relate to any of the three time periods which together compose the reasonable time for acceptance: the time for the offer to reach the offeree, the time for consideration of the offer needed by the offeree, and the time for the reply purporting to be an acceptance to reach the offeror.

Despite the foregoing, under certain circumstances, pursuant to Article 21 CISG, a late acceptance can lead to the conclusion of the contract. In this respect, Article 21 distinguishes between two different scenarios, according to the reasons for the lateness of the acceptance. While Article 21(1) sets forth a general rule potentially governing every late acceptance, irrespective of the grounds for the lateness, Article 21(2), which prevails as *lex specialis* over Article 21(1), addresses the case in which the lateness of the acceptance is due to a discernible delay in its transmission.

Pursuant to the general rule, a late acceptance is nevertheless effective as an acceptance if, without delay, the offeror orally so informs the offeree or dispatches a notice to that effect. Whether the approval is made "without delay" depends on the amount of time that elapses between the moment when the late acceptance reaches the offeror (or when the act indicating assent is performed) and the moment the approval is dispatched. It is irrelevant whether the approval ever reaches the acceptor. This means, on the one hand, that a withdrawal of the approval is not possible, and, on the other hand, that the acceptor bears the risk of loss of the approval, because the approval is effective even if it gets lost or reaches the acceptor late.

Where all requirements for an effective and valid approval are met, including those of the applicable domestic law, which governs the approval's validity, with the exception of its formal validity, the contract is deemed to have been concluded when the late acceptance reached the offeror or, in case of acceptance indicated by the performance of an act, at the time that act was performed.

The rule set forth in Article 21(1) applies where a late acceptance contained in a letter or other writing shows that it was sent under such circumstances that if its transmission had been normal, it would have reached the offeror in due time. In this line of cases, the late acceptance is effective as an acceptance unless, without delay, the offeror orally informs the offeree that he considers his offer as having lapsed or dispatches a notice to that effect. Thus, while pursuant to Article 21(1) a contract is not concluded when the offeror does not react at all to the late acceptance, a contract is concluded pursuant to Article 21(2) when the offeror remains inactive.

For the rule set forth in Article 21(2) to apply, the lateness must be caused by the abnormal transmission. The circumstances that may adversely affect transmission can relate to the transmission of a specific acceptance, such as a specific acceptance being misrouted at a post office, or may affect the transmission on a more general level, such as a general strike, inclement weather, blockage of a street, etc. Article 21(2) is not applicable where lateness is due to reasons other than delays in transmission, such as the use of an incorrect address. Article 21(2) also requires that the writing containing the acceptance shows that the acceptance would have reached the offeror on time if transmission had been normal. If the writing does not show that the lateness is due to a delay in transmission, Article 21(1) applies.

To the extent that the aforementioned requirements are met (*i.e.*, if the lateness is caused by a delay in the transmission and this can be derived from the writing containing the acceptance), a contract is concluded at the time when the late acceptance reaches the offeror. If the offeror wants to avoid the conclusion of the contract, the offeror must protest "without delay." For the protest of the offeror—which can be made both orally or in writing—to prevent the contract from being concluded, it is not necessary that it reach the acceptor; its dispatch is sufficient, from which one can easily derive the impossibility of a withdrawal of the protest. From this one can also derive that it is the acceptor who bears the risk of loss of the protest.

For a reply to an offer to qualify as acceptance, it is also necessary, as a general matter, that the terms of the acceptance fully correspond to those of the offer (Article 19(1)).[29] This requirement corresponds to the application of the "mirror–image–rule".[30] Article 19(2) contains, however, an exception to "mirror–image–rule", as it allows for a contract to be concluded even where the acceptance

---

[29] *See* RB Koophandel Tongeren (Belgium), 25 January 2005, available in English at http://cisgw3.law.pace.edu/cases/050125b1.html.

[30] *See* U.S. District Court [N.D. Ill.] 7 December 1999 (*Magellan International Corp. v. Salzgitter Handel GmbH*), available at http://cisgw3.law.pace.edu/cases/991207u1.html.

does not mirror the offer, provided that the points on which the acceptance differs from the offer do not materially alter the offer. In effect, as long as a reply to an offer that purports to be an acceptance contains only "additional or different terms which do not materially alter the terms of the offer", a contract can be concluded, unless the offeror, without undue delay, objects orally to the discrepancy or dispatches a notice to that effect.

Where a reply that purports to be an acceptance material differences vis–à–vis the offer, it is treated as a rejection, which in turn leads to the termination of the offer. At the same time, that reply constitutes a counter–offer, the acceptance of which is also governed by the provisions of the CISG.

The determination that an additional or different term is material depends on the circumstances of the particular case. Despite the wording of Article 19(3), pursuant to which "[a]dditional or different terms relating, among other things, to the price, payment, quality and quantity of the goods, place and time of delivery, extent of one party's liability to the other or the settlement of disputes are considered to alter the terms of the offer materially", a case–by–case approach is also required in relation to the terms explicitly listed in Article 19(3). This is due to the fact that Article 19(3) only sets forth a rebuttable presumption of the materiality of differences relating to those terms.[31] Therefore, as noted for instance by the Supreme Court of Austria,[32] it is possible "that alterations of these terms will be classified as immaterial due to special circumstances of the particular case, practices established between the parties, pre–contractual negotiations or usage."[33]

Modifications or alterations relating to terms other than the ones expressly listed in Article 19(3) are not presumptively material. This does not mean that they cannot be material. Alterations, for instance, that deal with questions not addressed in the offer and that adopt solutions contrary to those of the applicable law should be considered material alterations. A choice of law clause contained in a reply to an offer, leading to the application of a law that would not be applicable absent that choice, must also be considered a material alteration. For the same reason, a reply to the offer containing a penalty clause, or a right to revoke not generally granted in the same circumstances by the applicable law, does not constitute an acceptance. The same is

---

[31]   *See* U.S. District Court [S.D.N.Y.], 14 April 1992 (*Filanto S.p.A. v. Chilewich International Corp.*), available at http://cisg w3.law.pace.edu/cases/920414u1.html.

[32]   *See* OLG Naumburg (Germany), 27 April 1999, available in English at http://cisgw3.law.pace.edu/cases/990427g1.html.

[33]   Supreme Court of Austria, 20 March 1997, available in English at http://cisgw3.law.pace.edu/cases/970320a3.html.

true with respect to a reply containing an arbitration clause[34] or a choice of forum clause.[35]

If the offeror requires that the reply to the offer take a given form, noncompliance with that form requirement must be considered a material alteration of the offer.

If, however, the modifications contained in the offeree's reply to the offer are immaterial, and if the offeror does not object without undue delay to those modifications, the contract comes into existence with the content of the offer as modified by the (immaterial) modifications contained in the reply of the offeree.[36] The time of contract conclusion is the time when the acceptance containing the immaterial modifications reaches the offeror.

5. CONCLUSION OF THE CONTRACT AND EFFECTIVENESS OF STATEMENTS

Article 23 CISG sets forth the rule, in principle to be resorted to whenever in the CISG reference is made to the moment at which the contract is concluded,[37] pursuant to which a contract is

---

[34] *See* U.S. District Court [S.D.N.Y.], 14 April 1992 (*Filanto S.p.A. v. Chilewich International Corp.*), available at http://cisg w3.law.pace.edu/cases/920414u1.html.

[35] *See* Supreme Court of France, 16 July 1998, available in English at http://cisgw3.law.pace.edu/cases/980716f1.html.

[36] *See* Supreme Court of Austria, 20 March 1997, available in English at http://cisgw3.law.pace.edu/cases/970320a3.html.

[37] *See, e.g.*, Article 1(2); Article 9(2); Article 10(*a*); Article 33(*c*); Article 35(2)(*b*); Article 35(3); Article 42(1); Article 42(2)(*a*); Article 55; Article 57(2); Article 68; Article 71(1); Article 73(3); Article 74; Article 79(1); Article 100(2).

concluded when the acceptance becomes effective. This provision is somewhat superfluous, as the same result can be derived from Article 18, which, as mentioned previously, provides that an acceptance of an offer becomes effective and, therefore, leads to the conclusion of the contract (namely at the moment the indication of assent reaches the offeror or, if offeree may indicate assent by performing an act, at the moment the act is performed).

By opting for the moment when the acceptance becomes effective to determine the moment of conclusion of the contract, the drafters of the CISG favored the so–called "receipt–theory" over other theories that determine when a contract is concluded on the basis of a different moment in time, such as the "theory of declaration" (merely requiring that the offeree accepts the offer, irrespective of the acceptance being externalized), the "mail–box–rule" (requiring that the acceptance be dispatched and, thus externalized) and the theory on the basis of which the contract is concluded upon the offeror gaining knowledge of the acceptance. The drafters' adoption of the "receipt–theory" does not exclude that a contract cannot be concluded at a different point in time. This may be the case when the parties so agree, which they are certainly free to do, since Article 23 is not mandatory. Furthermore, the "receipt–theory" is not applicable when a contract is not concluded by means of the "traditional" approach, through offer and acceptance, since in this line of cases Article 23 is not applicable. In these cases, a contract is considered concluded when the parties have reached an agreement; to determine when this is the case, resort is to be had to the rules of interpretation set forth in Article 8.

Where the contract is concluded subject to a condition precedent, the contract is not concluded upon receipt of the acceptance by the offeror, but rather at the moment in time agreed upon by the parties, which, once again, is to be determined by resort to the rules of interpretation set forth in Article 8. In general, this will be the moment in time at which the condition is met.

The issue of when a contract is concluded that by law requires for its effectiveness the consent of a third party, such as a governmental entity or body, must be settled on the basis of the applicable domestic law, since this issue falls outside the CISG's scope of application. Where, however, it is the parties who have agreed on the effectiveness of the contract depending on the assent of a third party, the moment at which the contract is concluded depends on an interpretation of the parties' agreement pursuant to Article 8.

It is worth pointing out that the party relying upon the contract conclusion or upon the contract conclusion having occurred at a given point in time must prove the relevant facts.

While Article 23 determines when a contract is concluded, it does not determine the place where it is concluded. Proposals to that effect made during the drafting process were rejected as were the proposals made during the Vienna Diplomatic Conference. In these authors' opinion, one therefore has to resort to the applicable domestic law to determine the place of conclusion of the contract.

Although Article 23 states that a contract is concluded when the acceptance becomes effective, and Article 18 states that an acceptance of an offer becomes effective at the moment the indication of assent reaches the offeror, neither provision defines when an acceptance effectively "reaches" the offeror. A specification of what is required for a statement to "reach" its addressee can be found in Article 24, which, however, applies to a wider range of statements. In effect, the definition of when a statement "reaches" its addressee generally applies to any declaration relevant for the conclusion of the contract that needs to reach its addressee to be effective, such as offer, revocation of the offer, withdrawal of the offer, rejection of an offer, acceptance, and withdrawal of the acceptance. Of course, Article 24 does not come into play in respect of those declarations concerning the formation of contract which exceptionally become effective at a different point in time, such as an act indicating assent, which, pursuant to Article 18(3), becomes effective upon its performance, or an objection by the offeror to immaterial modifications and alterations contained in the acceptance, which, like the approval of a late acceptance, becomes effective upon dispatch.

As a general matter, Article 24 does not apply to statements concerning issues governed by Part III CISG either. Those statements are generally subject to the rule set forth in Article 27, pursuant to which they become effective upon their dispatch. This, however, does not mean that Article 24 cannot be applied by analogy where Part III expressly requires[38] that a declaration "reach" its addressee to be effective.

Article 24 distinguishes between declarations made orally and those made "by any other means", rather than making a distinction between direct and indirect means of communication. However, the latter distinction is not irrelevant, as it may be helpful in defining what constitutes an "oral" declaration. In light of the legislative history of Article 24 CISG, it seems that "oral" communication are only those that can be understood immediately and the "receipt" of which can instantly be ascertained. This means that declarations made over the phone or via radio have to be treated as "oral" declarations, because they immediately reach the ear of the addressee, while declarations left by a person on an answering machine cannot be treated as "oral" declarations in the sense of Article 24.

From what has just been said it also follows that declarations made by electronic means of communication (for instance through the internet) do not constitute "oral" declarations under Article 24.

---

[38]   See, e.g., Articles 47(2), 48(4), 63(2), 65(1), 65(2), 79(4).

A declaration made orally by an intermediary with power of representation to the addressee must be treated as an "oral" declaration under Article 24 and, therefore, "reaches" the addressee at the moment it is made. The question of who qualifies as an intermediary with power of representation must be answered on the basis of the applicable domestic law. If the intermediary lacks power of representation, declarations made by or to such an intermediary must be regarded as "non–oral" declarations.

"Oral" declarations reach the addressee when they are "made". It is not necessary that the addressee also gain knowledge of the declarations. This can be derived from the legislative history, since the theory pursuant to which a declaration becomes effective upon it being known by its addressee was expressly rejected during the drafting process.[39] This, however, does not mean that for an oral declaration to "reach" its addressee it is merely sufficient that the declaration be communicated. Rather, the declaration must be formulated (as regards both its content and language) in a way that would allow a reasonable person of the same kind as the addressee (and, therefore, with the same language skills as the addressee or as a reasonable person involved in the same trade as the addressee), and in the same circumstances (among which one must count the volume of the oral declaration) to gain knowledge of it. Where the declaring party has made such a

---

[39]   *See* IX UNCITRAL YEARBOOK 36 (1978).

declaration, the risk of the declaration being misunderstood lies with the addressee.

Those declarations which, irrespective of the means of communication used, do not constitute "oral" declarations must be considered declarations "delivered by any other means". These declarations "reach" the addressee when their delivery occurs. Delivery occurs when the declarations arrive within the addressee's "sphere of control" and, under normal circumstances, allows the addressee to gain knowledge of them. Whether the addressee actually gains knowledge of the declaration is irrelevant. Like the "oral" declaration, the declarations "delivered by any other means" must also be formulated in a way to allow a reasonable person in the same circumstances as the addressee to understand them.[40] This means, for instance, that the language used must generally be one that is known to the addressee. The fact that the addressee knows a given language may be derived, for example, from previous business relations between the declaring party and the addressee, or from the bargaining process. Likewise, where the language is one generally used by parties to contracts of the type involved in the particular trade concerned, its use does not affect the issue of whether the declaration has "reached" its addressee.[41]

---

[40]   *See* OLG Hamm (Germany), 8 February 1995, available in English at http://cisgw3.law.pace.edu/cases/950208g3.html.

[41]   *Id.*

Delivery by service of process can be, but does not have to be sufficient for a declaration to be considered as having reached its addressee.

Article 24 allows for delivery of non–oral declarations by different means without requiring, unlike Article 27 that sets forth the general rule applicable to declarations subject to Part III, that those means be "appropriate in the circumstances".

Non–oral declarations can be handed over personally to the addressee (or to the addressee's representative). Where the delivery occurs by handing over the non–oral declarations personally, the place of delivery is irrelevant; thus, delivery can occur in a hotel, at the addressee's place of business, at the addressee's place of sojourn, etc. Alternatively, delivery may take place at the addressee's habitual residence or mailing address. Therefore, a letter posted in the addressee's mailbox must be considered as reaching the addressee just as a letter inserted into the addressee's post office box or a message left on the addressee's answering machine. Similarly, a telefax reaches the addressee when the addressee's telefax machine prints the declaration, provided that the telefax machine is under the addressee's control. If the telefax machine is not under the addressee's control, the telefax reaches the addressee when a printed copy of the telefax is delivered to the addressee. If printing is not possible because the telefax machine ran out of paper, one has to assume that the declaration has nevertheless reached the addressee. The insertion of a notice into the addressee's mailbox informing the addressee about a registered mailed letter also qualifies as delivery under Article 24.

Delivery at the addressee's place of habitual residence, which corresponds to the habitual residence referred to in Article 10, amounts to a delivery that allows the declaration to "reach" the addressee for the purposes of Article 24 only where the addressee does not have a place of business or mailing address. If a declaration is delivered to the addressee's place of habitual residence despite the fact that the addressee has a place of business or a mailing address, the declaration is treated as if it had never reached the addressee. However, if the addressee, gains knowledge of the declaration, he may not invoke the fact that the declaration was delivered at the wrong place. This can be derived from the CISG's general principle of good faith.[42] The fact that the addressee gains knowledge of the declaration also entails that the declaring party is bound by the declaration, provided that delivery at the wrong place is to be imputed to the declaring party—this can be derived from the CISG's general principle pursuant to which it is prohibited to *venire contra factum proprium*.[43]

An issue closely related to the one of when a declaration reaches its addressee is that of delivery outside business hours. Some commentators hold that a declaration delivered outside business hours, such as a telefax received after the closing of the

---

[42]   *See supra* Chapter 1, Section 5.

[43]   *See supra* Chapter 1, Section 5.

store, reaches the addressee only at the beginning of the next business day. This view cannot be shared, because it would shift the risks relating to the communication from the addressee to the declaring party. Hence, under the CISG also declarations delivered outside business hours "reach" the addressee at the moment when they are delivered pursuant to Article 24.

What has been said in regards to non–oral declarations also applies to notices addressed to the offeror that an act indicating assent has been performed, where the notice is not superfluous on account "of the offer or as a result of practices which the parties have established between themselves or of usage" (Article 18(3)).

The drafters of the CISG did not lay down specific rules dealing with the addressee's conduct— consisting, for instance, of disconnecting a telefax, refusing to accept a letter, etc.—that results in a declaration not reaching the addressee. In these authors' opinion, this should not lead one to automatically resort to the applicable domestic law to resolve the issue. Rather, the issue is to be resolved on the basis of the general principles underlying the CISG, in particular, on the basis of that pursuant to which it is prohibited to *venire contra factum proprium*. Where the addressee consciously or intentionally prevents a declaration from reaching him, the declaration must be considered as having reached the addressee at the moment the declaration would have reached the addressee under "normal" circumstances.

6.   PRE–CONTRACTUAL LIABILITY

The largely prevailing opinion among legal scholars is that the CISG does not provide for a general duty to act in good faith in the course of negotiations. Therefore, it is assumed that the Convention does not deal with, and is therefore not applicable to, possible duties and consequent liabilities that may arise in the course of negotiations as a result as some kind of "pre–contractual liability" doctrine. This conclusion, however, may seem in contradiction with another largely shared opinion, *i.e.*, that the CISG applies to "preliminary agreements", at least to the extent that this expression describes agreements that anticipate in time (and somehow favor, envisage or provide for) subsequent contracts for the sale of goods. The contradiction would result from the application of the CISG to agreements primarily intended to govern the stage of the negotiations between the parties, which in itself is beyond the scope of the Convention.

The foregoing suggests that the issue requires further investigation and, in particular, it requires a more precise characterization of what is intended by "pre–contractual liability". Indeed, the mere description of an issue as falling under the law of pre–contractual liability can prove too simplistic and misleading. Instead, it seems appropriate to take as a starting point the various (yet different) circumstances in which a claim for pre–contractual liability can be brought, and then to evaluate each one of them separately. This approach thus makes it possible to assess more precisely which situations fall within the scope of the CISG, and which ones are to be governed by the domestic rules applicable by virtue of the conflict–of–law rules of the forum.

Although the CISG does not establish specific rules for the pre–contractual stage, it does deal with the phase of contract formation and the conduct of the parties throughout that phase. In addition, the Convention also deals with various pieces of information relevant to the contractual relationship, which may be exchanged before the contract is concluded. It is therefore appropriate to make a distinction between at least four different situations possibly leading to a claim for damages resulting from the contingent occurrences happening in the course of negotiations. The four situations may be described as follows: first, the claim brought by the plaintiff may be the result of damages to protected assets, such as life, limb, property, etc.; secondly, the claim may be brought as a result of fraudulent conduct on the part of the defendant; thirdly, the claim may be brought as a result of the breaking off of negotiations at a stage where the other party relies on the fact that the contract under discussion is about to be concluded; finally, the fourth situation to be considered occurs when the damages suffered by the claimant are caused either by misleading information provided by the other party during the negotiations, or by a failure to provide information which the other party possesses.

The first situation described above is a relatively simple one. The claim resulting from damages to protected assets, such as life, limb, property, etc. in the course of negotiations is clearly outside the scope of application of the CISG. This conclusion applies not only with respect to damages consisting of the death or personal injury of the claimant (which are explicitly excluded under Article 5 CISG), but also with respect to damages to other protected assets, insofar as the event under consideration occurs before the conclusion of the contract and the negotiations seem merely to be the contingent situation in the course of which the damage occurred. This matter is thus typically dealt with under the domestic law applicable by virtue of the conflict–of–law rules of the forum and, in most cases, the situation is characterized as falling under the law of tort.

Whenever a claim is brought as a result of a fraudulent conduct on the part of the defendant in the course of the negotiation of a sales contract of a kind falling within the scope of the CISG, two different issues arise. On the one hand, the fraudulent conduct could be invoked to claim that the resulting contract is invalid: the exclusion under Article 4 CISG thus comes into play, and the issue is to be solved under the domestic rules applicable by virtue of the conflict–of–law rules of the forum. On the other hand, the fraudulent conduct could also be invoked to claim damages under domestic law, which have often been requested in addition to those claimed in contract under the CISG.[44] The question

---

[44]   *See* U.S. District Court [S.D. Ohio], 10 October 2006 (*Miami Valley Paper, LLC v. Lebbing Engineering & Consulting*

thus arises as to whether the claimant can rely on domestic rules providing for damages on the basis of fraud, possibly in addition to other claims brought under the CISG; the crucial point, in this regard, is that the CISG does not address factual situations involving fraud, so that the source of the claimed damages appears to fall outside the scope of the Convention and back into the realm of domestic law.

The claim for pre–contractual liability connected to the formation of a contract falling under the scope of the CISG must be treated in a rather different way whenever that claim is brought as a result of the breaking off of negotiations. Indeed, irrespective of whether the possibly applicable remedies under domestic law are provided in contract or in tort, such remedies should be regarded as not available insofar as the CISG is applicable. This is because Articles 15 and 16 CISG deal with the issue of revocability of an offer (which implies that the issue is covered by the Convention) without providing for damages as a possible result of the revocation. The point is that under the CISG, two distinct situations are considered. If the offer is irrevocable, the remedy available to the offeree is that, notwithstanding the revocation, he can accept the offer, thus causing the contract to be concluded. The general rule, however, provides that the offer is freely revocable, without any liability possibly stemming from that revocation. For, whenever the

_____

GmbH), available at http://cisgw3.law.pace.edu/cases/090326u1. html.

general rule of free revocation of the offer applies under the CISG, the concurrent application of domestic rules affirming liability for breaking off negotiations is precluded.

In practical cases, however, the solution that has just been depicted can prove somewhat problematic. This is the case whenever it is not possible to conclude whether the contract under discussion will be of a kind governed by the CISG. For example, one can imagine a situation where it is unclear whether the contract under discussion will be performed by the seller through its place of business located in a non–contracting State, or that located in a contracting State (other than the one where the buyer is located): in the former case, the CISG would most likely not apply, whereas it would apply in the latter. Moreover, one can consider the situation where the discussion about the future contract is still open as to the services that the seller will provide in addition to the goods, so that the contract might be of a kind excluded under Article 3 CISG, insofar as the preponderant part of the obligation undertaken by the seller consists in the supply of services. In the cases which have just been described, it is unclear whether the contract under discussion is of a kind covered by the CISG. Therefore, there would seem to be the possibility of applying the domestic rules on liability for the breaking off of negotiations.

Finally, the fourth type of situation worth considering here occurs when the damages suffered by the claimant are caused either by misleading information provided by the other party during the negotiations, or by a failure of the other party to provide information available to him. Insofar as the misleading information is provided fraudulently, the solution should be the same one as that provided for other cases of fraud, thus leading to the application of domestic law. Some domestic courts[45] have adopted the same solution also with respect to situations where the misleading information was provided negligently, on the basis of the assumption that the remedies for negligent misrepresentation are provided for under the domestic law of tort. This approach, however, must be criticized in that it omits to consider which facts the alleged misrepresentation pertains to. In particular, whenever the misleading information relates to the goods, the situation may be deemed to fall within the scope of Article 35 CISG. As a result, the application of concurrent domestic rules should be precluded.

A similar analysis applies also to the situation where the claim for damages is brought under domestic law on the basis of an alleged breach of a pre–contractual duty to disclose information. The claim under domestic law is possible and may concur with an action brought under the CISG only insofar as the duty to disclose pertains to matters that are outside the scope of the Convention.

---

[45]   U.S. District Court [E.D. Kentucky], 18 March 2008 (*Sky Cast, Inc. v. Global Direct Distribution LLC*), available at http:// cisgw3.law.pace.edu/cases/080318u1.html.

CHAPTER 6

OBLIGATIONS OF THE SELLER

1. DELIVERY OF GOODS

Article 30 CISG outlines the obligations of the seller arising from a contract for the sale of goods. It states that "[t]he seller must deliver the goods, hand over any documents relating to them, and transfer the property in the goods, as required by the contract and this Convention". The rule thus clarifies that the obligations of the seller are primarily determined by the terms of the agreement between the parties, whereas the purpose of the default rules set forth in Sections I and II (Articles 31 to 44) of Chapter II of Part III CISG is to supplement the parties' will to the extent that the contract is silent on any relevant matter.

The main obligation to which the seller is bound is to deliver the goods promised to the buyer. As will be pointed out later, the obligation to deliver the goods may concur with that to transfer property in the goods; however, the latter obligation is merely possible and, in practice, will not require any action from the seller whenever the property already passed as a direct and immediate consequence of the conclusion of the contract. Therefore, the obligation to deliver the goods may, depending on the circumstances of the case, take the form of delivery of goods that are already owned by the buyer, or delivery of goods, the property of which the seller is further required to transfer to the buyer.

On the other hand, it is possible (although not frequent in practice) that the buyer be already in possession of the goods at the time of the conclusion of the contract. In this situation, it is apparent that the obligation to deliver the goods is devoid of any purpose and that the seller is not required to take any action other than the mere conclusion of the contract, which, as a general rule, will also cause the immediate transfer of property, according to the rule of the so–called "*traditio brevi manu*".

The most relevant issues regarding the obligation to deliver the goods relate to the place and time of delivery. These two issues are dealt with separately in the CISG, with Article 31 being devoted to the issue of the place of delivery and Article 33 dealing with the time of delivery. In practice, however, it has been pointed out that in most cases the "questions as to place and time will merge into a single issue: Did the goods get to the agreed place on time?" And the unitary answer to that question is most commonly drawn from the specific provisions that the parties include to that effect in their contract, either by drafting specific tailor–made rules, or by incorporating by reference rules dealing with the issue at hand, such as the INCOTERMS of the International Chamber of Commerce. This is quite clearly acknowledged by the opening sentence of Article 31 CISG, which lists the rules on the place of delivery that are applicable "[i]f the seller is not bound to deliver the goods at any other particular place". Conversely, should the parties not include any specific rule in their contract, the issues of the

place and time of delivery shall be governed by the
aforementioned rules of the CISG.

In addressing the question as to where the seller
must deliver the goods, Article 31 CISG makes a
distinction between contracts of sale involving
carriage (Article 31(1)(*a*) CISG), and sales not
involving carriage (Article 31(1)(*b*) and (*c*) CISG).
Although the rules applicable to sales involving
carriage will be dealt with in further detail in the
next paragraph, it is appropriate to consider here
the rule regarding the place of delivery in this type
of transaction. Under Article 31(1)(*a*) CISG, if the
contract of sale involves carriage, the seller's
obligation to deliver the goods consists in "handing
the goods over to the first carrier for transmission to
the buyer". As a prerequisite for the rule to apply,
the CISG refers to the circumstance that the
contract of sale "involves" carriage, whereas the
provision does not require that the parties have
"agreed" on the seller handing the goods over to the
carrier. This seems to imply a legal presumption
that, unless the contrary can be inferred from the
contract,[1] established practices between the
parties,[2] or relevant trade usages,[3] the seller's
obligation to deliver the goods includes the
obligation to dispatch the goods whenever carriage
is involved. Conversely, only to the extent that there
is a clear indication to that effect (either set out in

---

[1]   In particular in the light of the interpretative means set
forth in Article 8 CISG.

[2]   Under Article 9(1) CISG.

[3]   Under Article 9(2) CISG.

the contract, or inferable from established practices or trade usages), may one conclude that the buyer is to collect the goods from the seller.

The rule set forth in Article 31(1)(*a*) CISG has been held to apply ordinarily for sales at a distance.[4] However, it should be noticed that it applies only to the extent that an independent transport undertaking (a "carrier") is engaged by the seller, so that the seller surrenders custody and control of the goods when handing them over to the carrier. Therefore, the rule does not apply if transportation is performed directly by either one of the parties, or by any of their employees, internal divisions or agents, or under any other circumstances, under which the goods do not pass under the control of an independent carrier.[5] Similarly, the rule at hand does not apply in the event that the seller instructs his own supplier to deliver the goods directly to the buyer (so called "third–party deal"), unless (and until) the third party hands the goods over to an independent carrier for the purpose of transporting the goods to the final destination. On the other hand, the rule under Article 31(1)(*a*) applies in the event of multi–party or multi–modal transportation, as the rule itself specifies that delivery occurs upon the handing over of the goods to the "first carrier". Similarly, the handing over of the goods to a freight

---

[4] *See*, *e.g.*, AG Duisburg (Germany), 13 April 2000, available in English at http://cisgw3.law.pace.edu/cases/000413 g1.html.

[5] *See* Audiencia Provincial de Córdoba (Spain), 31 October 1997, English abstract available at http://cisgw3.law.pace.edu/cases/971031s4.html.

forwarder also satisfies the requirements of Article 31(1)(*a*) CISG, to the extent that control over the goods passes to an independent undertaking in view of transportation to the final destination.

If the place for delivery of the goods cannot be assessed on the basis of the rule discussed above, two alternatives are provided under Article 31 CISG. The first one, set forth in Article 31(1)(*b*) CISG, applies when three requirements are met: first, delivery must not involve carriage as per the preceding paragraph of Article 31 CISG, so that it must be the buyer's task to take possession of the goods; second, the goods must be "specific goods, or unidentified goods to be drawn from a specific stock or to be manufactured or produced"; third, both parties must have been aware at the time of conclusion of the contract that the goods were located at a particular place, or that they were to be manufactured or produced at a particular place. When the aforementioned requirements are met, the seller must deliver the goods to the buyer by placing them at the buyer's disposal at the very place where the goods were located at the time of the conclusion of the contract or where the goods were to be manufactured or produced. Moreover, the seller must also give notice to the buyer that the goods are placed at the buyer's disposal, ready for the taking of delivery by the buyer.

Finally, if neither Article 31(1)(*a*), nor Article 31(1)(*b*) apply to a specific case, and the parties have not otherwise agreed on the place of delivery, Article 31(1)(*c*) CISG comes into play as the residuary rule for determining the place of delivery. In particular, this situation occurs when the goods are not to be transported by an independent carrier and one or more of the requirements for the application of Article 31(1)(*b*) is not met. In this situation, the seller must deliver the goods by placing them at the buyer's disposal at the place where the seller had his place of business at the time of the conclusion of the contract. At the same time, he must also give notice to the buyer that the goods are placed at his disposal, ready for the taking of delivery by the buyer.

The determination of the place of delivery by the seller can have implications beyond just the substantive effect of that obligation. In fact, one of the most commonly litigated issues under Article 31 CISG has been whether a given court has jurisdiction to adjudicate a contract action governed by the Convention, based on jurisdictional rules that allow a plaintiff to bring a case at the place of delivery of the goods. In particular, in the member States of the European Union and in other jurisdictions that follow the same approach, in matters relating to a contract for the sale of goods a plaintiff may sue the defendant in the courts for the place "where, under the contract, the goods were delivered or should have been delivered".[6] This

---

[6]   *See* Article 5(1) of Reg. (EC) n. 44/2001 of 22 December 2000, on jurisdiction and the recognition and enforcement of judgments in civil and commercial matters ("Brussels I" Regulation). The Regulation substituted the previously applicable Brussels Convention of 27 September 1968 on the same matter. Moreover, as from 10 January 2015, the said

provision has caused some debate as to the meaning to be attached to the notion of "place of delivery" used in the European Regulation. On the one hand, there has always been general consensus that the notion has to be defined autonomously, without regard to domestic rules.[7] On the other hand, however, there has been disagreement as to the autonomous notion to be adopted, in particular in the event of sales of goods involving carriage, where the place of dispatch of the goods by the seller to the first carrier differs from the place of final destination and taking of possession of the goods by the buyer. At last, the interpretative issue has been solved by the European Court of Justice in a decision[8] whereby the court indicated that the place of delivery for jurisdictional purposes coincides with the place of delivery agreed upon between the parties in the contract.[9] Failing an agreement, however, the place of delivery for jurisdictional purposes coincides with the place of final destination of the goods. As a result, in the member

---

Regulation will be repealed by the new Regulation (EU) n. 1215/2012 of the European Parliament and the Council of 12 December 2012 on the same matter ("Brussels I recast" Regulation).

[7]   *See, e.g.*, Trib. Padova (Italy), 10 January 2006, available in English at http://cisgw3.law.pace.edu/cases/060110i3.html.

[8]   European Court of Justice, 25 January 2010, C–381/08 (*Car Trim GmbH v. KeySafety Systems Srl*).

[9]   For further clarifications on how the notion of place of delivery may be determined by agreement of the parties, *see* European Court of Justice, 9 June 2011, C–87/10 (*Electrosteel Europe SA v. Edil Centro Spa*).

States of the European Union and in other legal systems following the same approach, failing an agreement as to the place of delivery, the notion of "place of delivery" adopted for jurisdictional purposes differs from the one adopted under the CISG. Under the former, the place of delivery coincides with the place of final destination of the goods; whereas under the latter, the place of delivery in sales involving carriage coincides, as a default rule, with the place of dispatch of the product by the seller to the first carrier, typically in the country of origin where the seller is located.

Not only must the seller deliver the goods to the buyer at the place to be determined according to Article 31 CISG, but he must also deliver the goods on time. Article 33 CISG deals with the issue of the time for delivery and, not surprisingly, its subparagraphs (*a*) and (*b*) refer to the contract as the main source of rules governing this matter. The contract may, in fact, expressly or impliedly set a date for delivery, while absent an express indication, the date can also be inferred from the practices established between the parties or from applicable trade usages. In any event, the indication that may be drawn can refer to a fixed date, or to a period of time within which delivery is to take place. Article 33(1)(*a*) CISG provides that "if a date is fixed by or determinable from the contract", the seller must deliver the goods on that date. According to some court decisions, the provision at hand also applies when the parties did not originally fix the date for delivery, but instead agreed that the seller would deliver at the request of the buyer.[10]

Article 33(1)(*b*) accounts for the situation where the contract fixes or provides guidance to determine a period of time within which delivery must take place. In this situation, the seller must deliver the goods "within that period unless circumstances indicate that the buyer is to choose a date". The provision at hand has been applied by arbitral tribunals to clauses such as one providing for delivery "until: end December",[11] or another referring to delivery to be "effected in 1993–1994".[12] The seller was given the option to decide when exactly to deliver within the said period. Conversely, for the buyer to have the option to choose the date of delivery, a specific agreement to that effect is necessary, although at least in one case a court held that an agreement on delivery "ex factory" granted the buyer the right to specify the date for the taking of delivery at seller's premises.[13]

If the contract is silent on the date for delivery, the residuary rule under Article 33(1)(*c*) applies, which provides that in all circumstances not falling within the cases considered in the previous

---

[10]   OLG Hamm (Germany), 23 June 1998, available in English at http://cisgw3.law.pace.edu/cases/980623g1.html.

[11]   ICC Court of Arbitration, Arbitral Award n. 8786, ICC INTERNATIONAL COURT OF ARBITRATION BULLETIN 7 (2000).

[12]   ICC Court of Arbitration, Arbitral Award n. 9117, ICC INTERNATIONAL COURT OF ARBITRATION BULLETIN 83 (2000).

[13]   Supreme Court of Spain, 9 December 2008, English abstract available at http://cisgw3.law.pace.edu/cases/081209s4.html.

paragraphs, the seller must deliver the goods "within a reasonable time after the conclusion of the contract". What is reasonable depends on the specific circumstances of the case and the respective interests of the parties involved. In particular, it has been held that the time to be reasonably granted to the seller to deliver the goods may vary significantly based on whether the goods sold are held in stock, or they are manufactured or produced customized specifically for the buyer.[14]

2. SALES INVOLVING CARRIAGE AND INCOTERMS

As pointed out in the preceding paragraph, under Article 31(1)(a) CISG in the event of a contract for the sale of goods involving carriage the delivery obligation of the seller consists in "handing the goods over to the first carrier for transmission to the buyer". Unless the contrary can be inferred from the contract, as a general rule the seller is bound to dispatch the goods to the first carrier, whereas the exception to the rule (applicable only if agreed upon, or inferable from established practices or usage) requires the buyer to collect the goods from the seller. Sales involving carriage may, thus, imply several additional obligations and costs related to the transportation of the goods from the place of dispatch to the place of final destination. Only part of these additional issues, however, are addressed

---

[14]   RB Koophandel Kortrijk (Belgium), 3 October 2001, English abstract available at http://www.unilex.info/case.cfm?id= 948.

by the CISG, whereas other issues are left to the agreement of the parties, or are to be solved under Article 7(2) CISG, on the basis of the general principle on which the CISG is based according to which each party must bear the costs of his own performance.

With specific regard to sales of goods involving carriage, Article 32(1) CISG deals with the situation where, upon the handing over of the goods to the carrier, it is not possible to clearly identify the goods to the contract by markings, by shipping documents or otherwise. In these circumstances, "the seller must give the buyer notice of the consignment specifying the goods", so as to prevent the seller from identifying opportunistically the goods at a later stage, possibly after they have been lost or damaged. Article 32(2) CISG deals with the arrangements to be done in view of the carriage of the goods. However, it does not operate so as to allocate the costs of carriage. Instead, Article 32(2) CISG merely addresses the situation where the seller is bound "to arrange" carriage of the goods, which is the case both, when the seller has to dispatch the goods at buyer's costs (as under the general rule of Article 31(1)(a) CISG), and when the seller has to dispatch the goods and pay for the costs of transportation. In both cases, the seller "must make such contracts as are necessary for carriage to the place fixed by means of transportation appropriate in the circumstances and according to the usual terms for such transportation".[15] In practice, in most cases the seller will entrust a freight–forwarder with the task of concluding the contract of carriage.

The foregoing suggests, as a general rule, that since the seller is only bound to hand the goods over to the carrier (or to the freight–forwarder) for transportation and not bound to perform the transportation, he duly performs his obligation by merely dispatching the goods. Therefore, unless differently agreed in the contract, the seller is not required to pay for the costs of carriage, as those costs are to be borne by the buyer. If the parties intend to contract around this default rule, a practical and efficient way to agree on a different allocation of the costs of carriage, as well as on several other issues related to the terms of sale contracts involving carriage,[16] is to incorporate by reference into the agreement one of the INCOTERMS of the International Chamber of Commerce.[17] In particular, by including a "C–term",

---

[15] *See, e.g.,* Zhejiang Cixi People's Court (China), 18 July 2001, available in English at http://cisgw3.law.pace.edu/cases/ 010718c1.html, maintaining that a seller who is obliged to arrange for the transport of the goods does not fulfil his duty if he does not inform the carrier of the correct address of the buyer to whom the goods must be shipped.

[16] Including the allocation of customs duties and charges and costs of insurance, which will be dealt with later in this paragraph, and the allocation of the risk of accidental loss or damage of the goods, which will be dealt with in Chapter 8, Section 5.

[17] *See* the latest version of 2010 of INTERNATIONAL CHAMBER OF COMMERCE (ICC), *INCOTERMS® 2010*, ICC Publication No. 715E.

such as the acronyms "CPT" ("Carriage Paid To"), "CIP" ("Carriage and Insurance Paid To") or "CIF" ("Cost Insurance and Freight Paid To"), the parties cause the seller to undertake to pay the costs of the contract for the carriage of the goods. The same applies also if the parties include a "D–term" in their agreement, such as "DAT" ("Delivered at Terminal"), "DAP" ("Delivered at Place") or "DDP" ("Delivered Duty Paid"), under which the seller undertakes to perform transportation of the goods to the place of destination indicated in the contract. To the contrary, if the parties enter a sale contract under "EXW" ("Ex Works") terms, the seller performs his delivery obligations by merely placing the goods at the buyer's disposal at the seller's premises. Similarly, if the parties incorporate an "F–term", such as "FCA" ("Free Carrier"), "FAS" ("Free Alongside Ship") or "FOB" ("Free on Board"), the seller must bear the costs only until delivery to the named carrier, until placement of the goods alongside the named ship, or until the placing of the goods on board of the named vessel. Under an "F–term" the buyer must pay for carriage from the place of the handing over of the goods to their final destination.

As far as customs duties and charges are concerned, absent a contractual rule addressing this matter, their allocation between the parties in sales involving carriage may be assessed on the basis of the general rule that each party must bear the costs of his own performance. Accordingly, charges arising on export from the country of origin are to be borne by the seller, while charges on import into the country of destination are to be borne by the buyer. Also in this regard, however, the incorporation of an INCOTERM may result in a different allocation of costs. "Ex Works" sales, on the one hand, require the buyer to pay for customs duties and charges related to both the import and the export of the goods. On the other hand, sales involving carriage concluded under "DDP" ("Delivered Duty Paid") terms imply that the seller must pay for both, customs duties and charges on export from the country of origin and customs duties and charges on import into the country of destination.

Finally, with respect to insurance, it can be inferred from Article 32(3) CISG that the seller is not bound, as a default rule, "to effect insurance in respect of the carriage of the goods". Absent an obligation to buy insurance, the CISG imposes on the seller a less burdensome obligation, in that it provides that the seller "must, at the buyer's request, provide him with all available information necessary to enable [the buyer] to effect such insurance". Again, the parties may make different arrangements in their contract, or may affect the allocation of costs and duties relating to insurance by incorporating an INCOTERM into their contractual arrangements. In particular, "C–terms" that include the letter "I" (*i.e.* "CIP" and "CIF") specifically address the issue of insurance by providing that the seller must obtain insurance at his own expense. Conversely, under "D–terms" the seller has no obligation to the buyer to make a contract of insurance, and it is therefore for the parties to make contractual arrangements on this matter.

3.   HANDING OVER OF DOCUMENTS

Under Article 34 CISG, whenever the seller is bound to hand over documents relating to the goods, he must hand them over "at the time and place and in the form required by the contract". The CISG does not provide rules determining when the seller's obligation to hand over the documents arises; instead, it merely acknowledges that under certain circumstances the seller is bound to duly perform that obligation. Similarly, the CISG does not provide rules governing the time, place and form for the handing over of documents, but rather it refers to the rules agreed upon by the parties in their contract.

With respect to the circumstances under which the obligation to hand over the documents arises, it is apparent that this effect may be provided for in the contract itself, or may be inferred from the practices established between the parties, or from any applicable usage. It seems correct to affirm, however, that the need for the handing over of documents may also arise, absent all previously mentioned sources of the related obligation, from the specific facts that characterize the transaction. The seller may thus be deemed to be under a duty to hand over documents also if the transaction–specific circumstances of the case make it reasonable to consider the seller bound to such obligation, in addition to the duty to deliver the goods.

The "documents relating to the goods", to which the provision at hand applies, include negotiable documents for the carriage of goods, such as bills of lading and warehouse warrants,[18] as well as non–negotiable documents, such as duplicate consignment notes and delivery notes. Moreover, relevant documents may also include, among others, insurance policies, commercial invoices and certificates of origin, of quality and the like.[19] On the other hand, it has been held that the procurement of customs documents is incumbent upon the seller only if so agreed between the parties.[20]

If the obligation to hand over the documents applies, the time, place and form of performance of this obligation must be assessed on the basis of the contract. This rule applies without major difficulties when the parties expressly address the issue and provide tailor–made rules for the handing over of documents. However, the rule set forth in Article 34 CISG applies also in circumstances where the

---

[18] *See, e.g.,* KG St. Gallen (Switzerland), 12 August 1997, English abstract available at http://cisgw3.law.pace.edu/cases/970812s1.html.

[19] For a similar list, *see* Tribunal of International Commercial Arbitration of the Ukrainian Chamber of Commerce and Trade (Ukraine), Arbitral Award of 5 July 2005, available in English at http://cisgw3.law.pace.edu/cases/050705u5.html.

[20] KG St. Gallen (Switzerland), 12 August 1997, English abstract available at http://cisgw3.law.pace.edu/cases/970812s1.html.

parties did not expressly address the issue of the handing over of documents, and requires a case–by–case analysis of the structure of the transaction in order to infer implicit rules applicable to the obligation at hand. For instance, if the document is made out to order, the seller must hand it over to the buyer in endorsed form. If the sale involves carriage, the documents required by the buyer to take delivery of the goods must be handed over by the seller after dispatch, in such a manner that they reach the buyer prior to, or at the time of, arrival of the goods. If the transaction provides for the issuance of a documentary letter of credit by the buyer, the seller must hand over the relevant documents at the place of business of the nominated paying bank. More generally, it can be affirmed that if no other specific modalities are agreed or applicable, the seller must hand over the documents "in such time and in such form as will allow the buyer to take possession of the goods from the carrier when the goods arrive at their destination, bring them through customs into the country of destination and exercise claims against the carrier or insurance company."[21]

In all these circumstances, if the seller fails to tender the due documents, or hands over non–conforming documents, he commits a breach of contract, to which the normal remedies available to the buyer apply. This conclusion is confirmed in case law, although in one case a court held that the

---

[21]   UNCITRAL Secretariat, *Commentary* to (then) Article 32, p. 31, para. 3.

delivery of non–conforming (false) documents did not constitute a fundamental breach of contract (which would have justified the avoidance of the contract) to the extent that the buyer could easily "remedy the defect itself without difficulty by obtaining a correct document" from the producer.[22] On a different note, Article 34 CISG further grants to the seller a general right to cure any failure or defective tender of documents to the buyer, to the extent that the time for the handing over of documents under the contract has not elapsed. The buyer must thus accept the curing tender of documents, unless the exercise of the seller's right to cure causes the buyer "unreasonable inconvenience or unreasonable expense". In any event, if the first, non–conforming tender of documents from the seller caused the buyer to suffer a loss and such loss is not entirely eliminated by the subsequent conforming tender, then under Article 34 CISG the buyer "retains any right to claim damages" from the seller.

4. TRANSFER OF PROPERTY AND RETENTION OF TITLE

The other fundamental obligation of the seller, besides delivering the goods, is to transfer property in the same goods to the buyer. As already pointed out, however, due to the exclusion provided for under Article 4(1)(*b*) CISG, the Convention does not deal with the "effect which the contract may have on

---

[22] Supreme Court of Germany, 3 April 1996, available in English at http://cisgw3.law.pace.edu/cases/960403g1.html.

the property in the goods sold",[23] so that this issue is governed, absent a contractual rule agreed upon between the parties, by the domestic law applicable by virtue of the conflict–of–law rules of the forum. In this respect, it is common knowledge that the basic dichotomy as to the fundamental requirements that must be fulfilled in order to transfer ownership is due to the existence of legal systems where the property passes from the seller to the buyer by mere consent, as opposed to legal systems where the property passes at the moment of delivery of the goods. In the former model (based on the so–called "consensus principle"), which in its codified version goes back to the French 1804 *Code civil*,[24] the transfer of ownership (as a general rule, although coexisting with many relevant exceptions) takes place upon the execution of the contract of sale, even if the goods have not been delivered or the price has not been paid. This rule applies as long as the contract goods are specified goods belonging to the seller. According to the opposite general

---

[23] Article 4(1)(*b*) CISG; for further details on this provision, *see supra* Chapter 4, Sections 4 and 5.

[24] *See*, in particular, the general rule applicable to all contracts set forth in Article 1138 of the *Code civil*, as well as the special rule for sales provided in Article 1583 of the *Code civil*. The French approach towards transfer of ownership was adopted in many other countries, including (among many others) Italy, Belgium, Mexico, Quebec and Louisiana. Notably, the consensus principle applies also in England, under Section 18 of the 1979 Sale of Goods Act, absent a different intention of the parties in the contract, and to the extent that the sale is an "unconditional contract for the sale of specific goods in deliverable state."

principle (the so–called "principle of delivery"),[25] the transfer of ownership takes place at the time of delivery and primarily as an effect of delivery, although most legal systems following this rule add as a secondary requirement the consent of the parties to the proprietary effects, necessary to determine the purpose of delivery, which in itself could be ambiguous and, in particular, may not coincide with an intention of the parties to transfer ownership. In any event, irrespective of the default rule applicable to the issue of the passing of property, in all legal systems the parties are free to contract around the default rule and modify it, by preventing, in particular, the mere consensus or the delivery of the goods from determining the passing of ownership.

In the light of the foregoing, it is safe to affirm that the rule under the CISG, which provides for the seller's obligation to transfer property in the goods sold to the buyer, should be intended quite differently on the basis of whether or not property already passed as a result of the mere contractual consensus of the parties. If property in the goods already passed as a result of consensus, the obligation at hand is inoperative and the seller is not required to take any action. Conversely, if

---

[25]   The principle of delivery applies, albeit in different forms, in Germany, Greece, the Netherlands, Spain, Switzerland, Brazil and most other Latin American countries. This principle, most likely due to the German B.G.B.'s influence and Karl Llewellyn's reform campaign, also applies in the United States (with the exception of Louisiana), under Article 2–401(2) of the Uniform Commercial Code.

property in the goods has not passed as a result of the conclusion of the contract, the seller must take any action required to perform the obligation to transfer property in the goods. In most cases, such action coincides with the fulfillment of the other basic obligation of the seller, consisting of the delivery of the goods. Under special circumstances, however, the action required from the seller may be different from, or not limited to, the delivery of the goods. In particular, this provision covers situations where the transfer of property under the applicable domestic law requires a specific declaration of intention to transfer property. In this case, the seller is bound under Article 30 CISG to render that necessary declaration.

In the light of the alternative rules described above, one may argue that the seller will transfer ownership in the goods to the buyer, either when the contract of sale is concluded or when the goods are handed over to the buyer, depending on the rule of law applicable to the passing of property. However, if the seller agrees to postpone payment or if he accepts payment in instalments, thus financing the buyer's business, he does so at his own risk. In order to limit this risk the seller may request that the parties stipulate that the supply of the goods to the buyer takes place on the condition that the seller remains the owner of the goods (*i.e.*: retains title to them), although they are already in the hands of the buyer, until the purchase price is paid in full. This common contractual solution is referred to as a "retention of title" clause and it is available to the parties of a sale contract in any modern legal system, thus allowing the parties to agree on a postponement of the passing of property until the purchase price is paid in full. This leads to a structure of the transaction under which, at a prior stage, the goods are delivered to the buyer and the risk passes to him, but the ownership does not; whereas, at a later stage, payment is performed or completed and the title to the goods passes from the seller to the buyer.

The retention of title clause provides a security interest to the seller, who can recover the goods if the buyer fails to pay, and, given certain circumstances, can do so even if the goods are sold to a third party, or seized on behalf of another creditor, or if the buyer goes bankrupt. Since the retention of title clause is not governed by the CISG,[26] its legal operation and its validity against third parties depend on the applicable general domestic rules on property, enforcement and bankruptcy, which vary significantly in different jurisdictions. Indeed, each legal system requires the fulfillment of different formalities in order for the retention of title to be valid against third parties.

---

[26] *Accord* LG Freiburg (Germany), 22 August 2002, available in English at http://cisgw3.law.pace.edu/cases/020822 g1.html; *contra*, although only to a limited extent, Federal Court of Australia, 28 April 1995 (*Roder Zelt– und Hallenkonstruktionen GmbH v. Rosedown Park Pty. Ltd. et al.*), available at http://cisgw3.law.pace.edu/cases/950428a2.html, stating that the validity of a retention of title clause and whether the clause constituted a breach of the obligation to transfer property in the goods, had to be assessed on the basis of the CISG.

Since the issue is neither specifically governed by the CISG, nor by any other uniform law instrument currently in force,[27] whenever a retention of title clause is set forth in an international contract, in order to identify the applicable regulation, recourse is to be had to domestic law applicable by virtue of the conflict–of–law rules of the *forum*. However, the application of domestic substantive law with regard to international business transactions will lead to enormous problems. Indeed, in most jurisdictions matters related to security rights and property rights involving international situations are regulated by the domestic law to be identified according to the *lex rei sitae* criterion (also known as "*lex situs*–rule"). This means, with reference to moveable goods, that those matters may possibly be governed by two different laws in two different moments, depending on where the goods are located. The possible negative effect with reference to a retention of title clause is apparent: the recognition and enforcement of proprietary rights after a change of the *situs* depends on the domestic law of the new *situs* with regard to such rights. As a consequence, depending on the differences in the requirements of validity against third parties, it might be the case

---

[27] For a notable exception to the stated lack of uniform rules, although relevant only to a specific and limited category of goods, see the 2001 Cape Town Convention on International Interests in Mobile Equipment, along with the Protocols accompanying the Convention, namely the Protocol on Matters Specific to Aircraft Equipment (Cape Town, 2001), the Protocol on Matters Specific to Railway Rolling Stock (Luxembourg, 2007) and the Protocol on Matters Specific to Space Assets (Berlin, 2012).

that a proprietary right endowed according to the rules of one jurisdiction is deemed invalid in another jurisdiction requiring specific formalities. Consider, for example, the following hypothetical:[28] a seller in "Country A" gives credit to a company in that same jurisdiction for the purchase of a car. In order to secure the seller in the case of the buyer's insolvency, the parties enter into an agreement whereby the seller retains title in the car sold, thus obtaining a security interest. Nevertheless, possession of the car and the right to use it are transferred to the buyer, on the assumption that the existence of an agreement duly dated and executed in writing makes the retention of title clause valid against third parties. Indeed, this is the case under the law of "Country A". The car, however, is subsequently driven in "Country B", where it is seized by a creditor of the buyer. The seller claims cancellation of the enforcement order on the ground that he has a prior security interest in the car. However, the court in "Country B" applies its domestic law, it being the law of the (new) *situs* where the car is located and, on grounds that under the law of "Country B" the security interest must be characterized as a pledge and requires dispossession in order to be valid against third parties, rejects the seller's claim. It is apparent from the hypothetical

---

[28]   The hypothetical in the text is based on the case dealt with in a famous decision rendered by the Supreme Court of France, 8 July 1969, REVUE CRITIQUE DE DROIT INTERNATIONAL PRIVÉ 75 (1979), although it should be noted that in the meantime the French law on retention of title clauses has changed.

above that the lack of uniform regulation with regard to the validity against third parties of retention of title clauses may lead to results which, in practice, may prove discouraging for a seller who would otherwise be available to finance his buyer under the security of a retention of title.

5.   CONFORMITY OF THE GOODS AND NOTICE OF NON–CONFORMITY

As can be derived from Article 35 CISG, the seller has an obligation to deliver conforming goods. If the seller does not deliver such goods, the buyer may exercise certain rights or claim damages under Article 74 CISG, provided that the buyer gives an appropriate notice of the lack of conformity within a given period of time. If the buyer does not give such notice to the seller, "[t]he buyer loses the right to rely on [the] lack of conformity of the goods" (Article 39(1)). In other words, a failure to give proper notice generally prevents the buyer from being able to rely on the lack of conformity,[29] barring all remedies: a potential claim for damages, requiring performance by the seller, avoidance of the contract and reduction of the purchase price. Furthermore, pursuant to Article 39(2), "the buyer loses the right to rely on a lack of conformity of the goods if he does not give the seller notice thereof at the latest within a period of two years from the date on which the goods were actually handed over to the buyer." The

---

[29]   *See* OLG Düsseldorf (Germany), 10 February 1994, available in English at http://cisgw3.law.pace.edu/cases/940210 g1.html.

harsh consequences attached to a failure to give proper notice are, however, mitigated by the fact that Article 39 must not be read on its own but rather in a wider context. The CISG contains two provisions, Articles 40 and 44, which mitigate the rigor of the consequences of a failure to give proper notice. These provisions were introduced upon the insistence of the developing countries, which considered the loss of all rights and the absolute exclusion of all claims after two years as being too harsh a consequence for such failure.

At this point, it is important to examine when the buyer is required to notify the seller in order not to lose the right to rely on the lack of conformity. In this respect, Article 39 itself merely states that the need to notify is triggered when there is a "lack of conformity". Article 39 does, however, not define the "lack of conformity". Rather, one has to turn to Article 35 to find a uniform, autonomous, and broad definition, which takes the place of any domestic definition, when the CISG applies.

According to Article 35(1) CISG, there is a lack of conformity primarily where the goods do not conform with contract specifications requiring (either expressly or implicitly) that the goods have certain characteristics that, pursuant to the non-exhaustive list contained in Article 35(1) CISG, may relate to the quality, quantity, description and packaging of the goods sold. Whether the contract requires goods of a particular quantity, quality or description, or requires that the goods be contained or packaged in a particular manner, is to be determined on the basis of the general rules for determining the content and the interpretation of the parties' agreement, such as Article 8 CISG.

As just mentioned, the goods do not conform where they lack the qualitative characteristics agreed upon, independently of whether the quality of the goods is worse or better than that stipulated in the contract. It must be noted that for the purpose of establishing from a qualitative point of view whether the goods do conform with the contract requirements, it is irrelevant whether the lack of conformity relates to physical characteristics of the goods (that may concern the color of the goods, their composition, the ornaments that may be attached to them) rather than to more technical ones, such as their origin or they being accompanied by a certificate.[30]

The goods lack conformity also when they do not meet the quantitative requirements agreed upon, and it does not matter at all whether the quantity delivered is less or more[31] than that agreed upon. In other words, any quantitative discrepancy constitutes a lack of conformity and triggers the need for the buyer to notify the lack of conformity in order not to lose the right to rely on the lack of conformity, even where the discrepancy in quantity

---

[30]   *See* OLG München (Germany), 13 November 2002, English translation available at http://cisgw3.law.pace.edu/cases/021113g1.html.

[31]   *See* OLG Rostock (Germany), 25 September 2002, available in English at http://cisgw3.law.pace.edu/cases/020925 g1.html.

was apparent from the documents, such as the invoice.

Similarly, where the packaging does not correspond to that agreed upon, the goods lack conformity and the buyer has to give notice of that lack of conformity to avoid losing the right to rely on it. This certainly is true where the packaging itself adds value to the goods sold. Where, however, the packaging agreed upon merely constitutes a means to protect the goods during transport and the goods reach their destination undamaged, the buyer cannot rely on the packaging being damaged, as this would violate the principle of good faith upon which the CISG is based.

What, however, where the seller delivers an *aliud*, *i.e.*, goods entirely different from those specified in the contract? Even though the CISG does not expressly address the issue, unlike, for instance, the ULIS, it cannot be doubted that the notification requirement applies in this line of cases as well.[32] In these authors' opinion, the opposite solution contrasts with the rationale behind Article 39 CISG, which, as stated in case law,[33] requires that the seller be put in a position where he can examine the goods in order to be able to ascertain whether a claim is justified and, if so, cure any lack of conformity.

---

[32] *See* Supreme Court of Spain, 17 January 2008, available in English at http://cisgw3.law.pace.edu/cases/080117s4.html.

[33] *See, e.g.,* Supreme Court of Switzerland, 28 May 2002, available in English at http://cisgw3.law.pace.edu/cases/020528s1.html.

It should also be noted that even though Article 39 CISG merely refers to the "lack of conformity of *the goods*", it is here suggested that the notice requirement also applies where the defect relates to the documents rather than to the goods themselves.

When a contract does not contain any indication of the characteristics the goods must have (or when the indications are too imprecise or insufficient) and the characteristics cannot be derived from the practices established between the parties or the usages applicable pursuant to Article 9 CISG, it is Article 35(2) CISG that establishes the characteristics that the goods must meet for them not to lack conformity. In other words, Article 35(2) CISG lays down objective minimum requirements that the goods must meet. Of course, where the parties do not want to be bound by these minimum standards, they can agree not to be bound by them, since Article 35(2) CISG is dispositive in nature.

As regards the characteristics laid down in subparagraphs (*a*) and (*d*), it must be pointed out that they have to be met in any case, *i.e.*, whenever Article 35(2) applies. The requirements based on the criteria set forth in subparagraphs (*b*) and (*c*), on the other hand, have to be met only where certain preconditions to be addressed later are fulfilled. In these authors' opinion, this does not mean that where the preconditions for the application of subparagraphs (*b*) and (*c*) are fulfilled, the more "general" requirements do not have to be met; rather, the more general requirements have to be met on top of the more special ones covered by subparagraphs (*b*) and (*c*).

Pursuant to Article 35(2)(*a*), the goods must be fit for all purposes for which goods of the same description would ordinarily be used. In light of the circumstance that the CISG generally applies to contracts between business parties, the determination of whether the goods are fit for those purposes is to be based upon what a reasonable businessman of the same kind as the buyer would objectively have had reason to expect in the same circumstances. This means that the goods must primarily be fit for commercial purposes, which, in turn, requires them to be at least fit for resale.[34]

Article 35(2)(*a*) also requires that the goods sold have a certain duration; thus, it is not surprising that a French court decided that the delivery of goods that broke soon after they were put into operation constitutes a breach of the obligation deriving from Article 35(2)(*a*).[35]

Article 35(2)(*a*) CISG has triggered a dispute as to the regulatory and safety standards to be used to determine whether the goods are fit for the purpose for which goods of the same description would ordinarily be used. Most commentators correctly hold that the standards to be referred to are those applicable in the seller's country, except when the

---

[34]   *See* LG Trier (Germany), 12 October 1995, available in English at http://cisgw3.law.pace.edu/cases/951012g1.html.

[35]   *See* CA Grenoble (France), 15 May 1996, available in English at http://cisgw3.law.pace.edu/cases/960515f1.html.

seller has repeatedly delivered goods of the same kind to parties in the buyer's country,[36] where the seller knows or ought to know about the standards applicable in the buyer's country, or when the standards in the buyer's country are the same as those in the seller's country, that is to say, when there are "special circumstances" pursuant to which the seller knew or should have known of the standards applicable in the buyer's country.[37]

Since Article 35(2)(*a*) CISG obliges the seller to deliver goods that "are [merely] fit for the purposes for which goods of the same description would ordinarily be used", buyers cannot expect the goods to also be fit for particular purposes. In effect, as can easily be derived from Article 35(2)(*b*), goods must be fit for a particular purpose only if this "purpose [was] expressly or impliedly made known to the seller at the time of the conclusion of the contract, except where the circumstances show that the buyer did not rely, or that it was unreasonable for him to rely, on the seller's skill and judgment." From the text just quoted, one can derive that there is no need for an agreement relating to the fitness

---

[36]   *See* U.S. District Court [E.D. La.], 17 May 1999 (*Medical Marketing International, Inc. v. Internazionale Medico Scientifica, S.r.l.*), available at http://cisgw3.law.pace.edu/cisg/wais/db/cases2/990517u1.html.

[37]   *See* High Court of New Zealand, 30 July 2010 (*RJ & AM Smallmon v. Transport Sales Limited and Grant Alan Miller*), available at http://cisgw3.law.pace.edu/cases/100730n6.html; Supreme Court of Austria, 19 April 2007, available in English at http://cisgw3.law.pace.edu/cases/070419a3.html; Supreme Court of Germany, 2 March 2005, available in English at http://cisgw3.law.pace.edu/cases/050302g1.html.

for a particular purpose, as long as the particular purpose was made known to the seller. This means that the buyer can unilaterally determine the purpose for which the goods must be fit.

At this point one must also mention Article 35(2)(*c*), pursuant to which the seller has to deliver goods that also have all the qualities possessed by the goods which the seller has held out to the buyer as a sample or model, provided that the seller had not held out the goods "without obligation", *i.e.*, without the intention to be bound to deliver goods possessing the same qualities.

Article 35(2)(*d*) imposes upon the seller the obligation to deliver goods that "are contained or packaged in the manner usual for such goods or, where there is no such manner, in a manner adequate to preserve and protect the goods." This means that this subparagraph lays down the minimum standard applicable in those cases in which the parties have not agreed upon higher standards, thus allowing the buyer to receive the goods in good condition.

Where the seller delivers goods that do not possess the required characteristics, the goods lack a conformity that triggers the seller's need to notify the lack of conformity within the time period and in the manner specified in Article 39 CISG. A proper notice does, however, not necessarily lead to the seller's liability for breach of contract. In effect, pursuant to Article 35(3) CISG "[t]he seller is not liable under subparagraphs (*a*) to (*d*) of the preceding paragraph for any lack of conformity of the goods if at the time of the conclusion of the contract the buyer knew or could not have been unaware of such lack of conformity."

In these authors' opinion, the rule laid down in Article 35(3) CISG does not necessarily always apply when its requirements are met. When more blame falls upon the seller than the negligent buyer (e.g., when the seller hides the defects), Article 35(3) CISG does not apply. This solution is justified by the general principle underlying the CISG pursuant to which a negligent buyer deserves more protection than a fraudulent seller.[38]

Before discussing the time requirement for notice, one must focus, at least briefly, on Article 38 CISG. This dispositive provision is very closely connected to Article 39. This becomes apparent if one considers that it is Article 38(1) that, by laying down the rule according to which the buyer has the burden of examining the goods, or cause them to be examined, within as short a period of time as is practicable under the circumstances, determines the moment from which the buyer has only a reasonable period of time within which to notify the seller of the lack of conformity in order not to lose the right to rely on that lack of conformity. It must be pointed out, however, that even though the examination of the goods *generally* constitutes a prerequisite for the application of the notice requirement, and the buyer

---

[38]   *See* OLG Köln (Germany), 21 May 1996, available in English at http://cisgw3.law.pace.edu/cases/960521g1.html.

will generally examine them, the lack of an examination does *per se* not lead to the loss of the buyer's rights.

As far as the period of time is concerned within which the inspection must occur, it generally starts to run when the goods are at the buyer's disposal, generally with the delivery of the goods. In light of the wording of Article 38(1), the time within which inspection has to occur is flexible and to be determined on a case–by–case basis. Therefore, one should not try to establish presumptions or average periods of time within which the examination has to occur, as is done at times.[39]

As regards the circumstances to be taken into account in determining the period of time at hand, only objective ones have to be taken into account.[40] Such objective circumstances include the perishable nature of the goods, the difficulty of effecting the examination, the way the goods are packaged, the seasonal character of the goods, and the like.[41]

As far as the inspection itself is concerned, Article 38 CISG does not specify the methods of inspection

---

[39]   *See* Supreme Court of Switzerland, 7 July 2004, available in English at http://cisgw3.law.pace.edu/cases/040707s1.html; U.S. District Court [N.D. Ill.], 21 May 2004 (*Chicago Prime Packers, Inc. v. Northam Food Trading Co.*), available at http://cisgw3.law.pace.edu/cases/040521u1.html.

[40]   *See* OLG Köln (Germany), 21 August 1997, available in English at http://cisgw3.law.pace.edu/cases/970821g1.html; *contra* Supreme Court of Austria, 27 August 1999, available in English at http://cisgw3.law.pace.edu/cases/990827a3.html.

[41]   *See* also Supreme Court of Austria decision cited in the previous note.

required. It has been suggested that the buyer (or a member of the buyer's staff or even a third person authorized to do so) does not have to make extraordinary efforts or run into extraordinary expenses.[42] Rather, it is sufficient that in inspecting the goods the buyer acts diligently and in a reasonable manner, *i.e.*, in a manner consistent with the way in which a reasonable person involved in a contract of the same type in the particular trade concerned would, taking into account, among other things, the type of goods involved.[43] Indeed, "a party would not be expected to discover a lack of conformity of the goods if he neither had nor had available the necessary technical facilities and expertise, even though other buyers in a different situation might be expected to discover [the] lack of conformity."[44] From what has just been said about the thoroughness of the inspection, it follows for instance that where a large quantity of goods is delivered, it is not necessary to inspect all the

---

[42] *See* OLG Dresden (Germany), 8 November 2007, available in English at http://cisgw3.law.pace.edu/cases/071108 g1.html; Supreme Court of Austria, 27 August 1999, available in English at http://cisgw3.law.pace.edu/cases/990827a3.html; Supreme Court of Germany, 30 June 2004, available in English at http://cisgw3.law.pace.edu/cases/040630g1.html.

[43] *See* KG Schaffhausen (Switzerland), 27 January 2004, available in English at http://cisgw3.law.pace.edu/cases/040127 s1.html.

[44] OFFICIAL RECORDS OF THE UNITED NATIONS CONFERENCE ON CONTRACTS FOR THE INTERNATIONAL SALE OF GOODS. VIENNA, 10 MARCH—11 APRIL 1980, *supra* note 3, at 34.

goods;[45] rather, it is sufficient that the buyer performs spot checks, by inspecting an adequate number of goods.[46]

As mentioned earlier, for the buyer to avoid losing the right to rely on the lack of conformity, the buyer must send a proper notice of the lack of conformity to the seller "within a reasonable time", unless the parties have agreed on a specific period within which notice has to be sent, which they are allowed to do since Article 39(1) CISG is dispositive in nature, and unless a specific period is imposed by the practices established between the parties or by usages applicable pursuant to Article 9 CISG.[47]

As regards the burden at hand that is imposed upon the buyer for "the purpose of achieving clarity concerning whether performance was properly effected",[48] the most important issue in practice is that of determining the requirements a notice must meet in order to prevent the harsh consequences of the lack of a proper notice, *i.e.*, the loss of the right to rely on the lack of conformity.

One requirement is a time requirement. Notice has to be sent "within a reasonable time" after the

---

[45] *See* OG Kanton Luzern (Switzerland), 8 January 1997, available in English at http://cisgw3.law.pace.edu/cases/970108 s1.html.

[46] *See* OLG Köln (Germany), 12 January 2007, available in English at http://cisgw3.law.pace.edu/cases/070112g1.html.

[47] *See* Trib. Rimini (Italy), 26 November 2002, available in English at http://cisgw3.law.pace.edu/cases/021126i3.html.

[48] Supreme Court of Austria, 27 August 1999, available in English at http://cisgw3.law.pace.edu/cases/990827a3.html.

lack of conformity has been discovered or ought to have been discovered. This requires one to take a case–by–case approach in determining the "reasonable time" and look at the circumstances of each case.[49] The circumstances that can influence the determination of the reasonableness of a given time period include the nature of the goods, in particular whether they are perishable or closely related to a particular season. When the goods are perishable, or when they are seasonal, the "reasonable time" period must be shorter. Where the goods are neither perishable nor closely related to a particular season, the period for notice may be longer.

The flexibility of the "reasonable period of time" comes at a price: it may lead to diverging interpretations by courts from different countries. In these authors' opinion, these divergences are, however, not very worrisome, as they are nothing but a quite natural result of the application of language intentionally drafted to be very flexible and adjustable to the circumstances of the case. Much more worrisome are the divergences that derive from the differences in the approach taken to determine the "reasonable time" referred to in Article 39(1) CISG. In effect, rather than resorting to the case–by–case approach mandated in these authors' opinion by the text of Article 39(1), some

---

[49]   *See, e.g.*, U.S. District Court [S.D. Ohio], 26 March 2009 (*Miami Valley Paper, LLC v. Lebbing Engineering & Consulting GmbH*), available at http://cisgw3.law.pace.edu/cases/090326u1. html; Trib. Forlì (Italy), 16 February 2009, available in English at http://cisgw3.law.pace.edu/cases/090216i3.html.

courts resort to presumptive time periods to determine whether a notice was given within a "reasonable period of time". In these authors' opinion, recourse to presumptive periods should be avoided, as it does not reflect the flexibility of the "reasonable time" standard set forth in Article 39(1) CISG. Moreover, resorting to presumptive periods could have an effect on the allocation of the burden of proof, for example by creating the presumption that a notice not given within that presumptive period is untimely. This must be avoided.

In order to bar the loss of the right to rely on the lack of conformity, it is not sufficient, however, that the buyer notifies the seller in time (by using appropriate means of communication).[50] According to Article 39(1) CISG, the buyer must also specify (all) the non–conformities, and this is a way that allows the seller to get a picture of the situation and to decide how to react.[51] This does not mean that Article 39(1) imposes overly–demanding standards of specificity.[52] Still, a generic notice that merely states that the goods are defective cannot be considered a proper notice under Article 39(1).[53]

---

[50]   *See* Trib. Vigevano (Italy), 12 July 2000, available in English at http://cisgw3.law.pace.edu/cases/000712i3.html.

[51]   *See* Trib. Vigevano (Italy), 12 July 2000, available in English at http://cisgw3.law.pace.edu/cases/000712i3.html.

[52]   *See* Supreme Court of Austria, 8 November 2005, available in English at http://cisgw3.law.pace.edu/cases/051108 a3.html: "Although the requirements as to the content of the notice must not be exaggerated, the notice must be specific in that it must describe the non–conformity in detail."

[53]   *See* OLG Hamm (Germany), 2 April 2009, available at http://www.globalsaleslaw.com/content/api/cisg/urteile/1978.pdf.

Therefore, a notice concerning defective fashion items that says no more than "too soft", "not in order", "defective quality or delivery of wrong goods", "inferior and poor quality", or "poor workmanship and improper fitting" is not specific enough.

It is worth pointing out that even though the notice of lack of conformity has to meet both a temporal and a substantive requirement, it does not have to meet a formal one. Article 39(1) does not require that the notice take a given form.[54] Thus, it can be given in writing, orally, and also via phone. Where, however, notice is given via phone, the buyer has to prove the precise date of the call, the person who received it as well as the contents of the conversation.[55]

At this point, one must at least briefly mention that apart from the aforementioned flexible time period for notice required by Article 39(1), the CISG also contains a rigid cut–off limit of two years, beyond which no notice of lack of conformity, not even one which would satisfy all Article 39(1) requirements, can avoid the loss of the buyer's right to rely on the lack of conformity. This rigid two–year limit, the running of which cannot be suspended or interrupted, starts to run from the time the goods are actually physically handed over to the buyer.

---

[54]   See AG Bern (Switzerland), 11 February 2004, available in English at http://cisgw3.law.pace.edu/cases/040211s1.html.

[55]   See LG Kassel (Germany), 22 June 1995, available in English at http://cisgw3.law.pace.edu/cases/950622g1.html.

As mentioned earlier, an improper notice by the buyer bars the full range of the buyer's remedies. However, according to Article 40 CISG, an improper notice by the buyer does not lead the loss of the buyer's right to rely on the lack of conformity, if this lack of conformity relates to facts which the seller knew, or could not have been unaware of, and which he did not disclose to the buyer—and this is true even if more than two years from the date of delivery of the defective goods have passed. Thus, Article 40 relaxes the rigor of the consequences of an improper notice laid down by Article 39 CISG. In order for a missing disclosure to foreclose the seller from relying upon Article 39 CISG it is not necessary that the seller did not disclose the lack of conformity in bad faith: Article 40 CISG is applicable even when the seller is "merely" grossly negligent.[56]

Article 40 CISG is not the only provision by virtue of which the rigor of an improper notice of the lack of conformity is relaxed. Article 44 also does so, as it maintains the remedies of price reduction and compensatory damages, except for loss of profit, in cases where the buyer has a reasonable excuse for his failure to give the required notice. Article 44 CISG does not, however, affect the two–year cut–off period provided for in Article 39(2). Thus, after the expiration of two years after the delivery of the goods, the buyer, who has the burden to prove the prerequisites of the application of Article 44, loses

---

[56]   *See* OLG Celle (Germany), 10 March 2004, available in English at http://cisgw3.law.pace.edu/cases/040310g1.html.

his rights to rely on the lack of conformity, even though he may have a "reasonable excuse".

6.   FREEDOM FROM THIRD–PARTIES' RIGHTS, CLAIMS AND INTELLECTUAL PROPERTY RIGHTS

The obligation of the seller to deliver goods in conformity with the contract or the Convention is accompanied by the additional guarantee, which the seller owes to the buyer, that the goods be free from third parties' rights, claims and intellectual property rights. Article 41 CISG, in particular, lays down a general liability of the seller for defects in title resulting from third parties' claims based of proprietary or other rights, to the exclusion of rights and claims "based on industrial property or other intellectual property rights". The latter ones, in fact, are dealt with under Article 42 CISG. The seller's general liability for defect in title, on the other hand, does not operate if "the buyer agreed to take the goods subject to [the third party's] right or claim." A specific consensus of the buyer to this effect is required, whereas a mere generic acceptance of the goods "as they are" will not suffice to exempt the seller from liability.

The obligation set forth in Article 41 CISG cannot be regarded as a mere restatement or specification of the seller's basic obligation to transfer title in the goods. On the one hand, Article 41 CISG applies to third parties' rights and claims, whereas the general obligation of the seller to transfer property applies where the defect in title is dependent on the seller's remaining interest *in rem* hindering the buyer's full title. On the other hand, as already pointed out, the CISG does not provide rules dealing with the transfer of property, and this issue is therefore governed by the domestic rules applicable by virtue of the conflict–of–law rules of the forum. Accordingly, the seller's obligation to transfer property in the goods to the buyer operates only to the extent that property has not already passed to the buyer on the basis of the applicable domestic rules. These rules include rules on the transfer of property by contract, as well as rules on the transfer of property based on the *bona fides* purchaser rule. If the seller delivers to a *bona fides* buyer goods belonging to a third party, it may well be the case that the buyer acquires title in those goods on the basis of the applicable domestic law. In this situation, the seller is not in breach of his obligation to transfer property in the goods to the buyer; however, he is in breach of his obligation to "deliver goods which are free from any right or claim of a third party" under Article 41 CISG, notwithstanding the acquisition of title by the buyer. The buyer may therefore exercise all remedies available to him for the seller's breach of contract.

Third parties' rights which are relevant under Article 41 are primarily rights *in rem*, including any type of proprietary rights, usufruct, security interests, encumbrances, life temporary or remaining interests *in rem* and the like.[57]

---

[57]   *See, e.g.*, Juzgado Segundo de lo Civil y Mercantil de San Salvador (El Salvador), 28 February 2013, available at http://

Confiscation and other rights or measures of public authorities may also be relevant under the provision at hand.[58] Third parties' *in personam* rights or claims, on the other hand, may be relevant only to the extent that they can be claimed against the buyer.[59]

The language of Article 41 (not unlike that of the subsequent provision under Article 42) makes it clear that the guarantee owed by the seller to the buyer is not limited to situations where a third party has a well–grounded "right" on which his claim is based. The seller also guarantees freedom from third parties' "claims", irrespective of whether such claims are well–grounded. In fact, no matter how frivolous the third party's claim may be, unless the parties agreed on different contractual arrangements, the CISG allocates on the seller the burden of defeating the claim put forward by the third party, on the presumption that the seller is typically based in the same country as the third

---

www.cisgspanish.com/wp–content/uploads/2013/08/ElSalvador28 feb2013.pdf.

[58] *See, e.g.*, Arbitration Court for the Western Siberia Circuit (Russian Federation), 6 August 2002, available in English at http://cisgw3.law.pace.edu/cases/020806r1.html, dealing with the confiscation of goods by Customs authorities, due to the seller's failure to take necessary action in order to fulfill his obligations within the "temporary import" regime time limits.

[59] *See* Supreme Court of Austria, 6 February 1996, available in English at http://cisgw3.law.pace.edu/cases/960206a3.html, applying Article 41 CISG to a case where the seller's supplier had restricted the export of the goods.

party, and therefore is in the best position to deal with the case.

While Article 41 deals with defects in title resulting from third parties' rights and claims in general, Article 42 CISG deals more specifically with the guarantee that the seller is bound to give to the buyer that the goods are "free from any right or claim of a third party based on industrial property or other intellectual property". There is general consensus that, although Article 42 CISG uses the two concepts as if they were distinct, the notion of intellectual property ("IP") rights includes industrial property rights, as well as copyrights and other similar rights. The Convention does not define that notion. However, given the number and relevance of international conventions in the field of IP, it seems correct to refer to the definitions provided in those conventions, which are generally accepted in international commerce and coincide to a very large extent. This approach makes it possible to elaborate an articulated definition,[60] which certainly includes patents, copyrights, trademarks, industrial designs and models, names, trade–names, commercial names, logos, geographical indications, literary artistic and scientific works, know–how, and the like. Conversely, in these authors' view, third parties' rights and claims based on alleged unfair competition should fall under the general provision of Article 41, rather than under the special one set forth in Article 42. This is because

---

[60]   *See, e.g.,* the definition contained in the 1967 Convention establishing the World Intellectual Property Organization.

claims based on unfair competition are not as territorial–based as other IP rights are, whereas territoriality seems to be the main criterion that induced the drafters of the CISG to provide for a separate rule on liability for defects in title, when the defect consists of third parties' claims based on IP rights.

The provision at hand may be regarded as somewhat controversial in that, compared to the regime of strict liability set forth in Article 41 CISG, Article 42 operates so as to limit in several ways the liability of the seller for defects in title due to third parties' IP rights or claims.

First, the seller may be held liable only to the extent that "at the time of the conclusion of the contract [he] knew or could not have been unaware" of the third party's right or claim based on IP. A court held that the buyer bears the burden of proving this requirement of seller's liability,[61] which, in fact, transforms the regime of liability of the seller for the defects in title under consideration in a fault–based liability. But negligence in conduct is not the only element that limits seller's liability. In addition, in light of the fact that IP rights are territorial in nature, the seller is only liable if the third party's right or claim is based on the law of one of the States identified in Article 42(2)(*a*) or (*b*). As pointed out in a decision rendered by the Supreme Court of Austria, the seller merely has to

---

[61]   *See* Hof Arnhem (The Netherlands), 21 May 1996, available in English at http://cisgw3.law.pace.edu/cases/960521 n1.html.

"guarantee a corresponding conformity in certain countries, but not on a worldwide level [. . .] It is primarily liable for any conflict with property rights under the law of the State in which [the product] is being resold or in which it is supposed to be used, provided that the parties took this State into consideration at the time of the conclusion of the sales contract."[62] If the situation does not fall within the scope of the rule considered by the Supreme Court of Austria, then the seller guarantees freedom from third parties' IP rights, under Article 42(2)(*b*) CISG, only "under the law of the State where the buyer has his place of business."

An additional limitation of the possible liability of the seller arises from Article 42(2)(*a*), which excludes seller's liability if the third party's right or claim is one of which "[a]t the time of the conclusion of the contract the buyer knew or could not have been unaware". On the basis of this rule, for instance, the Supreme Court of France dismissed an appeal by a buyer on the grounds that, in his professional capacity as purchaser and reseller of shoes, he could not have been unaware that the shoes delivered by the seller had counterfeit ribbons.[63]

---

[62]   Supreme Court of Austria, 12 September 2006, available in English at http://cisgw3.law.pace.edu/cases/060912a3.html.

[63]   *See* Supreme Court of France, 19 March 2002, available in English at http://cisgw3.law.pace.edu/cases/020319f1.html; for a similar reasoning *see* also CA Colmar (France), 13 November 2002, available in English at at http://cisgw3.law.pace.edu/cases/021113f1.html.

Furthermore, the seller's liability is excluded under Article 42(2)(*b*) whenever the third party's rights or claims result from the seller's "compliance with technical drawings, designs, formulae or other such specifications furnished by the buyer." The rule, which appears to be based on the principle of assumption of risks, does not require fault on the part of the buyer furnishing specifications. Rather, it applies to the specific case under consideration. The general principle is that an obligee cannot rely on the obligor's breach to the extent that the breach was caused by the obligee's own act or omission. In a famous Israeli case in which the buyer instructed the seller to affix the "Levi's" trademark to the boots purchased, the court held that the seller was not liable to the buyer because the buyer had himself specified to the seller what symbol to affix to the boots.[64]

In a fashion that closely resembles the rule under Article 39, Article 43 CISG provides that the buyer loses the right to rely on the rules setting forth the seller's liability for defects in title (*i.e.*, Articles 41 and 42 CISG) if the buyer "does not give notice to the seller specifying the nature of the right or claim of the third party within a reasonable time after he has become aware or ought to have become aware of the right or claim." Much of what has been said with respect to the rule under Article 39 CISG can apply

---

[64]   Supreme Court of Israel, 22 August 1993, available in English at http://cisgw3.law.pace.edu/cases/930822i5.html. It should be noted that the CISG was not *per se* applicable to the contract in question, which, instead, was governed by ULIS; nonetheless, the court relied on Article 42 CISG to solve the case.

mutatis mutandis to the provision under consideration. In particular, the wording of the two provisions is significantly almost identical with respect to the modalities of giving notice of the defect. As a result, it is safe to affirm that, unless the parties make different contractual arrangements, the temporal requirement ("reasonable time") and the substantive one ("specificity") illustrated with respect to Article 39 apply in the very same manner also to cases falling under Article 43.[65] What differs, instead, at least to some extent, is the moment in time from which the notice period runs. Article 43 CISG refers to this effect to the moment when the buyer "has become aware" of the third party's right or claim, or when he "ought to have become aware". There is difference from the language of Article 39, which refers to the "discovery" of the defect. In these authors' view, however, the difference is primarily due to the different type of defects, and its consequences should not be overestimated. In one case, in fact, the defect is physical and the acquaintance thereof cannot but occur by "discovery"; in the other case, instead, the defect is legal and the acquaintance thereof takes the form of supervening "awareness".

---

[65] *See, e.g.*, LG Köln (Germany), 5 December 2006, available in English at http://cisgw3.law.pace.edu/cases/061205g1.html, rejecting the buyer's complaint based on the seller's delivery of goods that violated a third party's trademark on the basis that the buyer had failed to give the seller notice specifying the third party's right or claim within a reasonable time.

A more relevant difference between the two provisions at hand lays in that Article 43 CISG does not set forth a two–year cut–off period, like Article 39(2) does. This solution can be understood in light of the fact that defects in title can often become discernible only much later than physical ones. The absence of the two–year cut–off period, however, would not justify the conclusion that the buyer can bring a claim for defects in title without time limits. The issue of the limitation period applicable to causes of action available to the parties under the Convention is not dealt with under the CISG. Accordingly, the rule governing the limitation period applicable to a claim for defects in title must be drawn from the domestic law applicable by virtue of the conflict–of–law rules of the forum.

In spite of the buyer's failure to give timely notice, under Article 43(2) CISG the buyer retains his right to remedies based on the defect in title if the seller "knew of the right or claim of the third party and the nature of it". The rule is similar to that set forth in Article 40, in that both relax the rigor of the failure to give timely notice of defects. However, unlike Article 40, Article 43 CISG requires positive knowledge on the part of the seller and does not equate to that positive knowledge the mere negligent lack of knowledge. Also Article 44 CISG operates so as to relax the rigor of a failure to give proper notice of defect in title. It does so, in fact, by maintaining the remedies of price reduction and compensatory damages, except for loss of profit, in

cases where the buyer had a reasonable excuse for
his failure to give the required notice.

CHAPTER 7

OBLIGATIONS OF THE BUYER

1. PAYMENT OF THE PURCHASE PRICE

The characteristic obligations of the buyer who is party to a contract for the sale of goods governed by the CISG are identified in Article 53. This provision specifies that the buyer must "pay the price for the goods and take delivery of them as required by the contract and this Convention." Article 53 CISG is therefore the counterpart of Article 30, in that the latter sets forth the main obligations of the seller, whilst the former sets forth the main obligations of the buyer. In addition to the characteristic obligations identified above, the buyer may be contractually bound to other obligations, as made clear by the language of Article 62 CISG, which refers to "other obligations" in addition to the characteristic ones, in order to specify the contents of the claims for performance granted to the seller. However, additional obligations, other than those identified in Article 53, can be binding on the buyer only to the extent that he expresses his consent to make them part of the contractual undertakings. Some possible additional obligations are referred to in other provisions of the Convention. For instance, Article 3(1) CISG refers to the buyer's obligation to supply a (non–substantial) part of the materials necessary for the manufacture or production of the goods;[1] Article 65 CISG refers to circumstances under which the buyer must submit specifications regarding the form, measurement or other features of the goods. Of course, many other obligations can be agreed upon between the parties and are common in business practice, including, to give just one example, the obligation to provide security for a postponed payment or a payment in installment.

Unlike the obligation to take delivery, which under special circumstances may not be required (*e.g.*, when the buyer has already possession of the goods sold to him), the obligation to pay the purchase price is a fundamental obligation of any sales contract. Indeed, the payment obligation is required for the very existence of a contract of "sale" and if payment is entirely missing the contract is simply not a sales contract, at least under the CISG. On the other hand, the contract remains a sale if the parties agree to substitute for part of the payment obligation a different kind of performance. Moreover, even contracts that appear to be barter or countertrade transactions may be regarded as the combination of two sales contracts, to the extent that it can be argued that the parties agreed to two reciprocal sales and to the setting–off of the reciprocal credits.

Irrespective of any possible additional obligations that the parties may have agreed upon in their contract, under Article 54 CISG the buyer's

---

[1]   For further details on this provision, *see supra* Chapter 4, Section 2.

obligation to pay the purchase price "includes taking such steps and complying with such formalities as may be required under the contract or any laws and regulations to enable payment to be made." This provision deals with actions preparatory to payment and treats them as an integral part of the buyer's obligation to pay the purchase price. The most relevant consequence of this solution is that the failure to perform such preparatory actions can, in itself, be regarded as a breach of contract. Therefore, the seller can react to such failure by resorting not only to the remedies available for anticipatory breach of contract under Articles 71 and 72 CISG,[2] but also to the general remedies for breach of contract by the buyer set forth in Articles 61 et seq. CISG.[3] Another relevant consequence of the inclusion of preparatory actions within the framework of the buyer's characteristic obligations is that the buyer has to bear the costs implied by such activities and formalities.[4]

Article 54 CISG refers both to preparatory actions and formalities required under the contract to enable payment to be made and to those required by any laws and regulations. Preparatory actions required under the contract may include, among

---

[2]   For a comment on these provisions, *see infra* Chapter 9, Section 4.

[3]   *See* Supreme Court of Austria, 6 February 1996, available in English at http://cisgw3.law.pace.edu/cases/960206a3.html.

[4]   *See* LG Duisburg (Germany), 17 April 1996, available in English at http://cisgw3.law.pace.edu/cases/960417g1.html.

many others, the opening of a letter of credit,[5] and the establishment of security to guarantee payment.[6] However, actions that the buyer may be bound to perform can also include formalities required by "any laws and regulations". The provision at hand clearly makes reference to formalities under relevant domestic laws and regulations, including, for instance, foreign exchange and clearing rules. However, Article 54 CISG should not be constructed as a conflict–of–law provision, implying the application of conflict rules to determine which national legal system the parties should refer to in order to identify the formalities that the buyer is bound to fulfil. Instead, Article 54 sets forth a substantive rule, imposing on the buyer a duty to take actions so as to enable payment to be made, irrespective of the law under which obstacles to a smooth performance of payment exist. Therefore, although in most cases the relevant domestic laws and regulations that the buyer must consider are those of the buyer's home country, at times the buyer may also be required to abide by the laws and regulations of the seller's country or by those of a third country, to the extent that they govern the payment process. Furthermore, the prerequisites of payment that must be satisfied may include both measures of a commercial nature

---

[5]   See, e.g., ICC Court of Arbitration, Arbitral Award n. 11849 of 2003, available in English at http://cisgw3.law.pace.edu/cases/031849i1.html.

[6]   See, e.g., MKAC Arbitral Tribunal (Russian Federation), Arbitral Award of 25 May 1998, available in English at http://cisg w3.law.pace.edu/cases/980525r1.html.

and administrative measures imposed by local authorities. However, with respect to the latter measures, the buyer may be exempt from liability under Article 79 CISG,[7] dealing with the prerequisites and effects of force majeure circumstances. In fact, to the extent that the formalities imposed by the local authorities can be regarded as an impediment to payment, which is beyond the buyer's control, unforeseeable and insurmountable, the buyer may be exempted from the liability to compensate damages for his breach of contract, although the seller's right to require performance under Article 79(5) CISG remains unaffected.

The CISG does not provide rules dealing with the currency in which payment must be made. In most cases, the currency will be indicated by the parties in the contract,[8] either by means of a detailed provision dealing with the currency of payment, or by means of the simple use of the symbol (*e.g.*, "$", or "€") or acronym (e.g., "USD" or "EUR") indicating the currency next to the sum indicating the purchase price. In some cases, however, the currency may be unspecified in the contract and the question arises as to whether the CISG provides rules for determining the currency. In the absence of an express rule in the Convention, the prevailing

---

[7]   For further details about this provision, *see infra* Chapter 8, Section 6.

[8]   *Accord* Trib. Cantonal du Valais (Switzerland), 27 April 2007, available in English at http://cisgw3.law.pace.edu/cases/070427s1.html.

view in scholarly writing and case–law[9] is that the matter of the currency of payment is governed by the CISG, but not expressly settled in it. Therefore, under Article 7(2) CISG, the matter is to be settled, if possible, "in conformity with the general principles on which [the Convention] is based."[10] The relevant general principle applicable to the issue at hand can be drawn from Article 57(1)(*a*) CISG, under which, unless the parties differently agree, the buyer must pay the purchase price at the place of business of the seller. Hence, it can be inferred that also the currency of payment must be that of the place of business of the seller.[11] Moreover, to the extent that the currency of payment is determined on the basis of the seller's place of business, the rule under Article 57(2) CISG may also apply. Accordingly, the seller must "bear any increase in the expenses incidental to [the currency of] payment which is caused by a change in his place of business subsequent to the conclusion of the contract." The solution that has been proposed as to the currency of payment is to be preferred to the one that has been held by at least one court, albeit in more than one decision,[12] which is based on

---

[9]   *See, e.g.*, KG Berlin (Germany), 24 January 1994, available in English at http://cisgw3.law.pace.edu/cases/940124 g1.html.

[10]   For further details on the gap–filling rule under Article 7(2) CISG, *see supra* Chapter 1, Section 4.

[11]   *Accord* OLG Koblenz (Germany), 17 September 1993, available in English at http://cisgw3.law.pace.edu/cases/930917 g1.html.

[12]   Trib. Cantonal du Valais (Switzerland), 27 April 2007, available in English at http://cisgw3.law.pace.edu/cases/070427

the application of domestic law identified by virtue of the conflict–of–law rules of the forum. In fact, in most cases the latter solution leads to the application of the currency of the seller, at least whenever the law of the seller is the law applicable to the contract with respect to issues not governed by the CISG. However, in some circumstances a different law may be chosen by the parties, or applicable by virtue of other objective conflict–of–law criteria. When this is the case, making the currency dependent on the law applicable to the contract may lead to results, which are both inefficient and often inconsistent with the intent of the parties.

A different issue, which is of great practical relevance, is whether, in the presence of a contractual specification of the currency, the buyer can nonetheless discharge his debts in the currency of the place of payment. This question arises often in practice because many domestic jurisdictions set forth a similar provision and even consider it an overriding mandatory provision protecting public policy interests. However, as expressly maintained by the Supreme Court of Austria, under the CISG the buyer cannot claim his entitlement to pay the

---

s1.html; Trib. Cantonal du Valais (Switzerland), 27 October 2006, available in English at http://cisgw3.law.pace.edu/cases/061027 s1.html; Trib. Cantonal du Valais (Switzerland), 23 May 2006, available in English at http://cisgw3.law.pace.edu/cases/060523 s1.html; Trib. Cantonal du Valais (Switzerland), 27 May 2005, available in English at http://cisgw3.law.pace.edu/cases/050527 s1.html.

price in a currency other than that agreed upon in the contract or otherwise determinable as the currency of payment, since the possibility to pay in an alternative currency would necessarily require an agreement to that effect in the light of the pivotal role of parties' freedom of contract within the Convention.[13]

In most cases the parties expressly fix the price in the contract, or at least they make provision for determining the price. As a specification of this common occurrence, Article 56 CISG mandates that if the price is determinable on the basis of the weight of the goods, unless differently agreed upon by the parties (*e.g.*, by means of the term "gross for net"), "in case of doubt [the price] is to be determined by the net weight." For the purpose of the provision at hand, the net weight must be calculated at the time and place of performance of the delivery obligation.

If the parties omit to include in the contract any indication regarding the price and they don't make any provision for its determination, Article 55 CISG applies. According to this provision "the parties are considered, in the absence of any indication to the contrary, to have impliedly made reference to the price generally charged at the time of the conclusion of the contract for such goods sold under comparable circumstances in the trade concerned." The issue of open price contacts is dealt with in significantly

---

[13]   Supreme Court of Austria, 22 October 2001, available in English at http://cisgw3.law.pace.edu/cases/011022a3.html.

different ways in domestic legal systems, with a major distinction between legal systems that apply the principle of *pretium certum*, under which a fixed or determinable price is an essential term of the sales contract, and legal systems that provide legal criteria to supplement the contract if the price is not fixed. Article 55 CISG clearly adopts the latter solution and it refers to the price "generally charged at the time of the conclusion of the contract for such goods sold under comparable circumstances in the trade concerned". The criterion adopted under the CISG differs from the one that was provided under Article 57 ULIS, which made reference to the price generally charged by the seller at the time of the conclusion of the contract. The change introduced under the CISG is intended to add objectivity and predictability to the rule, although its application in practice can still prove rather problematic.

Article 55 applies to the extent that a valid sales contract governed by the CISG has been concluded. Accordingly, it has been held that the provision at hand does not apply if the transaction is not a contract of sale within the meaning of the Convention.[14] Furthermore, it has been also held that the provision cannot be applied if there is no evidence that a valid contract for sale has in fact been concluded.[15] This is, of course, primarily a

---

[14]   U.S. District Court [E.D. Pa.], 29 March 2004 (*Amco Ukrservice et al. v. American Meter Company*), available at http://cisgw3.law.pace.edu/cases/040329u1.html.

[15]   *See*, *e.g.*, Supreme Court of the Czech Republic, 25 June 2008, available in English at http://cisgw3.law.pace.edu/cases/080625cz.html.

matter of interpretation of the intention of the parties, to be conducted on the basis of Articles 8 and 9 CISG. However, the assessment may be further complicated by the difficulty to reconcile the rule laid out in Article 55 with the rule contained in Article 14 CISG. The latter provision sets the necessary requirements of a valid offer and includes the requirement that the proposal "expressly or implicitly fixes or makes provision for determining" the purchase price. No conflict exists between Article 14 and Article 55 whenever, in accordance with the reservation laid down in Article 92 CISG, either the application of Part II of the Convention (which includes Article 14) or the application of Part II of the Convention (which includes Article 55) is excluded. In most cases, however, the two provisions coexist and must therefore be reconciled.

Some court decisions have given precedence to the rule of Article 14 over that of Article 55 CISG,[16] thus affirming that a contract was not validly formed in the absence of a fixed or determinable price. Other court decisions have regarded the issue of the existence of a validly formed contract as an issue excluded from the scope of the Convention under Article 4 CISG. Accordingly, these decisions have relied on the domestic law applicable by virtue of the conflict–of–law rules of the forum.[17] However,

---

[16] *See, e.g.*, Supreme Court of Hungary, 25 September 1992, available in English at http://cisgw3.law.pace.edu/cases/920 925h1.html.

[17] *See, e.g.*, MKAC Arbitral Tribunal (Russian Federation), Arbitral Award of 30 May 2001, available in English at http://cisg w3.law.pace.edu/cases/010530r2.html.

in these authors' view neither one of the reported solutions is correct. The solution giving precedence to the rule of Article 14 is inconsistent with the intention of the parties, to the extent that the parties perform in whole or in part the contract, thus showing that they consider the contract to be in place, valid and effective. The solution leading to the application of domestic law seems inconsistent with the interpretative mandate of Article 7(1) CISG "to promote uniformity in [the Convention's] interpretation."[18] On the other hand, it can be argued effectively that Article 14 CISG sets forth the requirements for a valid offer, but, in accordance with Article 6, the parties can derogate to it expressly or implicitly. Accordingly, to the extent that the parties begin to perform the contract, although in the absence of a provision that "expressly or implicitly fixes or makes provision for determining" the purchase price, it can be argued that the parties have expressed their consensus to derogate to the rule under Article 14, thus relying on the application of the criterion laid out in Article 55 CISG.[19]

Also the issue of the means of payment is not dealt with explicitly by the CISG. Nonetheless, there should be no doubts that payments in cash

---

[18]   For further details on the rule on interpretation under Article 7 CISG, *see supra* Chapter 1, Section 2.

[19]   *See, e.g.*, Trib. Cantonal du Valais (Switzerland), 27 April 2007, available in English at http://cisgw3.law.pace.edu/cases/ 070427s1.html; Supreme Court of Austria, 10 November 1994, available in English at   http://cisgw3.law.pace.edu/cases/941110 a3.html.

always satisfy the requirements of the Convention. However, also "cashless" payments must be deemed permissible, since they can be deemed to be in conformity with a general usage of international trade. Therefore, international bank wire transfers represent a valid form of payment in international sales, permissible under the CISG, the performance of which is complete when the payment is credited to the benefit of the seller. Conversely, payment by cheque is always made on account of performance and the seller may thus legitimately reject such form of payment, unless it had been agreed upon in the contract. In any event, if the seller accepts the cheque and the cheque is thereafter cashed, payment must be deemed to have taken place upon the handing over of the cheque.

As far as the place of payment is concerned, Article 57(1) CISG, in conjunction with Article 6, refers primarily to the particular place indicated by parties in their contract. Failing a contractual agreement on this point, the place of payment may be determined on the basis of usages or contractual practices between the parties, under Article 9 CISG. However, if "the buyer is not bound [by agreement, contractual practices or usages] to pay the price at any other particular place," Article 57(1) differentiates the solution on the basis of whether or not the payment "is to be made against the handing over of the goods or of documents."

Under Article 57(1)(*b*) CISG, "if the payment is to be made against the handing over of the goods or of documents," the seller must pay the purchase price "at the place where the handing over takes place." In other words, the place of the handing over of the goods takes a bearing also as regards the place of payment. This rule applies, in particular, in conjunction with the general rule on the time of payment (Article 58(1) CISG), under which, unless differently agreed upon, payment is to be made concurrently with the handing over of the goods or of documents. Conversely, if the parties are not bound to perform their obligations simultaneously, the rule under Article 57(1)(*b*) does not apply.[20] This is often the case in sales of goods involving carriage, where the seller typically performs his obligation by handing over the goods to the first carrier, under Article 31(1)(*a*) CISG. When this is the case, the seller's performance typically precedes payment in that, under Article 58(1) CISG, the buyer is not required to pay the purchase price until the goods or documents controlling their disposition are placed at the buyer's disposal at destination.

The alternative rule under Article 57(1)(*a*) applies to cases where the buyer is bound to pay in advance, as well as to cases where the parties agree on a postponed payment. Moreover, it also applies to the sale of goods in transit, as well as to the sale of goods to be transported by a carrier who has no authority to collect the purchase price. In all these cases, as well as in any other cases where the payment is not to be made against the handing over

---

[20]   *See, e.g.,* ZG Kanton Basel–Stadt (Switzerland), 3 December 1997, available in English at http://cisgw3.law.pace.edu/cases/971203s2.html.

of the goods or of documents, the buyer must pay the purchase price "at the seller's place of business". In the event that the seller's place of business changes between the time of contract conclusion and the time of payment, the place of business at the time of payment is relevant. However, if the change in the place of payment causes an increase in the expenses incidental to payment, the seller must bear such additional expenses (Article 57(2) CISG). In practice, it is important to notice that the rule under Article 57(2) regarding the change in the seller's place of business also applies in the event that the seller assigns his claim for the price. Accordingly, when the assignment occurs, the buyer must perform payment to the place of business of the assignee; however, if this causes an increase in the expenses, the seller must bear such increase.

As already pointed out above, Article 58 CISG, along with Article 59, sets forth rules on the time of payment. Not unlike the place of payment, the time of payment may be determined, first of all, by agreement of the parties,[21] or by any relevant contractual practices or usages. If, however, "the buyer is not bound to pay the price at any other specific time," Article 58 CISG applies. Under this provision, as a general rule the buyer must pay the purchase price "when the seller places either the goods of the documents controlling their disposition at the buyer's disposal in accordance with the

---

[21]   This rule has been affirmed, *e.g.*, by Trib. Padova (Italy), 25 February 2004, available in English at http://cisgw3.law.pace. edu/cases/040225i3.html.

contract and this Convention." Therefore, Article 58 lays out the general rule of simultaneous exchange of goods and price, applicable unless the parties make different arrangements as regards the timing for performance of the reciprocal obligations.[22] Therefore, the time when payment is due is usually dependent on the place and time of the handing–over of the goods or documents under Article 31(1)(*b*) or (*c*).[23] Conversely, in the event of sale involving carriage under Article 31(1)(*a*) the seller fulfills his obligation by handing over the goods to the first carrier, but under Article 58(1) the buyer is not bound to pay the price until the goods or documents are handed over to him at destination.

In any event, the seller may make payment "a condition for handing over the goods or documents", as specified in general terms in the last sentence of Article 58(1) CISG, as well as in Article 58(2) with regard to sales of goods involving carriage. These provisions lay out a right of retention in favor of the seller, which is to be read in conjunction with the buyer's right to retain payment under Article 58(3) CISG. Under the latter provision, the buyer "is not bound to pay the price until he has had an opportunity to examine the goods." However, the

---

[22] *Accord*, among many others, Supreme Court of Switzerland, 18 January 1996, English abstract available at http://cisgw3.law.pace.edu/cases/960118s1.html; Supreme Court of Austria, 8 November 2005, available in English at http://cisgw3.law.pace.edu/cases/051108a3.html.

[23] *See, e.g.*, OLG Düsseldorf (Germany), 28 May 2004, available in English at http://cisgw3.law.pace.edu/cases/040528g1.html.

buyer's right to retain payment cannot be exercised in the event that "the procedures for delivery or payment agreed upon by the parties are inconsistent with" the buyer having the opportunity to examine the goods. This is the case, in particular, where the parties have agreed on payment terms such as "cash against documents" or similar. Furthermore, it has been held that during the time necessary to examine the goods the buyer may legitimately suspend payment in light of the general principle of simultaneous exchange of goods and price.[24]

Article 59 CISG lays out the rule under which the purchase price becomes due automatically on the date set for payment, without the need for a demand on the part of the seller, or for any other formalities. In particular, it has been held that this rule implies that the obligation to pay the purchase price is not conditional on the issuance of an invoice.[25] Although this view can be shared in principle, it should also be highlighted that relevant exceptions to it exist. In particular, it has often been held that the requirement that the seller send an invoice in advance may be drawn not only from the parties' agreement to this effect, but also from contractual practices or usages.[26] This conclusion, indeed, is

---

[24]   Supreme Court of Austria, 8 November 2005, available in English at http://cisgw3.law.pace.edu/cases/051108a3.html.

[25]   *See, e.g.*, Supreme Court of the Slovak Republic, 3 April 2008, available in English at http://cisgw3.law.pace.edu/cases/080403k1.html.

[26]   *See, e.g.*, OLG Köln (Germany), 3 April 2006, available in English at http://cisgw3.law.pace.edu/cases/060403g1.html.

reinforced in light of the fact that all INCOTERMS require that the seller issue a commercial invoice to the buyer, a provision that may be regarded as the restatement of a general usage in international trade.

The most relevant practical implication of the rule laid out in Article 59 CISG is that upon the buyer's failure to pay at the due date, he is in breach of contract. Therefore, the seller can resort to all remedies available for the buyer's breach of contract and may claim interest accrued in accordance with Article 78 CISG.[27] In fact, many court decisions have pointed out that the interest accruing on sums in arrears begins to accumulate as soon as the sum becomes due, without the need for any demand of other formalities.[28]

2.   OBLIGATION TO TAKE DELIVERY

Although the obligation to pay the purchase price is arguably the most relevant obligation of the buyer, Article 53 CISG indicates also another obligation among the characteristic ones, to which the buyer is bound. It is the obligation to take delivery, which is specifically addressed by Article 60 CISG. According to this provision, the obligation to take delivery consists not only in "taking over the goods" (Article 60(1)(*b*) CISG), but also in "doing all the acts which could reasonably be expected of him

---

[27]   For further details on this provision, *see infra* Chapter 8, Section 4.

[28]   *See, e.g.*, Trib. Padova (Italy), 31 March 2004, available in English at http://cisgw3.law.pace.edu/cases/040331i3.html.

in order to enable the seller to make delivery" (Article 60(1)(*a*) CISG).

Under the rule laid out in Article 60(1)(*a*) CISG, the buyer owes a duty to cooperate with the seller consisting in performing all acts reasonably necessary to enable the seller to deliver the goods. These ancillary obligations are often identified in the contract, either by means of tailor–made rules, or by incorporation by reference of INCOTERMS, which provide for several obligations of the buyer in addition to payment of the purchase price. Under "F–terms", for instance, the buyer must provide the seller with information about the carrier and the time and place of loading of the goods; under "C–terms", the buyer may be required to obtain an import license.[29] Moreover, it has been held that the obligation to perform preparatory acts enabling the seller to make delivery also includes preparatory measures for the manufacture of the goods, such as the supply of designs or data.[30] In any event, it should be pointed out that the buyer's obligation to cooperate is limited only to "acts which could reasonably be expected of" the buyer. This implies, in particular, that the seller can only expect cooperation from the buyer,[31] but he cannot expect

---

[29]   *See* MKAC Arbitral Tribunal (Russian Federation), Arbitral Award of 24 January 2002, available in English at http://cisgw3.law.pace.edu/cases/020124r1.html.

[30]   *Accord* U.S. District Court [S.D.N.Y], 10 May 2002 (*Geneva Pharmaceuticals v. Barr Laboratories*), available at http://cisgw3.law.pace.edu/cases/020510u1.html.

[31]   *See* Supreme Court of Austria, 6 February 1996, available in English at http://cisgw3.law.pace.edu/cases/960206a3.html.

the buyer to perform acts, which are due by the seller, in lieu of the seller. This is the case even where the buyer could perform such acts at significant lower costs than those to be borne by the seller.

Article 60(1)(*b*) CISG sets forth the buyer's obligation to take physical possession of the goods.[32] The place and time for performance of the obligation to take delivery are not specified in the CISG. This is due to the fact that these obligations are dependent on the procedures applicable to the delivery of the goods, according to the contractual arrangements or, in the absence of such arrangements, to the rules set forth in Article 31 CISG. The taking of delivery is an obligation of the buyer, to the effect that the latter has no legitimate choice as to whether or not to take delivery. As a result of this characterization of the taking of delivery, the performance of this obligation on the part of the buyer cannot be presumed to imply in itself the buyer's acceptance of the goods.[33] Therefore, notwithstanding the taking of delivery, the buyer retains the right to give notice of non–conformity under Article 39 CISG[34] and to resort to any available remedy for non–conformity of the

---

[32]   *Accord* OLG Brandenburg (Germany), 18 November 2008, available in English at http://cisgw3.law.pace.edu/cases/081118 g1.html.

[33]   *See* KG Schaffhausen (Switzerland), 27 January 2004, available in English at http://cisgw3.law.pace.edu/cases/040127s1 .html.

[34]   For further details on this provision, *see supra* Chapter 6, Section 5.

goods delivered to him, including contract avoidance, or substitution of the goods, if the non–conformity amounts to a fundamental breach under Article 25 CISG.[35]

Article 60 CISG clarifies that the buyer owes to the seller the obligation to take delivery of the goods. However, the provision at hand does not specify under what circumstances the buyer may reject the goods handed over to him by the seller. Other provisions of the Convention provide some guidance in this respect. Under Article 52(1) the buyer may reject the goods if they are delivered before the date fixed for delivery. Similarly, under Article 52(2) the buyer may refuse to take delivery of the quantity of goods in excess of what was contractually agreed. Other than in the foregoing circumstances, no express solution is provided in the CISG to the issue of the buyer's right to reject the goods. Therefore, the answer to the question as to whether the buyer has a right to reject the goods must be based on the analysis of the remedies available to the buyer in the given circumstances. Accordingly, it is beyond doubt that the buyer may reject the goods in the event of a delay or non–conformity amounting to a fundamental breach of contract. Indeed, under these circumstances the buyer has a right to avoid the contract, or a claim for substitute goods and it would be inconsistent

---

[35] For further details on the notion of "fundamental breach" under Article 25 CISG, *see infra* Chapter 9, Section 1; for details on the buyer's remedies of contract avoidance and substitution of goods, *see* Chapter 9, Sections 2 and 3.

with those remedies to deny the buyer's right to reject the goods delivered to him in fundamental breach of contract. Conversely, in the event of a non–conformity that does not constitute a fundamental breach, the buyer cannot reject the goods.[36] Instead, the buyer must take delivery of the non–conforming goods and resort to the remedies available to him, which include claims for repair of the goods, price reduction and damages.

It should be noted that, even if the buyer intends to reject the goods handed over to him by the seller, under Article 86(1) CISG he may be subject to the obligation to "take such steps to preserve [the goods] as are reasonable in the circumstances." This may even require that the buyer takes possession of the goods, in view of the reasonable steps necessary to preserve them. However, if this situation occurs the buyer is entitled to claim reimbursement of any expense encountered for the purpose of preserving the goods.[37]

3. PASSING OF RISK

The buyer owes the payment obligation to the seller in consideration for delivery of goods conforming to the contractual arrangements. However, it may happen that in the lapse of time between the conclusion of the contract and the time

---

[36] For a court decision supporting the view expressed in the text, *see* OLG Frankfurt (Germany), 18 January 1994, available in English at http://cisgw3.law.pace.edu/cases/940118g1.html.

[37] For further details on the parties' duty to preserve the goods, *see infra* this Chapter, Section 6.

of dispatch of the goods to the buyer at the agreed final destination accidental events occur, which cause damage to, or even the complete loss of the goods. The question thus arises as to whether, notwithstanding the damage or loss of the goods, the buyer is still bound to pay the purchase price. The foregoing is commonly referred to as the issue of the passing of risk, which addresses the question of the moment in time when the risk of accidental loss of or damage to the goods passes from the seller to the buyer, and allocates the burden resulting from the accidental event on the basis of the timing of the passing of risk. The CISG devotes to this matter the rules set out in Chapter IV ("Passing of Risk") of Part III, which includes Articles 66 to 70. The issue is of great practical significance because of its potential harsh consequences. Legal rules provided for with regard to the allocation of the risk of loss of or damage to the goods determine whether the seller has to provide substitute goods or may claim payment of the purchase price from the buyer. Moreover, the same rules also determine whether the buyer has to pay the price for the goods and take delivery, despite the fact that they are partially damaged or totally destroyed. Reference is obviously made to the accidental loss or damage of the goods, since whenever the loss or damage is due to one party's breach of a statutory or contractual duty, the counterpart is granted other specific contractual remedies.

The traditional rule, which still applies in many legal systems, states that the risk of loss follows the title, according to the rule that "*res perit domino*" (*i.e.*, "the thing is lost to the owner"). However, in spite of this common link between ownership (and the passing of property) and risk (and the passing of risk), under Article 4(*b*) the CISG expressly excludes from its scope of application the issue of transfer of property,[38] whereas it provides for rules on the transfer of the risk of loss or damage of the goods. Therefore, the former matter is governed by the domestic law applicable by virtue of the conflict–of–law rules of the forum. The issue of the passing of risk, instead, is not linked to the passing of property and it is autonomously governed by the provisions in Articles 66 to 70 CISG.[39]

Article 66 CISG describes the effects of the passing of risk by specifying that "[l]oss of or damage to the goods after the risk has passed to the buyer does not discharge him from his obligation to pay the price, unless the loss or damage is due to an act or omission of the seller." The provision at hand illustrates only the effects that the rules on the passing of risk have on the buyer's payment obligation. It does not deal with when the risk passes. The time of the passing of risk is established by the CISG's provisions that follow, namely Articles 67 to 69. However, under Article 6 CISG the parties may derogate to the rules on the time of the

---

[38]   For further details on the scope of the exclusion under Article 4(*b*) CISG, *see supra* Chapter 4, Section 4.

[39]   *Accord* U.S. District Court [S.D.N.Y.], 26 March 2002 (*St. Paul Guardian Ins. Co. v. Neuromed Medical Systems & Support GmbH*), available at http://cisgw3.law.pace.edu/cases/020326u1. html.

passing of risk, and in practice commercial operators often do so by means of the incorporation into the agreement of trade terms, like the INCOTERMS of the International Chamber of Commerce.[40] In the presence of a contractual regulation of the time when risk passes, the parties' arrangements prevail and they exclude the application of Articles 67 to 69 CISG. On the other hand, they do not exclude, but rather trigger, the application of Article 66. Accordingly, if it is established (either contractually, or by the applicable CISG's rules) that the goods were lost or damaged before the risk passed from the seller to the buyer, the seller's failure to deliver or his delivery of non–conforming goods amounts to a breach of contract on the part of the seller.[41] Therefore, the buyer may claim any remedy available to him in the given circumstances for breach of contract by the seller. Conversely, if it is established that the goods were lost or damaged after the risk passed from the seller to the buyer, the buyer is required to pay the purchase price, unless the loss or damage is due to an act or omission of the seller.[42]

The final sentence of Article 66 CISG contains an exception to the general rule laid out in that provision. Accordingly, the buyer may be discharged

---

[40]   For further details, *see infra* this Chapter, Section 5.

[41]   *See, e.g.,* OLG Köln (Germany), 9 July 1997, available in English at http://cisgw3.law.pace.edu/cases/970709g3.html.

[42]   *See, e.g.,* District Court Comarno (Slovak Republic), 12 March 2009, available in English at http://cisgw3.law.pace.edu/cases/090312k1.html.

from his obligation to pay the purchase price if "the loss or damage is due to an act or omission of the seller". It must be noticed that the provision at hand does not refer to a breach of contract committed by the seller, but rather to his "act or omission". This suggests that even acts or omissions of the seller that do not constitute a breach of contract may nonetheless procure the discharge of the buyer from his payment obligations. This is the case, for example, with respect to seller's conduct that is unlawful in tort, although it may not be relevant in the light of the parties' contractual arrangements.

The risk dealt with in the provisions under consideration is the risk of accidental loss or damage to the goods. The notions of loss and damage are not provided in the CISG, but several decisions suggest that both notions are to be constructed in a rather extensive fashion. Accordingly, it has been held that the notion of loss also includes cases where the goods are stolen.[43] On the other hand, the notion of damage includes not only physical damages, but also complete destruction, deterioration, or shrinkage of the goods during carriage or storage.[44]

Another relevant issue on which the CISG is silent is who has the burden of proof regarding the passing of risk. There is vast consensus in legal

---

[43] *See*, *e.g.*, OLG Hamm (Germany), 23 June 1998, available in English at http://cisgw3.law.pace.edu/cases/980623g1.html.

[44] *See*, *e.g.*, Cámara National de Appelaciones en lo Comercial (Argentina), 31 October 1995, available in English at http://cisgw3.law.pace.edu/cases/951031a1.html.

writing that the question at hand concerns a matter governed by the CISG, but not expressly settled in it. Accordingly, the gap must be filled in accordance with Article 7(2) CISG,[45] by resorting primarily to the general principles on which the CISG is based. Two relevant general principles can be identified in this respect, which can be drawn, among other provisions, from Article 79(1) CISG: the general principle that the party who wants to derive beneficial legal consequences from a legal provision has to prove the existence of the factual prerequisites of the provision,[46] in other words, *"ei incumbit probatio qui dicit, non qui negat,"* and the general principle according to which the party claiming an exception has to prove the factual prerequisites of that exception.[47] The application of the foregoing general principles to the issue of the burden of proof regarding the passing of risk leads to relevant conclusions. A seller claiming payment of the purchase price must prove that the goods were in conformity with the contractual arrangements at the time of the passing of risk.[48]

---

[45]   For further details on this provision, *see supra* Chapter 1, Section 4.

[46]   *See* Trib. Cantonal du Valais (Switzerland), 28 January 2009, available in English at http://cisgw3.law.pace.edu/cases/090128s1.html; Supreme Court of Switzerland, 13 November 2003, available in English at http://cisgw3.law.pace.edu/cases/031113s1.html.

[47]   *See* Trib. Vigevano (Italy), 12 July 2000, available in English at http://cisgw3.law.pace.edu/cases/000712i3.html.

[48]   *See, e.g.*, LG Bamberg (Germany), 23 October 2006, available in English at http://cisgw3.law.pace.edu/cases/061023 g1.html.

Conversely, a buyer claiming remedies for the seller's alleged failure to deliver the lost goods, or for alleged non–conformity of the goods delivered damaged, must prove that the accidental loss of or damage to the goods occurred before the time when risk passed to him.[49]

Some court decisions seem to suggest that under certain circumstances a shift of the burden of proof may occur. In particular, it has been held that if the buyer duly gives notice of non–conformity to the seller according to Article 39 CISG, the seller then bears the burden to prove conformity of the goods at the time of passing of risk, whereas the burden shifts back to the buyer if he accepts without complaint.[50] In these authors' view this opinion cannot be shared. The consequence of the buyer's failure to duly give notice of non–conformity under Article 39 CISG is that he loses the right to rely on the lack of conformity of the goods. Therefore, the allocation of the burden of proof regarding the alleged non–conformity at the time of the passing of risk is irrelevant. Conversely, if the buyer wants to claim any remedy for the alleged breach on the part of the seller, he must not only give proper notice under Article 39, but also prove that the non–conformity existed at the time of the passing of risk. The buyer may base his proof on presumptions in

---

[49] *See, e.g.,* U.S. Court of Appeals [7th Cir.], 23 May 2005 (*Chicago Prime Packers, Inc. v. Northam Food Trading Co.*), available at http://cisgw3.law.pace.edu/cases/050523u1.html.

[50] AG Bern (Switzerland), 11 February 2004, available in English at http://cisgw3.law.pace.edu/cases/040211s1.html.

this regard; however, he cannot rely on a shift of the burden of proof on the seller.

In establishing when the risk of accidental loss of or damage to the goods passes from the seller to the buyer the CISG distinguishes between three different hypotheses. Article 67 provides rules on the passing of risk in sales involving carriage. Article 68 deals with sales of goods in transit. Article 69 provides the residual rules applicable to all cases not falling within Articles 67 and 68.

Article 67 CISG deals with sales involving carriage and makes a distinction based on whether or not the seller is bound to hand over the goods at a particular place. In both cases the risk passes when the goods are handed over to the carrier, or to a freight forwarder,[51] provided that the carrier or freight forwarder is an independent business operator and not an employee or branch of the seller. However, if the seller is bound to hand over the goods at a particular place, the passing of risk occurs upon the handing over to the carrier or freight forwarder at that place. If the seller is not bound to hand over the goods at a particular place, the risk passes to the buyer when the goods are handed over to the first carrier or to the freight forwarder for transportation.[52] The handing over

---

[51] For a court decision holding that delivery to a freight forwarder is equivalent to delivery to a carrier, *see, e.g.,* LG Saarbrücken (Germany), 26 October 2004, available in English at http://cisgw3.law.pace.edu/cases/041026g1.html.

[52] *See* AG Duisburg (Germany), 13 April 2000, available in English at http://cisgw3.law.pace.edu/cases/000413g1.html.

implies the transfer of custody to the carrier, thus
suggesting that the transfer of risk under the CISG
is linked to the physical control and custody of the
goods. However, it should be noted that Article 67
CISG requires that the handing over be "in
accordance with the contract of sale." This means
that the rule under consideration applies only if the
carriage of goods by a third party carrier was
stipulated in the contract. Conversely, it does not
apply if under the contract transportation of the
goods was to be performed by either one of the
parties, even if, in practice, the party bound to
transport the goods avails himself of a third party
carrier.[53] On the other hand, the rule under Article
67 applies, and the risk passes upon the handing
over of the goods to the carrier, irrespective of who
is contractually responsible for arranging transport
and insurance.[54]

The passing of risk under Article 67(1) is
conditional upon the clear identification of the goods
to the contract of sale. Indeed, under Article 67(2)
CISG failure of a clear identification results in the
risk not passing. Identification can take multiple
forms. In a non–exhaustive list the provision under
consideration mentions "markings of the goods,"
"shipping documents," or "notice given to the buyer."
The list, however, is open, as made clear by the

---

[53] *See, e.g.,* OLG Karlsruhe (Germany), 20 November 1992,
available in English at http://cisgw3.law.pace.edu/cases/921120
g1.html.

[54] Accordingly, Audiencia Provincial de Córdoba (Spain), 31
October 1997, English abstract available at http://cisgw3.law.
pace.edu/cases/971031s4.html.

language of Article 69(2), which indicates that the identification can also be effected "otherwise."

Article 68 CISG provides rules on the time when risk passes from the seller to the buyer if goods are sold while in transit. When this situation occurs, risk passes at the "time of the conclusion of the contract."[55] However, the provision at hand goes on by saying that "if the circumstances so indicate, the risk is assumed by the buyer from the time the goods were handed over to the carrier who issued the documents embodying the contract of carriage." The precondition for the retroactive effect laid out in the second sentence of Article 68 is rather vague. Arguably, the most relevant situation where "the circumstances [. . .] indicate" that the risk is assumed by the buyer retroactively occurs when transportation insurance exists. In fact, if transport insurance is in place, it will normally cover the period of time between the handing over of the goods to the carrier and the conclusion of the contract, thus providing indemnification to the buyer in the event that the goods were lost or damaged prior to the conclusion of the contract. In any event, the retroactive operation of the provision at hand is precluded if "at the time of the conclusion of the contract of sale the seller knew or ought to have known that the goods had been lost or damaged and did not disclose this to the buyer."

---

[55]   *See* China International Economic and Trade Arbitration Commission (CIETAC), Arbitral Award of 1 April 1997, available in English at http://cisgw3.law.pace.edu/cases/970401c1.html.

Residual rules for cases not within Article 67 or 68 are set forth in Article 69 CISG. This provision makes a distinction based on whether or not the buyer is bound to take over the goods at the place of business of the seller. If the buyer is bound to take over the goods at the place of business of the seller, Article 69(1) CISG applies, according to which "the risk passes to the buyer when he takes over the goods." This rule applies also if the buyer arranges for a third party carrier to take over the goods, provided that the contractual agreement was that the buyer would take over the goods.[56] Article 69(1) CISG also addresses the situation where the buyer fails to take over the goods in due time. When this happens, the risk passes to the buyer "from the time when the goods are placed at his disposal and he commits a breach of contract by failing to take delivery." However, it should also be noted that under Article 69(3) CISG, not unlike under Article 67(2), the goods cannot be considered to be placed at the buyer's disposal, unless "they are clearly identified to the contract."[57]

Article 69(2) CISG deals with all cases not within Article 67 or 68, in which the buyer is not bound to take over the goods at the place of business of the

---

[56]   *See* OLG Schleswig–Holstein (Germany), 29 October 2002, available in English at http://cisgw3.law.pace.edu/cases /021029g1.html.

[57]   For a decision applying the rule in Article 69(3) CISG, although with regard to Article 69(2), rather than 69(1) CISG, *see* OLG Hamburg (Germany), 14 December 1994, English abstract available at http://cisgw3.law.pace.edu/cases/941214g1.html.

seller.[58] Cases falling within the scope of Article 69(2) include sales of goods stored at a third party's warehouse, sales providing for delivery at the buyer's place of business, and sales providing for delivery to a third party.[59] When Article 69(2) CISG applies, risk passes "when delivery is due and the buyer is aware of the fact that the goods are placed at his disposal at that place."

4. RISK AND LIABILITY

The rules on the passing of risk apply to the extent that the loss of or damage to the goods is the result of an accidental event. If the loss or damage is the result of the seller's breach of contract, then Article 36(1) CISG applies, according to which the seller is liable "for any lack of conformity which exists at the time when the risk passes to the buyer, even though the lack of conformity becomes apparent only after that time." Moreover, under Article 36(2) the seller is also liable for any lack of conformity which occurs after the time when the risk passes to the buyer and "which is due to a breach of any of his obligations, including a breach of any guarantee that for a period of time the goods will remain fit for their ordinary purpose or for some particular purpose or will retain specified qualities of characteristics."

---

[58]   Accordingly, U.S. District Court [Colorado], 6 July 2010 (*Alpha Prime Development Corp. v. Holland Loader*), available at http://cisgw3.law.pace.edu/cases/100706u1. html.

[59]   *See, e.g.*, CJ Genève (Switzerland), 20 January 2006, available in English at http://cisgw3.law.pace.edu/cases/060120 s1.html.

As already pointed out, the rules on the liability of the seller under Article 36 do not correspond exactly with the scope of the last sentence of Article 66(1) CISG, which provides that the buyer is discharged from the obligation to pay the purchase price if "the loss or damage is due to an act or omission of the seller." Indeed, the act or omission of the seller, relevant under the said provision may consist of an unlawful act or omission that, in itself, does not constitute a breach of contract. It has been held, for instance, that the distinction under consideration may be relevant in the event of a "FOB" transaction, under which the risk passes to the buyer upon the loading of the goods on the vessel at the port of shipment. If the seller damages the goods when recovering the container at the port of destination, the seller's act or omission does not constitute a breach of contract. However, not only may his conduct be relevant under the applicable domestic law of tort, but it is also relevant in that the buyer is discharged from his payment obligation, although the risk of accidental loss of or damage to the goods has already passed.

The relationship between rules on the passing of risk and liability rules may pose puzzling questions in the event that the seller delivers non–conforming goods, but after delivery and the taking over of the goods on the part of the buyer (*i.e.*, after the risk passes to the buyer) an accidental event occurs, which causes the loss of the goods, or further negatively affects the fitness of the goods for the purposes envisaged in the sales contract. Under such circumstances, the application of the liability rules would give the buyer the right to retain payment of the purchase price and exercise the remedies available under the given circumstances. These remedies would include, in particular, contract avoidance, or a claim for substitute goods, provided that the failure to deliver conforming goods amounts to a fundamental breach.[60] Furthermore, they would include repair of the goods, price reduction and damages, irrespective of the fundamental or non–fundamental nature of the breach.[61] Conversely, if, in the same circumstances considered above, the rules on the passing of risk were to apply, then the occurrence of the accidental loss of the goods after the passing of risk to the buyer would cause the buyer to be bound to pay the purchase price even though the seller delivered non–conforming goods.

The relationship between rules on the passing of risk and liability rules is addressed by Article 70 CISG, which states that "[i]f the seller has committed a fundamental breach of contract, [the rules on the passing of risk] do not impair the remedies available to the buyer on account of the breach."[62] This provision provides two relevant rules, to be distinguished on the basis of whether or not the breach committed by the seller amounts to a

---

[60] For further details on remedies for fundamental breach of contract under the CISG, *see infra* Chapter 9.

[61] For further details on remedies for non–fundamental breach of contract under the CISG, *see infra* Chapter 8.

[62] Interestingly, there seems to be no reported case–law on this provision.

fundamental breach of contract. On the one hand, if the seller commits a fundamental breach of contract, the rule expressly laid out in Article 70 CISG grants to the buyer the right to claim remedies resulting from that breach, irrespective of the consequences of the subsequent accidental event. Therefore, even if the goods are lost as a result of the subsequent accidental event, the buyer is not bound to pay the purchase price and may claim either avoidance of the contract, or delivery of substitute goods.[63] In this respect, the practical effect of the rule laid out in Article 70 CISG is to shift the risk of accidental loss of or damage to the goods back to the seller.

On the other hand, if the breach committed by the seller does not qualify as a fundamental breach, the operation of the rules on the passing of risk is not precluded. Accordingly, if the goods are lost because of an accidental event after the passing of risk to the buyer, the latter must pay the purchase price even though the goods delivered by the seller failed to conform to the contractual specifications. Moreover, the buyer cannot declare the contract avoided, nor can he claim substitute goods. He may claim repair of the goods, as this remedy is available also in the event of non–fundamental breaches of contract; however, the remedy of repair is highly unlikely to be beneficial in a situation where the goods are lost

---

[63] For further details on the claim for substitute goods due to a fundamental breach of the sale contract, *see infra* Chapter 9, Section 2. For further details on contract avoidance, *see infra* Chapter 9, Section 3.

or destroyed due to the accidental event occurring after the passing of risk to the buyer. Conversely, as the buyer must pay the purchase price, he may have an interest in claiming price reduction, a remedy which is available to him under Article 50 CISG in the event of a non–fundamental breach of contract committed by the seller.

Article 70 CISG specifically addresses the issue of the relationship between rules on the passing of risk and liability rules in the event of a breach of contract committed by the seller. However, it should be noted here that the buyer's breach of contract may also affect the way in which the rules on the passing of risk operate. This is the case, in particular, when the buyer commits a breach of contract consisting of the failure to take delivery of the goods. Indeed, as an alternative to the passing of risk based on the taking over of the goods by the buyer, Article 69(1) CISG provides that the risk passes to the buyer also if he "commits a breach of contract by failing to take delivery," although the seller duly placed the goods at the buyer's disposal. There is broad consensus that the rule at hand lays out a general principle applicable also to situations that do not strictly fall within the scope of Article 69(1). The general principle posits that risk passes to the buyer if the seller cannot fulfill the requirements for the passing of risk because of the buyer's breach of contract. The said general principle may apply to situations not covered by Article 69(1) CISG, like buyer's failure to give necessary instructions for the dispatch of the goods.

5.   PASSING OF RISK AND INCOTERMS

It has already been mentioned that the rules on the passing of risk can be freely derogated from by the parties, in accordance with the principle of supremacy of the parties' freedom of contract affirmed in Article 6 CISG. Although articulated tailored–made clauses on the passing of risk are not a rare occurrence in business practice, in a very significant number of cases parties to an international contract of sale intending to derogate from the default rules on the passing of risk do so by incorporating in their agreement one of the INCOTERMS drafted by the International Chamber of Commerce, whose most recent edition was published in 2010.[64] However, the relevance of the INCOTERMS with respect to the regulation of the passing of risk is not limited to cases where the parties have expressly incorporated by reference one of ICC's trade terms into the agreement. Indeed, the wide knowledge and regular observance of the INCOTERMS as a source of rules on the passing of risk in international contracts for the sale of goods has led several courts to apply them as trade usages, applicable on the grounds of Article 9 CISG,[65] irrespective of their express incorporation in the agreement.

---

[64]   ICC, *INCOTERMS®* 2010, ICC Publication No. 715E. For an overview of the impact to the INCOTERMS of the International Chamber of Commerce on the obligations of the seller, *see supra* Chapter 6, Section 2.

[65]   For cases applying the INCOTERMS of the International Chamber of Commerce as trade usages under Article 9(2) CISG, in the absence of an explicit reference by the parties to that

In other cases, however, courts have regarded trade terms such as "CIF", or "FOB" included in the contract as an agreement between the parties consistent with (rather than derogating from) the relevant CISG's rules on the passing of risk, in particular those laid out in Article 67 CISG.[66] However, although at times there may be coincidence between the rules implied by an INCOTERM and the corresponding rules laid out in the CISG, this is not always the case and in many instances the inclusion of an INCOTERM in the contract produces a derogation to the otherwise applicable default rule on the passing of risk set forth in the CISG. In the light of the foregoing it seems appropriate here to provide a short overview of the impact of the various INCOTERMS on the rules on passing of risk.

In contracts of sale concluded under "EXW" ("Ex Works") terms, the seller delivers the goods to the buyer by merely placing them at the disposal of the buyer at the named place of delivery. The time of

---

source of interpretation of the trade term used in the agreement, *see, e.g.,* U.S. Court of Appeals [5th Cir.], 11 June 2003 (*BP Oil International v. Empresa Estatal Petroleos de Ecuador*), available at http://cisgw3.law.pace.edu/cases/030611u1.html (with respect to a "*CFR*" term); Supreme Court of Austria, 6 February 1996, available in English at http://cisgw3.law.pace.edu/cases/960206 a3.html (with respect to a "*FOB*" term).

[66] *See, e.g.,* Shangai No. 2 Intermediate People's Court (China), 25 December 2006, available in English at http://cisg w3.law.pace.edu/cases/061225c1.html, interpreting a "FOB" term in the sales contract involving carriage as being consistent with Article 67 CISG.

delivery also constitutes the moment when the risk of accidental loss of or damage to the goods passes from the seller to the buyer. The rule at hand basically corresponds to the one laid out in Article 69 CISG. The rule provided in the Convention, however, contains a distinction which is unknown to the INCOTERMS, in that it distinguishes between situations where the buyer is bound to take over the goods at the seller's place of business (Article 69(1) CISG), and situations where the buyer is bound to take over the goods at a place other than the seller's place of business (Article 69(2) CISG). In fact, an "Ex Works" sale can correspond to either one of the two cases considered by the CISG, depending on whether the named premises where the goods are placed at the disposal of the buyer coincide or not with the seller's place of business as defined under Article 10 CISG. Moreover, it should also be noted that, for the purpose of identifying the time of the passing of risk, Article 69(1) CISG refers primarily to the taking over of the goods on the part of the buyer and supplements that provision with an additional rule dealing with the buyer's failure to take delivery; the "EXW" INCOTERM, instead, refers only to the placing of the goods at the disposal of the buyer for delivery on the part of the seller.

The notion of delivery is pivotal also in respect of the rules on passing of risk in contracts of sale subject to an "F–term", including "FCA" ("Free Carrier") and "FOB" ("Free On Board"). Indeed, under these trade terms the risk of accidental loss of or damage to the goods passes to the buyer at the time the goods have been delivered. Delivery, in turn, is completed at different times depending on the circumstances of the case. In "FCA" contracts, if the place named for delivery is the seller's premises, delivery is completed when the goods are loaded on the means of transport provided by the buyer. If the place named for delivery is another one, delivery is completed when the goods are placed at the disposal of the carrier on the seller's means of transportation ready for unloading. Also in "FOB" contracts, the risk passes to the seller upon delivery, which occurs when the goods are placed on board the vessel nominated by the buyer. Moreover, in all "F–term" contracts, if the buyer fails to nominate the carrier or vessel, or if the carrier or vessel fails to arrive on time or to take the goods in charge, then the risk of accidental loss of or damage to the goods passes to the buyer on the date agreed for delivery, or upon the expiry of the period agreed for delivery. The rules on the passing of risk under "F–terms" largely correspond to the rule contained in Article 67(1), second sentence, CISG. Furthermore, similar exceptions to the general rule on the passing of risk are provided with respect to the event that the goods are not "clearly identified to the contract," a situation which prevents the risk of accidental loss of or damage to the goods from passing to the buyer.

Contracts of sale subjected to "C–terms", including "CPT" ("Carriage Paid To") "CIP" ("Carriage and Insurance Paid To") and "CFR" ("Cost and Freight"), do not differ significantly from "F–term" contracts as regards the rules on the passing of risk. In fact, the distinction between these different groups of INCOTERMS lays in that in "C–term" contracts the seller must contract for and pay the costs of carriage, freight and possibly insurance to the named port of destination. Not unlike under "F–term" contracts, however, delivery takes place at the port of shipment and the risk of accidental loss of or damage to the goods passes to the buyer when the goods are handed over to the carrier or loaded on the vessel. Also the "C–terms" are thus consistent with Article 67 CISG, although the latter is silent on some of the costs that are allocated under "C–terms".

If the parties to a sales contract want the seller to be bound to take care of carriage, insurance and possibly import customs formalities, they may include in their agreement one of the trade terms of the "D–term" group, which in the 2010 edition of the INCOTERMS of the International Chamber of Commerce consists of "DAT" ("Delivered At Terminal") "DAP" ("Delivered At Place") and "DDP" ("Delivery Duty Paid"). "D–terms" are "destination" terms, in that delivery occurs at the named place of destination of the goods. Moreover, in "DAT" contracts (unlike in "DAP" or "DDP" contracts) the seller is also bound to unload the goods from the arriving means of transport. The risk of accidental loss of or damage to the goods passes to the buyer upon completion of delivery. This rule implies that under "D–term" contracts the seller bears the risk of loss of or damage to the goods throughout the entire transportation to the named place of destination.

The cases contemplated in "D–terms" fall within the scope of Article 69(2) CISG, although the latter residual rule in the Convention also applies to cases completely unrelated to "D–term" contracts. However, it should be noted that both the INCOTERMS under consideration here and the said rule of the CISG provide for the passing of risk of accidental loss of or damage to the goods upon placing the goods at the disposal of the buyer at the named place of destination.

6. PRESERVATION OF THE GOODS

Section VI of Part III of the CISG provides rules on "Preservation of the goods", setting forth duties of preservation, which at times are imposed on the party who is in possession of the goods when the goods should be in the hands of the other party. Therefore, a duty of preservation arises in addition to the characteristic obligations of the parties, on the grounds that, although the goods should not be in his hand, failure of the party in possession of the goods to take measures to preserve them would result in the loss, damage or deterioration of the goods. Therefore, the CISG deals with the issue at hand by providing guidance with respect to both the measures that the party in possession of the goods may adopt, and the self–defenses and claims for reimbursement of costs that he can put forward as a result of the adoption of those measures. It should be noted at the outset that the rules on preservation of the goods laid out in the CISG's Section under consideration apply by default even if the parties have not included expressly any reference to duties of preservation in their contract. Conversely, given the general prevalence of the principle of parties' freedom of contract expressed in Article 6 CISG, it must be affirmed that the parties to a contract for the sale of goods governed by the CISG may derogate from the Convention's provision on preservation of goods, or may exclude their application.

Two different situations are considered in the CISG, both of which may result from the conduct of the buyer, although one of them leads to the seller's duty to take measures to preserve the goods, and the other one leads to the buyer's duty to take such measures. The first situation is considered in Article 85 CISG and it occurs in the event of the buyer's delay in taking delivery of the goods, or his failure to pay the price, when payment of the price and delivery of the goods are to be made concurrently. Under these circumstances, it is likely that the seller finds himself either in possession of the goods or otherwise able to control their disposition. If this is the case, then the seller "must take such steps as are reasonable in the circumstances to preserve" the goods.

The foregoing, of course, does not imply that the seller cannot claim the remedies available to him for the breach of contract committed by the buyer. Indeed, the buyer's failure to take delivery and the buyer's failure to pay the purchase price constitute breaches of contract leading to the seller's right to claim performance in kind or to his right to declare the contract avoided and claim damages. However, notwithstanding the existence of a breach on the part of the buyer, the seller is also bound by the obligation indicated in Article 85, which requires that the seller take reasonable steps to preserve the goods. It should be noted that the seller's obligation to preserve the goods is conditional upon the seller's possession of the goods, or his ability to control their disposition. However, if the foregoing prerequisite is fulfilled, the seller is bound to take such steps as are reasonable in the circumstances to preserve the goods, irrespective of the express inclusion of this duty in the agreement between the parties.

Reasonable steps to preserve the goods under Article 85 CISG are identified in Article 87 and Article 88 CISG, although these two provisions do not exhaust the possible measures that may be taken to preserve the goods. Under Article 87, a seller who is bound to take steps to preserve the goods "may deposit them in a warehouse of a third party at the expense of the [buyer] provided that the expense incurred is not unreasonable."[67] Under Article 88, in conjunction with Article 85, if the seller is bound to preserve the goods, he "may sell them by any appropriate means if there has been an unreasonable delay by the [buyer] in taking possession of the goods [. . .] or in paying the price or the cost of preservation, provided that reasonable

---

[67] For an arbitral award applying the rules under Article 85 and 87 CISG, *see* MKAC Arbitral Tribunal (Russian Federation), arbitral Award of 25 April 1995, case No. 142/1994, available in English at http://cisgw3.law.pace.edu/cases/950425r2.html.

notice of the intention to sell has been given to the [buyer]."

Therefore, in the event of a buyer's refusal to take delivery, the seller must be held to be under a duty to preserve the goods, but he may also be held to have the right to preserve them by reselling them at market price.[68] The only prerequisite that the seller must fulfill to this effect is to give reasonable notice to the buyer.[69] Other than for the foregoing prerequisite, several court decisions have applied the provision under Article 88(1) CISG rather liberally. One court, for instance, held that the seller was entitled to resell the goods on the grounds that the buyer had unreasonably delayed acceptance of delivery in a situation where the buyer had improperly rejected the goods.[70] Other courts, however, have adopted a stricter approach, noting, for instance, that the buyer's failure to pay in full the contract price would not justify the seller's initiative to sell to a third party a key component that the seller had retained, the more so as the

---

[68]   *See* Second Intermediate People's Court of Shanghai (P.R. China), 22 June 1998, available in English at http://cisgw3.law. pace.edu/cases/980622c1.html.

[69]   *See* Audiencia Provincial de Navarra (Spain), 22 January 2003, English abstract available at http://cisgw3.law.pace.edu/ cases/030122s4.html.

[70]   *See* U.S. District Court [E.D. Ca.], 19 May 2008 (*The Rice Corp. v. Grain Board of Iraq*), available at http://cisgw3.law.pace. edu/cases/080519u1.html.

component in question was not subject to fast deterioration.[71]

In fact, further guidance as to the circumstances under which the seller in possession of the goods may preserve them by selling them to a third party is provided by Article 88(2) CISG. This provision deals with goods that "are subject to rapid deterioration", as well as with goods whose "preservation would involve unreasonable expense". Under these circumstances the party bound to preserve the goods has not merely an option, but rather a duty to sell the goods,[72] whereas the delivery of notice to the other party is not regarded as a precondition, but rather as an informative act to be performed only "to the extent possible."

Article 86 CISG deals with various additional situations where the duty to preserve the goods arises. Unlike under Article 85, under Article 86 CISG the party bound to take appropriate measures to preserve the goods is the buyer. This happens if the buyer has received the goods and intends to exercise any right under the contract or the Convention to reject the goods. Furthermore, this also happens if goods dispatched to the buyer have been placed at his disposal at their destination and

---

[71]   Trib. Cantonal de Vaud (Switzerland), 17 May 1994, available in English at http://cisgw3.law.pace.edu/cases/940517 s1.html.

[72]   For a decision denying the application of the rule under consideration on the grounds that the goods (meet) could be preserved from deterioration by freezing, *see* OLG Braunschweig (Germany), 28 October 1999, available in English at http://cisg w3.law.pace.edu/cases/991028g1.html.

the buyer exercises the right to reject them. Under these circumstances the buyer is required to take such steps to preserve the goods "as are reasonable in the circumstances."[73] In particular, under Article 86(2) CISG if the goods are placed at the disposal of the buyer at destination, although he might intend to reject them, the buyer must take possession of the goods on behalf of the seller, "provided that this can be done without payment of the price and without unreasonable inconvenience or unreasonable expense." Moreover, the buyer's duty of preservation under Article 86(2) does not apply if the seller or a representative of the seller is present at destination.

Not unlike with the seller's obligation to preserve the goods under Article 85, a rejecting buyer's duty of preservation under Article 86 CISG is further detailed in Article 87 and Article 88 CISG. Therefore, most of what has been said with respect to Articles 87 and 88 in conjunction with Article 85 CISG may be applied *mutatis mutandis* to the buyer's obligation to preserve the goods under Article 86, in conjunction with Articles 87 and 88 CISG.

Thus, under Article 87, a buyer who is bound to take steps to preserve the goods "may deposit them in a warehouse of a third party at the expense of the [seller] provided that the expense incurred is not

---

[73]   *See, e.g.*, Higher Court Ljubljana (Slovenia), 14 December 2005, available in English at http://cisgw3.law.pace.edu/cases/051214sv.html.

unreasonable."[74] Under Article 88, in conjunction with Article 86, if the buyer is bound to preserve the goods, he "may sell them by any appropriate means if there has been an unreasonable delay by the [seller] in [. . .]taking [possession of the goods] back [. . .] or in paying [. . .] the cost of preservation, provided that reasonable notice of the intention to sell has been given to the [seller]."

In all circumstances where the goods should be in the hands of the one party to the contract, but the other party is in possession of the goods and owes a duty to take steps to preserve them, then the party in possession is entitled to retain the goods until he has been reimbursed his reasonable expenses by the other party. Moreover, if the party in charge of preserving the goods sells them, then his right of retention can no longer be exercised on the goods, but can be exercised on the proceeds of the sale of the goods. In particular, under Article 88(3) CISG, the party selling the goods "has the right to retain out of the proceeds of sale an amount equal to the reasonable expenses of preserving the goods and of selling them. He must account to the other party for the balance."

---

[74] For a court decision dealing with the allocation of costs resulting from the storage in a warehouse, *see*, *e.g.*, Trib. Forlì (Italy), 11 December 2008, available in English at http://cisgw3. law.pace.edu/cases/081211i3.html.

CHAPTER 8

GENERALLY AVAILABLE REMEDIES AND EXEMPTION

1. NON–FUNDAMENTAL BREACH OF CONTRACT

The binding force of a contract implies that each party must perform the obligations undertaken in a manner that conforms to the agreement. Earlier in this work, reference was made to the obligations of the parties and the distinction between the obligations of the seller[1] and those of the buyer.[2] In fact, this distinction mirrors one upon which the text of the CISG is based. In effect, the CISG sets forth rules relating to the obligations of the seller in Chapter II of Part III and rules applicable to the obligations of the buyer in Chapter III of the same Part. The CISG also makes a distinction between remedies available to the buyer for breach of contract by the seller (which are dealt with in Section III of Part III, Chapter II), and remedies available to the seller for breach of contract by the buyer (Section III of Part III, Chapter III). However, the remedies listed in the aforementioned Chapters are not the only ones available to an aggrieved party in case of breach by the opposing party. Additional remedies are listed in the Chapter dedicated to the provisions common to both parties (Part III, Chapter V), which also contains provisions relating

---

[1] *See* Chapter 6.

[2] *See* Chapter 7.

to what constitutes, in practice, the most relevant remedy for breach of contract, namely damages.

Although reference will be made throughout this Chapter to the different remedial claims available to the seller and to the buyer respectively, the way the issue of remedies for breach of contract will be dealt with follows a somewhat different approach. The discussion of the various remedies available in case of breach will distinguish the remedial schemes available to the aggrieved party on the basis of the requirements that need to be fulfilled in order for a party to be able to avail itself of a specific remedy. This approach leads to the need to make a distinction between generally available remedies, to be addressed in this Chapter, and remedies available only in the event of a fundamental breach of contract, to be discussed in the following Chapter.

The foregoing distinction relates to the standard of performance that the obligor in a sales contract has to abide by in order to discharge himself from the contractual obligations to which he is bound. In fact, the issue at hand may be addressed either in positive terms, focusing on what the obligor is required to do in order to be discharged from his obligations, or in negative terms, focusing on what degree of lack of performance triggers negative legal consequences for the non–performing party. The latter aspect will be discussed here.

The basic dichotomy as to the performance of contractual obligations may be described as the alternative between requiring perfect tender and being satisfied by substantial performance. Pursuant to the perfect tender rule the debtor is discharged from his contractual obligations only if performance is fully and perfectly in conformity with what was agreed upon; pursuant to the substantial performance rule discharge from the contractual obligations occurs to the extent that performance by the debtor substantially satisfies the creditor in the light of what was promised.

The traditional rule, common to most legal systems, imposes on the debtor the obligation of perfectly fulfilling all contractual obligations in order to be discharged. Under this traditional rule, whenever an inconsistency, even a very minor one, occurs between the terms of the promise and the concrete performance of the obligation, the performance is not deemed satisfactory and the debtor is not deemed discharged from the obligation to perfectly and fully perform. However, this traditional solution has been criticized because it promotes strategic behavior and moral hazard on the part of the creditor. The creditor may opportunistically take advantage of the possibility to reject any tender which is less than perfect, in order to refuse a substantially correct performance, whenever he seeks to free himself from the obligations promised in consideration of the debtor's full performance. In the alternative, the debtor's performance may be evaluated according to a substantial performance standard. While this alternative solution reduces the possibility of strategic behavior on the part of the creditor, it enhances that of strategic behavior of the debtor, who may opportunistically perform in a way that, although substantially fulfilling the required standard, ranges below the average standard performance. The foregoing dichotomy is reflected in the text of the CISG, which impliedly differentiates, in positive terms, between perfect tender and substantial performance. In fact, the CISG distinguishes, in negative terms, between consequences deriving from a simple, non–fundamental breach of contract, and remedies available only in the event of a fundamental breach.

Indeed, in all circumstances where a party has not fully performed his contractual obligations, the party will be deemed to be in breach of contract. Thus, liability under the CISG is based on a regime of strict liability, under which the promisor is deemed liable on the basis of the mere non–occurrence of what was promised or guaranteed, without any need for fault or negligence on the part of the promisor or any other prerequisite to affirm liability. Similar to the 1964 Hague Conventions, the CISG distinguishes between "fundamental breach" and "non–fundamental breach", although only the former notion is defined by the CISG in Article 25, and it is primarily based on the detrimental effects for the aggrieved party of the non–compliance with the contractual obligations, provided that those effects are foreseeable by the party in breach[3]. The category of simple breaches

---

[3]   Article 25 CISG is analyzed in greater details later in this work, in Chapter 9, Section 1.

can, therefore, be defined *a contrario* as that including any breach of contract other than those that are so severe as to amount to a fundamental breach. The importance of the distinction between simple and fundamental breach is rather evident. Only a fundamental breach entitles the aggrieved party to avoidance of the contract. This is made clear by both Article 49 CISG, as regards avoidance declared by the buyer due to a fundamental breach of contract by the seller, and Article 64, as regards avoidance declared by the seller due to a fundamental breach by the buyer. Moreover, with respect to the buyer's remedies, only in the case of fundamental breach can the buyer reject non–conforming goods, make a claim for delivery of substitute goods (Article 46 CISG), and still be entitled to remedies after the passage of the risk to him (Article 70 CISG).

Conversely, in regards to the type of non–compliance, the CISG adopts a unitary notion of breach, in that it does not make any express distinction based on the type of non–performance, its consequences, or the like. As a consequence, when dealing with the issues of performance and non–performance, the CISG does not rely on distinctions such as those between absolute non–performance, late performance, incomplete (or partial) performance, and non–conforming performance. Nonetheless, these distinctions may prove useful in dealing with the different available remedies and it seems therefore appropriate to consider them more closely.

By using a quantitative criterion of evaluation, the degree of performance of each contractual obligation can be described as having been completed to an extent ranging from 0% (zero percent) to 100% (one hundred percent), that is, from absolute non–performance to complete performance, with several degrees of partial performance in between the two extremes. However, it should be noted that absolute non–performance (zero percent performance) does not necessarily amount to a final and definitive (and, thus, fundamental) breach of contract, in that the possibility exists that the debtor still intends to perform, but is late in fulfilling his contractual duties. In this situation, although the degree of completion of performance is null, it is unlikely that a delayed performance can immediately qualify as a fundamental breach, unless the time for performance must be regarded as of the essence under the contract terms or the applicable usages.

On the other hand, by using a qualitative criterion of evaluation, a contractual performance can be described as conforming or non–conforming with the explicit or implied terms of the agreement, such as, for instance, the products' quality specifications. This distinction, of course, applies primarily to the seller's obligation to deliver conforming goods under Article 35 CISG. However, this distinction can also be used to evaluate some of the ancillary obligations of the parties, as well as the payment obligation of the buyer, to the extent that an issue arises as to the fitness of a certain means of payment other than the currency of the country of the creditor.

Further in relation to the distinction between simple and fundamental breach, some remedial schemes available to the aggrieved party in the event of the other party's breach of contract (namely, contract avoidance and substitution of the goods) are made available by the CISG only in the event that the non–performance qualifies as a fundamental breach of contract. This notion and the remedial consequences stemming therefrom will be considered at a later stage of this work. This Chapter, instead, will focus on generally available remedies, that is, remedies that the aggrieved party may resort to in any event of non–performance, irrespective of the seriousness of the consequences resulting therefrom. For the sake of clarity, it may be appropriate to specify that, while remedies for fundamental breach of contract are not available to the aggrieved party in the event of a breach that is not fundamental, the contrary cannot be maintained. General remedies provided by the CISG for a simple breach are available not only in the event of a breach that does not qualify as fundamental, but also in the event of a fundamental breach.

In particular, from a quantitative perspective, the unsatisfied creditor can claim performance in full in the event of late performance, or completion of performance in the event of partial performance. On the other hand, from a qualitative perspective, the buyer who receives non–conforming products can claim either repair of the goods, or reduction of the price so as to reproduce the original equilibrium of the agreement, whereas he cannot claim substitution of the goods unless the non–conformity amounts to a fundamental breach of contract. Moreover, in the event that the performance that is delayed is the payment of the purchase price (or any other payment due under the sales agreement), in addition to the amount due as contractually agreed upon, the creditor can also claim interests accrued on that sum. Finally, in all cases considered above, and irrespective of the type and severity of the breach, the aggrieved party has a claim for damages, unless the other party's non–performance can be excused under the CISG's exemption provision (Article 79 CISG).

2.   CLAIM FOR PERFORMANCE AND SPECIFIC PERFORMANCE

In light of the foregoing, one can safely affirm that under the CISG the aggrieved party can react to any kind of non–performance by requiring full performance in kind, irrespective of the severity of the breach committed by the non–performing party. This assertion, which suggests that the claim for performance is the basic generally available remedy under the CISG, is confirmed both by the basic provision dealing with the buyer's right to performance in the event of a breach committed by the seller (Article 46(1) CISG), and the parallel provision dealing with the seller's right to performance in the event of breach by the buyer

(Article 62 CISG). Indeed, in both cases the applicable CISG rule provides that the aggrieved party "may require" performance in kind (with the additional clarification, as regards the buyer's breach, that the latter may be required to either "pay the price, take delivery or perform his other obligations"). The only exception to this is that the aggrieved party cannot claim performance in kind if "[he] has resorted to a remedy which is inconsistent with this requirement". This limitation applies primarily in the event that the aggrieved party previously resorted to the remedy of contract avoidance, which is clearly incompatible with a later claim for performance. Absent a clear provision to that effect under the CISG, some court decisions have further limited the availability of the claim for performance in kind by stating that the buyer's right to claim performance in kind extinguishes in the event that performance becomes impossible, such as in the event that unique contract products are destroyed.[4] Conversely, in these authors' view, the availability of a claim for performance is not affected by the occurrence of an event qualifying for an exemption under Article 79 CISG. This is not only because of the clear language of Article 79(5), which clarifies that only the claim for damages is barred by the exemption, but also because the exempting event does not impact on the right to claim performance, but may only impact on the availability of a judgment for specific performance,

---

[4] *See* U.S. District Court [S.D.N.Y.], 20 August 2008 (*Hilaturas Miel, S.L. v. Republic of Iraq*), available at http://cisg w3.law.pace.edu/cases/080820u1.html.

which is to be assessed—as will be pointed out in greater details later in this paragraph—on the basis of the domestic law of the forum.

In light of the different possible types of non-performance, the rule granting a right to performance in kind may be read in a variety of different manners. If either the seller or the buyer fails to perform his obligation entirely, the aggrieved party has the right to require the entire performance; similarly, if performance is partial, the aggrieved party can claim the outstanding portion of performance. On the other hand, if a party (typically, but not necessarily, the seller) performs his obligation in full, but the performance fails to comply with the requirements agreed upon (*i.e.*, if the breach takes the form of delivery of non-conforming goods, or the goods are delivered to a place other than that agreed upon by the parties), the aggrieved party has the right to require that the performance be adjusted to make it comply with the contractual arrangements. In all cases, the remedy accessible to the aggrieved party aims toward the perfect completion of the contractual bargain as originally agreed upon by the parties.

As far as the remedies available to the buyer are concerned, Article 46 CISG provides the buyer with a general right to require performance from the seller. This right may take different forms, depending on the type of breach committed by the seller. If the seller fails to perform his obligation in its entirety, the buyer has the right to claim full performance of that obligation. On the other hand, if the seller delivers goods that do not conform with the contractual agreement, the buyer has the right to require substitute goods (if the non–performance amounts to a fundamental breach) or repair of the non–conforming goods. In the first situation (failure to perform the contractual obligation in its entirety) the aggrieved party may require performance while simultaneously triggering the *Nachfrist* mechanism,[5] which may possibly lead to the buyer's avoidance of the contract if the seller does not cure the breach within the additional period of time of reasonable length granted by the buyer. The seller is, thus, given the alternative to either perform, or be subject to contract avoidance, thus losing the possibility to obtain the payment of the contract price. Alternatively, the buyer may require performance in kind without triggering the *Nachfrist* mechanism, and he can do so irrespective of the severity of the consequences of the seller's non–performance whenever his choice is to claim performance in kind, rather than to avoid the contract and claim damages. Moreover, it should be highlighted that the *Nachfrist* mechanism, possibly leading to contract avoidance, is available only in the event of absolute non–performance. It cannot be resorted to in the event of partial performance, or non–conforming performance.

A claim for performance is also available to the seller in the event of a buyer's breach of his contractual obligations. In this regard, it is

---

[5]   For further details on the so–called *Nachfrist* mechanism, *see* Chapter 9, Section 3.

apparent that the most relevant obligation owed by the buyer is, in most cases, the payment of the purchase price. The generic nature of money makes it less problematic to compel performance of this obligation, as the mechanics of enforcement of performance in kind in this case are largely the same as those used for the purpose of enforcing recovery of damages and interests. However, as already pointed out, Article 62 CISG makes it clear that the seller's right to claim performance in kind applies not only in the event that the buyer fails to pay the purchase price, but also in the event of a breach of the obligation to take delivery or a breach of any other obligation of the buyer.

While in case of failure to receive the performance expected under the agreement, both the seller and the buyer have a right to claim the outstanding performance, it is apparent that the right to claim performance is of limited benefit if that right is not accompanied by legal tools making the enforcement of that right possible. Indeed, the party willing to compel his right to obtain performance in kind needs to resort to the force of public authorities whenever the obtainment of the due performance requires the participation of the obligor and the obligor is not willing to cooperate in order to accomplish the obligee's request. As applied to the right to require performance of the contract in the event of a breach, the foregoing makes it necessary to consider the availability of judicial intervention of domestic courts in contractual matters, in the form of a judgment for specific performance. A judgment of this kind constitutes the necessary link between the abstract recognition of a party's substantive right to claim performance and the concrete possibility to invoke public force to take all necessary steps to obtain performance in kind. The latter stage refers to the enforcement of the right. However, enforcement in modern societies would not be possible without prior recognition of the existence of the right in the concrete case by the competent adjudicating court, which has the power to order the domestic public officials to make use of public authority in order to fully implement the creditor's right.

As a very general rule, one may state that, given the same circumstances, specific performance is more likely to be granted by courts located in Civil Law countries, while Common Law courts are more inclined to uphold a claim for damages, but more reluctant to enter an order for specific performance. In this respect, some authors and arbitral decisions have maintained that the CISG adopts a Civilian approach in that it makes the claim for performance generally available and concurrent with a claim for damages.[6] Quite interestingly, however, the most cited case (and one of the very few ones, in fact)

---

[6] For a similar statement, *see*, *e.g.*, ICC Court of Arbitration, Arbitral Award n. 12173, available in English at http://cisgw3.law.pace.edu/cases/041217i1.html.

resulting in a judgment for specific performance comes from a Common Law court.[7]

In light of the somewhat inaccurate understanding of the importance of specific performance in Civil Law and Common Law countries, the drafters of the CISG faced the challenging task of providing for a compromise solution, which would not leave anyone too dissatisfied. The task was made even more challenging by the very fact that the uniform rules provided by the CISG are to be applied by the courts of different contracting states. The problem had already arisen with respect to the solution adopted under the ULIS, whose Article 16, in conjunction with Article VII of the Convention setting forth that Uniform Law, expressly excluded that a domestic court would be bound "to enter or enforce a judgment for specific performance except in cases in which it would do so under its law in respect of similar contracts of sale not governed by the Uniform Law".

The compromise reached under Article 28 CISG, according to which a national court "is not bound to enter a judgment for specific performance unless the court would do so under its own law in respect of similar contracts of sale not governed by" the CISG, very closely resembles that of its predecessor. The result of the provision set forth in Article 28 CISG is a gap in the uniform instrument. This conclusion is

---

[7]   U.S. District Court [N.D. Ill.], 7 December 1999 (*Magellan International Corp. v. Salzgitter Handel GmbH*), available at http://cisgw3.law.pace.edu/cases/991207u1.html.

confirmed by the change in the language of the provision that was introduced at the Diplomatic Conference in Vienna, where the word "would" was substituted for the word "could". Domestic courts are thus urged to proceed in the very same manner they "would" with respect to a domestic contract, rather than entering a judgment for specific performance whenever there is a possibility to do so (*i.e.*, if they "could") under domestic law. The provision at hand, however, is not useless, in that it defines the scope of the gap, in light of the purpose pursued by the drafters. Indeed, what the drafters intended to leave outside the scope of the CISG is only the procedural aspect of the enforcement, by resort to public force, of the right to claim performance, which is reflected in each legal system in the possibility for domestic courts to enter a judgment for specific performance. As a consequence of the gap being based on procedural grounds, one has to acknowledge the difference between the gap in question and other substantive external gaps found in the CISG, such as that regarding validity under Article 4(1)(*a*) CISG. Unlike substantive external gaps, which generally have to be filled by resort to the substantive rules applicable by virtue of the private international law rules of the forum,[8] the reference to the law of the forum ("its own law") contained in Article 28 does not include private international law.[9] A different interpretation of the

---

[8]   *See supra* Chapter 1, Section 4.

[9]   The conclusion reached in the text is in line with that reached in case law; *see, e.g.*, Supreme Court of Sweden, 27

rule (*i.e.*, one supporting resort to the private international law rules of the forum) would frustrate the very purpose of the compromise reached under Article 28. The fact that divergent solutions may be reached, depending on where the dispute is adjudicated, can certainly be regarded with some regret from the perspective of the parties to a sales transaction. However, it should be acknowledged that Article 28 serves well the goal which was assigned to this provision, that is, to leave to the forum State the competence to decide the extent to which its domestic courts should actively intervene in contractual matters. Accordingly, the availability of specific performance in practice may be restricted to the extent that specific performance is not available under the domestic law of the forum.[10] Conversely, the interpretation of Article 28, which has been rejected here (requiring regard to the private international law rules of the forum) would deprive the domestic lawmakers of that competence, in that it might lead to the application of a foreign law, based on different policy considerations. At the same time, that interpretation would not enhance uniformity and predictability of the final outcome of the decision. This is because in most cases one would

---

December 2010, reported in English at http://cisgw3.law.pace.edu/cases/101227s6.html.

[10] For a court decision qualifying the provision of Article 28 CISG as a "restriction" to the general rule of the availability of a claim for performance, *see* HG Bern (Switzerland), 22 December 2004, available in English at http://cisgw3.law.pace.edu/cases/041222s1.html.

still need to determine under what conditions the court in the forum State would be bound to apply the foreign applicable law providing for a right to specific performance, in cases where that court would not enter a judgment for specific performance "under its own law" with respect to similar contracts governed by the law of the forum.

To sum up, one can safely state that even if the failure to perform on the part of the breaching party does not amount to a fundamental breach, under the CISG the aggrieved party has the right to claim performance. This statement applies both to the claim of the buyer if the seller fails to perform (*i.e.*, mainly if he fails to deliver the goods), and to the claim of the seller if the buyer fails to pay the purchase price, to take delivery or to perform any additional obligations due under the agreement in place. Moreover, if the aggrieved party claims performance in kind of the contractual obligation and the obligor fails to spontaneously satisfy that request, the aggrieved party may bring his claim to court, seeking for a judgment compelling performance, possibly by making use of public authority. It is apparent, however, that while any jurisdiction provides means for compelling a payment obligation, the situation is more differentiated as regards the buyer's claim for specific performance of the seller's duty to deliver the contract products. In this respect, the acknowledgment by the CISG of a general right to claim performance must be reconciled with the rule under Article 28 CISG, which makes the availability of a judgment for specific performance conditional upon the availability of a judgment of that kind in the same circumstances under the domestic law of the forum.

3.   REPAIR OF THE GOODS AND PRICE REDUCTION

We shall now focus on the specific remedies available to the buyer in the event of a breach of contract committed by the seller. This requires one to focus, *inter alia*, on what happens when the seller delivers the very quantity of the goods agreed upon, but their quality does not meet the contractual specifications. In this situation, only if the delivery of non–conforming goods qualifies as a fundamental breach of contract can the buyer avoid the contract or claim substitute goods. Where the breach does not result in a detriment that substantially deprives the buyer of the benefits that he was entitled to expect under the contract, the remedies just mentioned are not available to the buyer. In particular, to the extent that the buyer wishes to obtain performance in kind, as originally agreed upon in the contract, he can only require the repair of the goods by the seller under Article 46(3) CISG. Yet, this remedy is also subject to limitations in terms of both timing and reasonableness of the request.

First, the buyer can request the repair of the non–conforming goods only to the extent that he puts forward that request within a relatively short period of time. Indeed, the request for repair of the goods must be made in conjunction with the notice of non—conformity that the buyer must give to the seller under Article 39 CISG,[11] or within a reasonable time thereafter. The time limit, therefore, is linked to the time of the notice of non—conformity; accordingly, it seems reasonable to affirm that if the parties derogate from rule under Article 39 CISG by providing for an extended period of time within which the buyer can give notice of the non—conformity, such contractual agreement will have an impact also on the availability of the claim for repair of the goods. Therefore, when the foregoing derogation to Article 39 occurs, the aggrieved buyer may put forward a claim for repair of the goods within a reasonable time from the notice of non—conformity given in accordance with the contractual agreement. In practice, the time limit may become relevant more than once within the same single contract for the sale of goods. This may happen if, following the first request for repair, the seller does intervene and repair the goods, but after some time the same or a different quality defect appears, with respect to which the buyer will have a new, or renovated, claim for repair. In this situation, as stated in relevant case law,[12] the buyer must give a new notice of non—conformity under Article 39 and, in conjunction with the latter or shortly thereafter, must request the new repair of the goods.

---

[11]   For further details on the notice of non—conformity under Article 39 CISG, *see* Chapter 6, Section 5.

[12]   *See* CA Versailles (France), 29 January 1998, available in English at http://cisgw3.law.pace.edu/cases/980129f1.html.

Besides the said time limits, the CISG further limits the availability of the remedy of repair of the goods by providing that the remedy is available to the aggrieved party only to the extent that the repair is not "unreasonable having regard to all the circumstances" of the case. Reasonableness is, therefore, a relevant limitation to the availability in practice of the remedy of repair. It is a notion introduced to protect the position of the seller and it is from the subjective perspective of the seller that the criterion of reasonableness must be evaluated. Therefore, a request for repair of the goods will prove unreasonable if it triggers costs that can be regarded as excessive compared to the availability of alternative remedies, including price reduction and damages. The evaluation must be made at the time the remedy is requested and must take into account the concrete circumstances of the case at that very moment. Accordingly, one should not give too much weight to the contract price, which may not reflect the situation at the time when the remedy is requested. Moreover, one court held that the request for repair was unreasonable in a situation where the buyer could easily repair the goods himself and then recover the related costs.[13]

Of course, an additional general limitation to the availability of the claim for repair of the goods applies in consideration of the fact that the remedy at hand is but a special kind of request for performance. Accordingly, also the request for

---

[13]   OLG Hamm (Germany), 9 June 1995, available in English at http://cisgw3.law.pace.edu/cases/950609g1.html.

repair of the goods is subject to the same general limitations identified for requests for performance in general, including the limitation consisting of the variable availability of specific performance under Article 28 CISG, which requires the analysis of whether the competent court would issue a judgment for specific performance compelling the request for repair of the goods under its domestic law. If the answer to this question is negative, then the buyer is prevented from successfully putting forward a claim for repair of the goods.

In light of the many limitations that may come into play with respect to the availability of the remedy of repair of goods, it is apparent that, in practice, in many circumstances the buyer will not be able to resort to that remedy. When this is the case, the remedy of price reduction is the sole remedy compelling performance of the agreement generally available to the buyer for any kind of non–performance committed by the seller. In fact, the remedy of price reduction can be claimed by the aggrieved buyer irrespective of the severity of the breach. Moreover, even if the seller can claim an exemption under Article 79 CISG, that exemption precludes the availability to the buyer of a claim for damages, but it does not preclude the claim for price reduction. This statement requires further clarification. Indeed, the CISG's legal patterns leading to the alternative remedial schemes seems to be inspired by the overall purpose to reduce, as much as possible, the costs deriving from the failure of the breaching party to comply with the original contractual arrangements. Hence, avoidance of the contract is restricted in light of the costs of a potential restitution. The same rationale seems to underlie the limited availability of the right to require substitute goods, which may be exercised only in the event of a fundamental breach, given the costs of restitution of the defective goods and those of delivery of the substitute ones. Repair of the goods may be required only if not "unreasonable".

In line with the rationale which underlies the remedies just mentioned, the CISG's favor for the completion of the contractual bargain should not be intended as necessarily fostering the adoption of remedies which compel the performance of the parties' obligations as originally agreed upon. Instead, the very nature of the goal pursued by the CISG's remedial scheme appears when one considers the last remedial option left to the buyer in the event of a breach committed by the seller. Indeed, should the non–conformity of the goods delivered not amount to a fundamental breach (thus preventing avoidance, or a claim for substitute goods), and should it prove unreasonable to claim for repair of the goods, the only option left to the buyer (besides a claim for damages) is the remedy of price reduction. This remedy may be resorted to even if the reasonable time period within which the contract must be declared avoided under Article 49(2) CISG has expired.[14] However, not unlike any other remedy available to the buyer, the remedy of

---

[14]   OLG Koblenz (Germany), 14 December 2006, available in English at http://cisgw3.law.pace.edu/cases/061214g1.html.

price reduction requires a timely notice of non–conformity to be given to the seller in accordance with Article 39 CISG.[15]

Price reduction is considered one of the most efficient remedies available to the buyer. On the one hand, this remedy may be adopted in the form of self–defense on the part of the aggrieved party. Indeed, Article 50 CISG makes it clear that the buyer may make a declaration to the effect of reducing the price "whether or not the price has already been paid." This solution seems particularly appropriate in that it not only prevents a subsequent claim for restitution of part of the price paid, but it also induces the parties to further negotiate to find the wealth–maximizing settlement, and it is thus likely to prevent the costs of an international dispute. Consistently, the only statutory limitation to the exercise of the remedy of price reduction applies in the event that the seller spontaneously cures the non–conformity, taking advantage of what, under the CISG, is not regarded as a mere possibility, but rather as a full–fledged right to cure.

On the other hand, the remedy in question is an efficient one in that—in a situation where the buyer is not substantially deprived of what he was entitled to expect—it imposes on the parties to rearrange the

---

[15]   Audiencia Provincial de Barcelona (Spain), 12 September 2001, available in English at http://cisgw3.law.pace.edu/cases/010912s4.html; Federal Court of Australia, 24 October 2008 (*Hannaford v. Australian Farmlink Pty Ltd*), available at http://cisgw3.law.pace.edu/cases/081024a2.html.

terms of the contract on the basis of the new situation created by the seller's non–performance. As a consequence, the CISG favors the completion of the contractual bargain, but it does so by favoring an adaptation of the contract to the new contingencies. The foregoing seems confirmed by the criterion adopted by the CISG in order to adjust the terms of the contract. The price may be reduced in the same proportion "as the value that the goods actually delivered had at the time of the delivery bears to the value that conforming goods would have had at that time." It may be debatable whether the criterion adopted by the CISG to measure the price reduction is a sound and efficient one. Of the two terms of the comparison, one is the actual market value of the non–conforming goods at the time of delivery. As to the other term of the comparison, this value is necessarily a hypothetical one, given that it cannot but refer to the value of conforming goods, which were in fact never delivered. However, this value may be determined at two different moments in time, and with regard to two different parameters. In particular, the value may be determined either with respect to the time of conclusion of the contract, or to the time of delivery. While the problem as to the time seems to be soundly settled by the CISG, which refers to the time of delivery, one may wonder whether the value should reflect the market value that conforming goods would have had, or the value of the promised goods as determinable on the basis of the terms of the contract. In these authors' view, the solution adopted by the CISG is correct. In fact, it is true that in a situation where the buyer obtained a favorable price for the goods, the price reduction under Article 50 CISG may undercompensate the loss suffered as a consequence of the seller's breach. However, one should bear in mind that the remedy of price reduction—as all other remedies leading to the performance of the contract (either in its original fashion or in an adapted form)—coexists with, and does not displace, the possibility for the aggrieved party to claim damages, should the loss suffered exceed the benefits obtained by virtue of the remedy resorted to by the aggrieved party.[16]

On a different note, if at the time of delivery the delivered goods have no value at all, the buyer can reduce the price to zero, thus retaining the payment of the purchase price originally due under the contract.[17]

Although the remedy of price reduction is the most prominent example of contract–adaptation under the CISG, it is not the only one. A similar rationale significantly underlies the seller's right to "make specification" under Article 65 CISG. This remedy is available in the event that the buyer fails to specify the "form, measurement or other features of the goods". This specification, in particular, may be needed in the event that the contract left some

---

[16] HG Zürich (Switzerland), 25 June 2007, available in English at http://cisgw3.law.pace.edu/cases/070625s1.html.

[17] An option confirmed in case–law by Supreme Court of Western Australia, 17 January 2003 (*Ginza Pte. Ltd. v. Vista Corp. Pty. Ltd.*), available at http://cisgw3.law.pace.edu/cases/030117a2.html.

terms open, but provided that those terms would be specified by the buyer. Of course, these terms may not refer to the quality and quantity of the goods; however, they may refer to other elements in the absence of specification of which the seller is not in the position to perform in accordance with the contract. Therefore, absent specification, one might argue that the contract is not complete, and therefore invalid or inexistent. Alternatively, one might be tempted to conclude that, in the absence of specification on the part of the buyer, the seller faces the alternative either to wait, or to avoid the contract, possibly after an additional period of time granted to the buyer to make the specification. Neither one of these alternatives is adopted under the CISG. Conversely, the CISG grants the right to the seller to make the specification, thus favoring the completion of the contractual bargain although in a form that does not reflect that originally agreed upon by the parties.

4.   INTERESTS ON SUMS IN ARREARS

As already pointed out, where the buyer defaults on his obligation to pay the purchase price in full or in part, the seller may put forward a claim for performance by requiring payment. Moreover, as a result of the delay in obtaining payment, the seller may also claim interests on the sums in arrears due to him under Article 78 CISG. Although the right to interests on sums in arrears does not only relate to late payments of the purchase price, but rather to the late payment of any sum of money, late payment of the purchase price triggers the right to interest more often than the late payment of any other sum of money.

The rule set forth in Article 78 CISG may seem a rather simple and straightforward one, in that it provides that in the event of failure to pay any sum, the creditor "is entitled to interest on it, without prejudice to any claim for damages recoverable under article 74". The issue of interests on sums in arrears and, in particular, what interest rate to apply, was one of the most debated issues during the Vienna Diplomatic Conference and it still creates difficulties under the CISG.

I light of the foregoing, it cannot come as a surprise that Article 78 CISG limits itself to merely providing for the general entitlement to interest, and it does so independently from any damage caused by the late payment, as also pointed out by several court and arbitral decisions.[18] Indeed, Article 78 CISG makes it clear that the entitlement to interest does not exclude the possibility to claim damages on the grounds of Article 74 CISG Article. What Article 78 CISG does not address, however, is the interest rate to be applied (or a way to identify said interest rate).

---

[18]   *See, e.g.*, Polimeles Protodikio Athinon (Greece), docket n. 4505/2009 (no date indicated), available in English at http://cisgw3.law.pace.edu/cases/094505gr.html; Supreme Court of Switzerland, 28 October 1998, available in English at http://cisgw3.law.pace.edu/cases/981028s1.html; ICC Court of Arbitration, Arbitral Award n. 8962, available at http://www.Unilex.info/case.cfm?pid=1&do=case&id=464&step=FullText.

Article 78 CISG establishes, however, when the creditor is entitled to interest, thus overriding all domestic provisions on this specific issue. From the text of the provision one can easily gather that the creditor is entitled to interest as soon as payment is due but is not effected. As regards the payment of the purchase price, it generally is due at the time agreed upon in the contract; failing such agreement, resort is to be had to Article 58 CISG to identify when payment has to be effected. Pursuant to this provision, the purchase price is generally due at the time "when the seller places either the goods or documents controlling their disposition at the buyer's disposal in accordance with the contract and [the CISG]."

As regards sums other than the purchase price, it must be assumed that payment is due immediately when the claim arises. As regards the interest on damage claims, which also fall under Article 78 CISG, this means that they are due from the time the loss occurred, as also stated in case law.[19]

Apart from the aforementioned requirement, no further requirement is to be met for the creditor to be entitled to interest on a given sum. This means, *inter alia*, that the right to interest on a sum in arrears does not depend, unlike under some domestic laws, on any additional formality to be fulfilled.

---

[19]   *See, e.g.*, HG Zürich (Switzerland), 5 February 1997, available in English at http://cisgw3.law.pace.edu/cases/970205 s1.html.

The lack of a specific formula to calculate the rate of interest on sums in arrears has led some courts and commentators to consider that issue as being an internal gap (also referred to as a gap *praeter legem*), *i.e.*, as being governed by (but not expressly settled in) the CISG, whereas other courts and commentators consider the issue at hand as falling outside the scope of application of the CISG, *i.e.*, as being an external gap (or gap *intra legem*). This necessarily leads to diverging solutions, since under the CISG, the aforementioned kinds of gaps have to be dealt with differently. According to Article 7(2) CISG, internal gaps have to be filled by resorting to the general principles on which the CISG is based or, in the absence of such principles, by having recourse to the law applicable by virtue of the rules of private international law. On the contrary, if an issue is considered as falling outside the CISG's scope of application, *i.e.*, if it is considered an external gap, it must be solved in conformity with the law applicable by virtue of the rules of private international law, *i.e.*, without any tentative recourse to the "general principles" of the CISG.[20]

On the one hand, it has been said that the issue of determining the rate of interest is not at all governed by the CISG and that it is, therefore, governed by the applicable domestic law. Although many scholars hold this view, they appear not to agree on how to determine the applicable domestic law. Indeed, some scholars favor the view according

---

[20]   *See* Trib. Padova (Italy), 31 March 2004, available in English at http://cisgw3.law.pace.edu/cases/040331i3.html.

to which the applicable domestic law is to be determined by virtue of the rules of private international law of the forum, thus making applicable, in general, the subsidiary law applicable to the sales contract. Other scholars, however, argue in favor of either the application of the law of the creditor, independently from whether this is the *lex contractus,* or the application of the law of the debtor. Other authors have suggested applying the *lex fori* or the *lex monetae.*

On the other hand, there are commentators holding the opposite view, pursuant to which the issue at hand has to be dealt with as an internal gap, thus requiring the preliminary search for a general principle within the CISG, leading to a truly uniform solution as regards the rate of interest. This is why some commentators suggest that the interest to be paid should be defined in accordance with the basic function of damages, that is to put the seller in the same position he would have been, had the sum been paid in time. In these authors' opinion, this solution must be criticized, as it does not allow one to draw a clear line between damages and interest, which Article 78 has expressly drawn. In recent times, some commentators have suggested resort to the UNIDROIT Principles of International Commercial Contract on the grounds that they constitute "general principles" under Article 7(2) CISG. However, this assumption is incorrect, insofar as they do not really constitute "general principles on which [the CISG] is based" within the meaning of Article 7(2) CISG. Thus, this solution, too, is untenable.

The aforementioned dispute is not merely a doctrinal one, as evidenced by the number of different solutions adopted by courts and arbitral tribunals.[21] The different solutions that apply in those instances where the parties have not reached an agreement on the rate to apply can be divided mainly into two categories: those favoring the view that the rate of interest has to be calculated on the basis of domestic law, and those holding that the issue *de quo* must be resolved by taking into account the "need to promote uniformity in the application" of the CISG and, thus, resorting to the general principles of the CISG or at least to a uniform solution.

In relation to the latter category, it is worth mentioning several Argentinean decisions,[22] which invoked Article 9 CISG in order to solve the issue of the applicable rates of interest and invoked relevant trading customs, without reference to any domestic law. On the other hand, two Austrian arbitral awards maintained that "the applicable interest rate is to be determined autonomously on the basis of the general principles underlying the

---

[21]   *See, e.g.*, ICC Court of Arbitration, Arbitral Award n. 7585, available at http://www.unilex.info/case.cfm?pid=1&do= case&id=134&step=FullText, providing an overview of the various solutions suggested by courts and arbitral tribunals.

[22]   *See, e.g.*, Juzgado Nacional de Primera Instancia en lo comercial n. 7, Buenos Aires (Argentina), 23 October 1991, available in English at http://cisgw3.law.pace.edu/cases/911023 a1.html.

Convention",[23] on the grounds that the recourse to domestic law would lead to results contrary to those promoted by the CISG, at least in those cases where the applicable domestic law would be that of a country which expressly prohibits the payment of interest. This is why in the foregoing awards the issue of the rate of interest was solved by resorting to the general principle of full compensation, which led to the application of the law of the creditor. It is the creditor who is expected to resort to bank credit as a result of the delay in payment and should therefore be entitled to interest at the rate commonly practiced in its country with respect to the currency of payment. However, this solution not only contrasts with the legislative history of Article 78 CISG, but it also overlooks the line which Article 78 CISG expressly draws between the damages to be awarded on the basis of Article 74 *et seq.* CISG and interests on sums in arrears, a line that many other tribunals have acknowledged. More recently, several arbitral tribunals have applied the interest rate (the LIBOR) laid down in the UNIDROIT Principles of International Commercial Contracts on the grounds that these Principles lay down general principles upon which the CISG is based.[24] As

---

[23]   *See* the following awards rendered by the Internationales Schiedsgericht der Bundeskammer der gewerblichen Wirtschaft in Österreich (Austria): Arbitral Award n. 4366, available in English at http://cisgw3.law.pace.edu/cases/940615a3.html; Arbitral Award n. 4318, available in English at http://cisgw3.law .pace.edu/cases/940615a4.html.

[24]   *See* ICC Court of Arbitration, Arbitral Award n. 6653, available in English at http://cisgw3.law.pace.edu/cases/936653i1. html; note, however, that this arbitral award was annulled by the

mentioned earlier, in these authors' opinion, this is not tenable, because the aforementioned "Principles" must be considered "external" principles in respect of the CISG, and because the drafters intentionally did not resolve the issue of the rate of interest. Also, some decisions simply apply a "commercially reasonable" rate of interest,[25] without indicating on what CISG provision the application of that rate is based. Other (arbitral) tribunals simply applied the EURIBOR,[26] at times without even trying to justify their choice.

As far as those court decisions and arbitral awards are concerned that resolve the issue by resorting to domestic law, on the grounds that the issue of the rate of interest falls outside the CISG's scope of application,[27] a distinction must be made.

CA Paris (France), 6 April 1995, available in English at http://cisgw3.law.pace.edu/cases/950406f1.html, on the grounds that the international trade usages do not provide rules to determine the applicable interest rate. For the application of the LIBOR by other tribunals, see China International Economic and Trade Arbitration Commission (CIETAC), Arbitral Award in case No. CISG/2007/05 (no date indicated), available in English at http://cisgw3.law.pace.edu/cases/070100c1.html.

[25]   *See* China International Economic and Trade Arbitration Commission (CIETAC), Arbitral Award of 18 April 2003, available in English at http://cisgw3.law.pace.edu/cases/030418 c1.html.

[26]   *See* Foreign Trade Court of Arbitration attached to the Serbian Chamber of Commerce (Serbia), Arbitral Award of 16 March 2009, available in English at http://cisgw3.law.pace.edu/cases/090316sb.html.

[27]   For this statement, *see*, *e.g.*, U.S. District Court [N.J.], 15 April 2009 (*San Lucio, S.r.l. et al. v. Import & Storage Services,*

There are cases applying the domestic law of a specific country by virtue of the rules of private international law;[28] in other cases, however, the domestic law of the creditor was applied[29] without it being necessarily the law made applicable by virtue of the rules of private international law (of the forum). It must be pointed out that there are also a few cases in which the *lex monetae* was applied;[30] and a few other cases where other criteria were applied (based on the rate of the country of payment, that of the country of the debtor, the rate of the forum state, or the rate of the "rate of the European Central Bank").[31]

Despite the many different solutions mentioned above, there seems to be the tendency to apply the *lex contractus*, *i.e.*, the law that would be applicable to the sales contract if it were not subject to the

---

LLC et al.), available at http://cisgw3.law.pace.edu/cases/090415 u1.html.

[28]   *See*, *e.g.*, Cámara Nacional de Apelaciones en lo Comercial de Buenos Aires (Argentina), 7 October 2010, available at http://turan.uc3m.es/uc3m/dpto/PR/dppr03/cisg/sargen18.htm; U.S. District Court [W.D. Penn.], 25 July 2008 (*Norfolk Southern Railway Company v. Power Source Supply, Inc.*), available at http://cisgw3.law.pace.edu/cases/080725u1.html.

[29]   *See*, *e.g.*, RB Koophandel Hasselt (Belgium), 20 September 2005, available in English at http://cisgw3.law.pace.edu/cisg/wais/db/cases2/050920b1.html.

[30]   *See*, *e.g.*, Audiencia Provincial de Alicante (Spain), April 2009, available at http://www.globalsaleslaw.org/content/api/cisg/urteile/2086.pdf.

[31]   *See* RB Koophandel Hasselt (Belgium), 10 May 2006, available in English at http://cisgw3.law.pace.edu/cisg/wais/db/cases2/060510b1.html.

CISG. Thus, in respect of the formula to calculate the rate of interest, the interest rate of the country of the seller generally applies (at least where the rules of private international law of the forum are based upon criteria comparable to those set forth by the Rome Convention, the Rome I Regulation, or the 1955 Hague Convention). *Quid iuris*, however, where the seller's domestic law does prohibit the payment of interest? In this line of cases, the claim does not become unenforceable as suggested by several authors. It is suggested here, that the principle laid down in Article 78 CISG remains valid even in this line of cases, but that in order to determine the amount of interest to be paid one has to look into whether that domestic law provides for rules that are functionally equivalent to Article 78 CISG and allow one to identify a rate of interest.

5. DAMAGES FOR BREACH OF CONTRACT

The CISG devotes a specific Section of Chapter V of Part III (namely Section II, Articles 74 to 77) to the issue of damages, with the provision of Article 74 CISG setting forth the basic principles applicable to the remedy at hand. It should be noted, however, that Articles 74 *et seq*. CISG merely provide the criteria to be used to calculate the damages for which the aggrieved party may claim compensation, whereas the legal grounds for affirming the right to damages must be sought elsewhere in the CISG. In particular, Article 45(1)(*b*) CISG grants to the buyer the right to "claim damages as provided in Articles 74 to 77" in the event that "the seller fails to perform any of his obligations under the contract or this Convention". Similarly, Article 61(1)(*b*) CISG grants the same right to "claim damages" to the seller "[i]f the buyer fails to perform any of his obligations under the contract or this Convention."

The right to claim damages for breach of contract constitutes a common remedy, which the aggrieved party in a sale contract resorts to in order to obtain compensation for the detrimental consequences suffered as a result of the other party's breach of contract. As a general rule the right to claim damages can concur with any other remedy. This is made clear by the wording of Articles 45(2) and 61(2) CISG, both of which state that the aggrieved party "is not deprived of any right he may have to claim damages by exercising his right to other remedies." Accordingly, in the event of absolute non–performance by the seller, the buyer may claim performance and damages (for the delay) concurrently. In the event of partial performance by the seller, the buyer may claim the outstanding portion of performance or price reduction, along with damages. In the event of a non–conforming performance, the buyer may request repair of the goods, if reasonable, (or their substitution, to the extent that the non–conformity amounts to a fundamental breach) and at the same time he can claim damages. On the other hand, in the event that the buyer fails to pay the purchase price, to take delivery, or to perform any of his other obligations, the seller may concurrently require performance of the relevant obligations and claim damages resulting from the breach.

Although this Chapter deals only with remedies available in the event of non–fundamental breaches, it should be noted that also in the event of contract avoidance due to the fundamental breach of the one party, the other party is entitled to claim damages resulting from the avoidance.[32] In other words, Article 74 CISG applies to damages for breach of contract irrespective of the severity of the breach. Conversely, in accordance with the rule set forth in Article 5 CISG, the provision at hand does not apply to tortious claims for compensation for damages consisting of "death or personal injury caused by the goods to any person", as confirmed in numerous court decisions,[33] and does not apply, in general, to tortious product liability claims, which are governed by the domestic law of torts applicable by virtue of the conflict–of–law rules of the forum. Conversely, Article 5 CISG does not exclude losses for damages to property other than the goods purchased, as also confirmed in case law.[34] Moreover, at least some court decisions affirmed that damages available under Article 74 CISG include also the loss of

---

[32]   An occurrence that will be examined more closely in Chapter 9, Section 5.

[33]   *See, e.g.*, US District Court [S.D.N.Y.], 10 May 2002 (*Geneva Pharmaceutical Technology Corp v. Barr Laboratories Inc.*), available at http://cisgw3.law.pace.edu/cases/020510u1. html.

[34]   HG Kanton Zürich (Switzerland), 26 April 1995, available in English at http://cisgw3.law.pace.edu/cases/950426s1.html.

reputation or goodwill, to the extent that the aggrieved party can prove such loss.[35]

With respect to the loss that the aggrieved party may seek compensation for under Article 74 CISG, the CISG relies on the general principle of full compensation,[36] and states that damages "consist of a sum equal to the loss, including loss of profit, suffered by the [aggrieved] party".[37] Therefore, the claim for damages is made available for any kind of breach, even of minor relevance, and notwithstanding whether any other remedy is available to the aggrieved party. It is always a monetary claim, aiming at what courts often refer to as the "positive interest", *i.e.* everything the damaged party would have obtained, had the contract been duly performed, including costs and expenses borne in view of the contract, as well as the loss of profits.[38] Accordingly, the overall compensable losses include both the reduction in the assets that existed at the time of the conclusion of the contract, and the increase in assets that

---

[35] *See, e.g.*, Helsingin Hoviokeus (Finland), 26 October 2000, available in English at http://cisgw3.law.pace.edu/cases/001026f5. html; CA Grenoble (France), 21 October 1999, available in English at http://cisgw3.law.pace.edu/cases/991021f1.html.

[36] For a court decision referring to the principle of "full compensation" as one of the "general principles on which [the CISG] is based" under Article 7(2) CISG, *see, e.g.*, Trib. Padova (Italy), 25 February 2004, available in English at http://cisgw3. law.pace.edu/cases/040225i3.html.

[37] Article 74 CISG.

[38] *See, e.g.*, Polimeles Protodikio Athinon (Greece), docket n. 4505/2009 (no date indicated), available in English at http://cisg w3.law.pace.edu/cases/094505gr.html.

performance of the contract would have made possible, but that the breach prevented. The reduction of assets compensable as damages certainly includes the reasonable expenditures incurred in preparation for, or as a consequence of, a contract that has been breached,[39] such as, for instance, costs for handling and storing non–conforming goods,[40] banking fees for retransfer of payments,[41] or costs for repair by the buyer of non–conforming goods.[42] An issue which has often been discussed in court decisions is whether the aggrieved party may recover the fees of an attorney hired to collect a debt. Decisions by national courts are rather split on this matter, which is somehow complicated by the fact that different legal systems adopt different solutions as regards the availability of the "loser pays" rule for attorney's fees, and that the issue is typically addressed by the procedural rules of the forum, rather than by the substantive rules on damages. In these authors' view, extra–judicial costs that can reasonably be regarded as aiming at mitigating the damages should be treated

---

[39]   *See, e.g.*, Supreme Court of Germany, 25 June 1997, available in English at http://cisgw3.law.pace.edu/cases/970625 g2.html.

[40]   Tribunal of International Commercial Arbitration at the Russian Federation Chamber of Commerce, Arbitral Award n. 375/1993 of 9 September 1994, English abstract available at http://www.unilex.info/case.cfm?id=249.

[41]   *See, e.g.*, ZG Kanton Basel–Stadt (Switzerland), 8 November 2006, available in English at http://cisgw3.law.pace.edu/cases/061108s1.html.

[42]   U.S. Court of Appeals [2nd Cir.], 6 December 1995 (*Delchi Carrier v. Rotorex*), available at http://cisgw3.law.pace.edu/cases/951206u1.html.

as part of the incidental loss recoverable as damages under Article 74 CISG. Conversely, with respect to judicial costs (including both court's and lawyer's fees), if the national procedural laws of the forum State exclude the "loser pays" rule, the reimbursement of legal fees cannot be claimed under Article 74.[43]

Lost profits include all those increases in assets that the breach of contract prevented. In determining the amount of the loss in question, courts are called upon to make a hypothetical comparison between the situation resulting from the breach and what the same situation would have been in the event that the contract had been duly performed. Accordingly, just to give a few examples, a court decision awarded the buyer damages for delivery of defective equipment, which included the difference between the unit costs for producing products using the defective equipment and the costs had the equipment not been defective.[44] Another decision took the common profit margins of the buyer into consideration in order to award the

---

[43] For a court decision adopting the same solution, *see* U.S. Court of Appeals [7th Cir.], 19 November 2002 (*Zapata Hermanos Sucesores, S.A. v. Hearthside Baking Company, Inc. d/b/a Maurice Lenell Cooky Company*), available at http://cisgw3.law. pace.edu/cases/021119u1.html.

[44] *See* ZG Kanton Basel–Stadt (Switzerland), 8 November 2006, available in English at http://cisgw3.law.pace.edu/cases/061108s1.html.

buyer damages caused by a non–delivery resulting in the unavailability of products for resale.[45]

The principle of full compensation also implies, *a contrario*, that under the CISG the aggrieved party cannot be granted a sum of money that exceeds the loss suffered, thus overcompensating the recipient of the sum. In this respect, when liquidating the damages to be awarded to the aggrieved party, courts must take into account not only any possible satisfactory result that the latter may have obtained as a result of the concurrence of any other remedy exercised, but also any positive effects or savings of costs resulting from the breach of contract for which damages are sought. Accordingly, by way of example, on the one hand, if the buyer successfully compels performance in kind, repair of the goods, or price reduction, the amount of damages that he can claim must be reduced in proportion to the benefit resulting from the concurrent remedy. On the other hand, if the buyer receives partial delivery or delivery of non–conforming goods, as a result of which he has lower costs of transportation or processing, that reduction of costs must be considered in the calculation of damages.

Not all damages suffered by the aggrieved party on the occasion of a breach of contract by the other party can give rise to a claim for compensation. In fact, compensable damages have to pass the test of remoteness, as is made clear by the language of the

---

[45]   *See* Supreme Court of Switzerland, 17 December 2009, available in English at http://cisgw3.law.pace.edu/cases/091217 s1.html.

provision, which refers to the loss being a "consequence" of the breach. The very fact that the test of remoteness is coupled with the requirement of "foreseeability" of damages—which plays a pivotal role in the assessment of the sum of money to be granted to the aggrieved party—suggests that there is no need to interpret the notion of remoteness in any stricter sense than in accordance with the general "but–for" rule (*condicio sine qua non*), leading to the inclusion of both direct and indirect consequences. To put it differently, the test of remoteness under the CISG is based on two different, although closely related, considerations. First, one has to determine whether the damages are a consequence of the breach; secondly, one has to assess whether the damages were foreseeable at the time of the conclusion of the contract. Thus, the assessment of foreseeability largely overlaps with the determination of causality and makes it less urgent to adopt a strict notion of causation, given that the limits to the possibility to recover damages derive from the notion of foreseeability.

The notion of "foreseeability" of damages is alien to many domestic jurisdictions that make a distinction, as to the damages recoverable, based on the subjective intention of the party in breach. Under the requirement at hand, as repeatedly affirmed by court decisions,[46] the damages obtainable by the aggrieved party under the CISG

---

[46]   *See*, among many others, Shanghai High People's Court (China), 21 September 2011, available in English at http://cisg w3.law.pace.edu/cases/110921c1.html.

are limited to those that were "foreseeable" to the breaching party at the time of the conclusion of the contract. More specifically, Article 74 CISG states that damages for breach of the contract "may not exceed the loss which the party in breach foresaw or ought to have foreseen at the time of the conclusion of the contract, in light of the facts and matters of which he then knew or ought to have known, as a possible consequence of the breach of contract." Therefore, it is of no relevance whether the debtor intentionally breached the obligation, or did not comply with the contractual requirements simply because of mere negligence.[47] Instead, the foreseeability requirement operates under the CISG as the legal criterion to be used in order to assess the amount of damages that the aggrieved party may recover, in a fashion that may be predictable also to the party in breach, so as to make it possible for the latter to pre–estimate *ex ante* the risk and consequences resulting from the breach.

The "foreseeability" may therefore be regarded as favoring an "efficient breach" on the part of the promisor, who is in the position to determine *ex ante*—on the basis of what is foreseeable at the time of conclusion of the contract—what amount of damages he is going to be held liable for, should he decide to breach the contract. Although such a conclusion is, in itself, correct, it should also be reconciled with the possible availability to the

---

[47]   *See* Supreme Court of Switzerland, 14 January 2002, available in English at http://cisgw3.law.pace.edu/cases/020114a3 .html.

aggrieved promissee of a judgment for specific performance, which would in fact frustrate the promisor's reasons for efficiently not fulfilling his contractual obligations. The very possibility of different solutions under Article 28 CISG, based on the location of the forum where the dispute is adjudicated, is therefore to be regarded with some regret, in that it also affects the concrete answer to the question as to whether a debtor may commit a breach when that conduct proves to be efficient in economic terms.

The notion of "foreseeability" must be interpreted autonomously on the sole basis of the text of the CISG. Accordingly, in these authors' view, one cannot share the opinion expressed in a U.S. court decision, according to which the notion at hand "is identical to the well–known rule of *Hadley v. Baxendale,* [. . .] such that relevant [domestic] interpretations of that rule can guide the Court's reasoning regarding proper damages".[48] Indeed, notwithstanding some possible similarities, the contents and goals of the two provisions compared by the quoted court are different. Under Article 74 CISG, the foreseeability of damages must be considered exclusively from the perspective of the party in breach, whereas under the traditional common law rule the limitation of damages is determined on the basis of the reasonable contemplation of the parties (so called:

---

[48] *See* U.S. District Court [S.D.N.Y.], 12 August 2006 (*TeeVee Tunes, Inc. et al. v. Gerhard Schubert GmbH*), available at http://cisgw3.law.pace.edu/cases/060823u1.html#ii1.

"contemplation rule"). It is therefore apparent that the domestic notion cannot be referred to when interpreting the requirement under the CISG, as also pointed out by at least one court decision.[49]

To say that the foreseeability must be considered from the perspective of the breaching party does not mean that the notion at hand is to be treated as a purely subjective one. To the contrary, the requirement of foreseeability consists of two separate, yet concurring, elements: a subjective one and an objective one. First and foremost, the limitation of the attribution of loss operates on the basis of objective standards, which require the interpreter to consider what a reasonable promisor "ought to have foreseen" as a possible consequence of the breach in light of the facts and matters that he "ought to have known" at the time of the conclusion of the contract.[50] In addition to the objective standard, the CISG also requires the interpreter to apply a subjective standard, to the effect that, irrespective of what a reasonable promisor ought to have foreseen in the given circumstances, the promisor must be held liable for all damages that he foresaw in the concrete circumstances of the case at hand. In practice, with respect to the breach of contract committed by the seller, it has been correctly maintained that the

---

[49]   Trib. Forlì (Italy), 12 November 2012, INTERNATIONALES HANDELSRECHT 161 (2013).

[50]   For a court decision providing an exhaustive overview of the requirement of foreseeability, *see* Supreme Court of Austria, 14 January 2002, available in English at http://cisgw3.law.pace.edu/cases/020114a3.html.

latter should foresee that a retail buyer would resell the contract products.[51] With respect to the breach committed by the buyer, who failed to establish the agreed letter of credit, it has been held that he should foresee that the seller could legitimately refrain from chartering the vessel and would therefore not be in the condition to use it.[52]

Regardless of the grounds on which the claim for damages is based, a possible reduction of the damages recoverable may derive, under Article 77 CISG, from the aggrieved party's failure "to take measures as are reasonable under the circumstances to mitigate the loss." The duty to mitigate is one imposed in many jurisdictions and it is therefore not surprising that the CISG also imposes on the aggrieved party a duty to mitigate the loss. Accordingly, in the event of a breach the aggrieved party is not allowed to remain passive as damages are being caused by the breach, and to comfortably rely on the possibility to thereafter sue the party in breach and recover the entire amount of the damages suffered. To the contrary, the aggrieved party has a duty to activate himself and take all reasonable steps in order to reduce the damages already produced, or to prevent further

---

[51]   *See, e.g.,* OLG Köln (Germany), 21 May 1996, available in English at http://cisgw3.law.pace.edu/cases/960521g1.html.

[52]   *See* Supreme Court of Queensland (Australia), 17 November 2000 (*Downs Investments v. Perwaja Steel*), available at http://cisgw3.law.pace.edu/cases/001117a2.html.

damages from materializing.[53] The costs of taking reasonable steps to mitigate damages may be claimed as part of the aggrieved party's damages under Article 74 CISG, although at least one court decision made such recovery of costs subject to giving prior notice to the party in breach of the steps to be taken to mitigate the loss.[54] Should the aggrieved party fail to mitigate, the party in breach is entitled to claim a reduction of the damages recoverable under Article 74. It is worth noticing, in this respect, that Article 77 CISG sets forth a remedy available to the party in breach in the event of the aggrieved party's failure to mitigate. This remedy, however, is to be regarded as independent from any other remedy available under the CISG for breach of a contractual obligation. In particular, the remedy available to the party in breach may only take the form of a reduction of the damages payable, to the exclusion of the possibility of compelling the obligation to mitigate under the provision at hand.

In accordance with the general provision contained in Article 6 CISG, the parties may derogate from or vary the effects of the most provisions,[55] including those on damages. This implies, in particular, that the parties may agree either on exemption clauses and limitations of liability, or on penalties and liquidated damages

---

[53]   *See, e.g.,* Supreme Court of Austria, 6 February 1996, available in English at http://cisgw3.law.pace.edu/cases/960206 a3.html].

[54]   *See* LG Darmstadt (Germany), 9 May 2000, available in English at http://cisgw3.law.pace.edu/cases/000509g1.html.

[55]   *See supra* Chapter 1, Section 5.

clauses. By means of an exemption clause or a limitation of liability clause the parties exclude any liability for damages, or limit the liability to a certain maximum amount or only to a certain type of losses. These clauses are not governed by the CISG and their validity falls under the exclusion of Article 4(1)(*a*) CISG, thus being governed by the domestic law identified by virtue of the conflict–of–law rules of the forum. Similarly, party autonomy may also play a relevant role in determining the amount due by the promisor upon breach of contract. Indeed, the parties may have different reasons to determine in advance the amount of damages: they may want to avoid the harshness of providing proof of the exact amount of damages, or they may want to coerce the debtor into performance. Furthermore, at times the parties merely want to limit the liability of the debtor. In the first situation the parties genuinely pre–estimate the likely loss, thus making the "liquidated damages" more readily enforceable by means of clauses that are widely regarded as entirely valid and enforceable. In other circumstances, however, the parties stipulate "penalty" clauses, conceived to operate "*in terrorem*", as a threat intended to coerce the debtor into performing his obligation. Again, the validity of these clauses is not governed by the CISG, but must be monitored in accordance with the substantive domestic law applicable by virtue of the conflict–of–law rules of the forum.

6.   EXEMPTION FOR NON–PERFORMANCE

As a general rule, under the CISG a promisor in breach of contract is liable and must compensate the aggrieved party for damages suffered as a result of the breach. As pointed out above, the harshness of this general rule is somewhat mitigated by the foreseeability requirement under Article 74, according to which only damages that were foreseeable at the time of the conclusion of the contract must be compensated. The rationale behind this rule is that the promisor must be, when entering the agreement, in the position to measure the risk that he is taking in order to price the contract and possibly to buy insurance for the risk he takes. In line with this rationale, another fundamental provision of the CISG is the one set forth in Article 79(1) CISG, according to which "[a] party is not liable for a failure to perform any of his obligations if he proves that the failure was due to an impediment beyond his control and that he could not reasonably be expected to have taken the impediment into account at the time of the conclusion of the contract or to have avoided or overcome it or its consequences". Thus, according to the provision at hand and coherently with the rationale of Article 74 CISG, the promisor cannot be held liable for non–performances that at the time of the conclusion of the contract were not foreseeable and that are due to an unpredictable impediment, which is beyond the scope of the risk that the promisor undertook by contract.[56]

The very fact that the rule at hand operates so as to exempt from liability the promisor who had not accepted to undertake the risk of occurrence of the exempting event makes it clear that the rule only plays a role to the extent that the relevant event would otherwise trigger the promisor's liability. Accordingly, the rule under Article 79 CISG must be coordinated with the rules on the passing of risk under Articles 66–70 CISG,[57] to the effect that, in particular, the need for the seller to rely on the possibility of an exemption under Article 79 lasts only until the risk of accidental loss or damage of the goods passes to the buyer under the rules on passing of risk.

Although the wording of Article 79 CISG closely resembles that of many domestic provisions dealing with exemptions for *force majeure*, frustration, or similar doctrines, it is apparent that the notion of exemption under the CISG, not unlike most other notions,[58] must be interpreted autonomously. Moreover, unlike under most domestic legal systems, the rule under Article 79 CISG operates so as to exclude only the obligation of the party in

---

[56] For a court decision reading the provision of Article 79 CISG as a rule on risk allocation between the parties, *see, e.g.*, Supreme Court of Germany, 24 March 1999, available in English at http://cisgw3.law.pace.edu/cases/990324g1.html.

[57] For a detailed analysis of these provisions *see supra* Chapter 7, Section 3.

[58] For further details on the autonomous interpretation of the CISG, *see supra* Chapter 1, Section 2.

breach to pay damages. This conclusion can safely be drawn from the wording of Article 79(5) CISG, under which "[n]othing in this article prevents either party from exercising any right other than to claim damages under this Convention". Accordingly, notwithstanding the occurrence of an event qualifying as an exemption under Article 79, all remedies for non–performance available under the CISG, other than damages, remain entirely available to the parties, provided that the prerequisites (if any) for each remedy are met. Therefore, either party may still avoid the contract to the extent that the non–performance caused by the supervening impediment qualifies as a fundamental breach. Either party may claim performance (possibly also consisting of a buyer's claim for substitute goods in the event of fundamental breach, or for repair of the goods if not unreasonable). Furthermore, as a result of the impeded performance, the aggrieved party may claim price reduction, or interests in sums in arrears.

The exemption under Article 79 CISG applies to any kind of breach, irrespective of whether it consists of the non–performance of obligations of the seller or of the buyer and of whether it relates to the non–performance of characteristic obligations of the parties, or of merely ancillary ones. Under Article 79(3) exempting impediments that temporarily prevent performance relieve the promisor from liability for damages for his temporary failure to perform. It is debated, on the other hand, whether the exemption can be called upon only with respect to absolute or partial non–performances, or also with respect to defective performances, primarily consisting of the non–conformity of the goods. The solution excluding exemption for non–conformity is at times maintained on the grounds that the liability for non–conformity operates objectively, as a warranty, thus making the call for an exemption irreconcilable with the very notion of the liability in question. In these authors' view, however, in line with relevant court decisions on this matter,[59] Article 79 CISG applies also in the event of delivery of non–conforming goods. However, it must be stressed that the exemption cannot be invoked in cases where the event, which allegedly impeded perfect performance, was within the scope of the risks assumed by the promisor. This conclusion is of great relevance in practice with respect to chains of sales, where the seller downstream in the chain claims an exemption for delivery of non–conforming goods on the grounds that he cannot be blamed for a defect that is due to a prior seller upstream in the chain.[60] In similar cases, one must recall that the liability for breach under the CISG is based on a no–fault, strict liability system,[61] so that the alleged

---

[59]   *See, e.g.*, although in somewhat problematic terms, Supreme Court of Germany, 9 January 2002, available in English at http://cisgw3.law.pace.edu/cases/020109g1.html.

[60]   For a similar scenario, leading to a wrong decision, *see* Trib. Besançon (France), 19 January 1998, available in English at http://cisgw3.law.pace.edu/cases/980119f1.html.

[61]   *See, e.g.*, Supreme Court of Austria, 21 April 2004, available in English at http://cisgw3.law.pace.edu/cases/040421 a3.html.

lack of blameworthiness in the promisor's conduct must be treated as entirely irrelevant and the possible application of the exemption under Article 79 CISG must entirely rest on the occurrence of an impediment falling beyond the scope of the risk assumed by the promisor. This means that the promisor could not reasonably be expected to have taken the impediment into account or to have avoided or overcome it or its consequences.

Under Article 79(2) the promisor is liable for the conduct of third persons who are engaged to perform the whole or part of the contract. As a court decision pointed out, the provision at hand "has as its scope maintaining the responsibility of the seller if he relies on third parties for the total or partial execution of the contract. The seller's employees and suppliers are not considered third parties according to the CISG, though they are subjects who, autonomously or as independent parties, fulfill a part of the whole of the contract. More generally, the individuals that are charged—by the seller and after the conclusion of the contract—with the fulfillment of the existing obligations toward the buyer are considered third parties according to the CISG. They are, in particular, the carriers that deliver the merchandise to the seller and the subcontractors that are assigned by the seller to carry out the finish work".[62] In such situations, the promisor can rely on an exemption due to an

---

[62]   Trib. App. Lugano (Switzerland), 29 October 2003, available in English at http://cisgw3.law.pace.edu/cases/031029 s1.html.

uncontrollable supervening event affecting the performance of the third person only insofar as he can prove that the event constituted an impediment that was unforeseeable and insurmountable for the promisor himself, and that the third person engaged would also have been exempted under Article 79(1) had he been the promisor.[63]

Article 79 CISG exempts the party in breach from the obligation to pay damages to the extent that that party can prove concurrently three different circumstances: first, that the reason for the breach lies in an impediment beyond his control; second, that the impediment could not be taken into account at the time of conclusion of the contract; and third, that the party in breach could not reasonably be expected to avoid or overcome the impediment or its consequences.

The first notion that needs to be defined is that of "impediment", which consists of an event that must be proved by the obligor to be the direct cause of his "failure to perform". Although the event qualifying as an impediment does not need to be such as to cause an objective and absolute impossibility of performance, it is apparent that it would be unacceptable to extend the notion of impediment to include also circumstances that merely alter even to a minor extent the equilibrium of the contract as a result of a change of the circumstances in which the

---

[63]   See, e.g., ICC Court of Arbitration, Arbitral Award n. 8128/1995, available in English at http://cisgw3.law.pace.edu/cases/958128i1.html, stating that "seller's responsibility for his supplier is an integral part of the general risk of supply of goods".

performance must be rendered. Accordingly, one can safely affirm that any event that makes performance objectively and absolutely impossible qualifies as an impediment under Article 79 CISG. However, also supervening events that do not make performance absolutely impossible may qualify as impediments, as evidenced, *a contrario*, by the fact that even events such as natural disasters (earthquakes, volcanic eruptions, etc.), wars, or acts of the authorities may leave performance physically possible, although no one would seriously question that those events qualify as impediments.

In case law, several court decisions applied Article 79 CISG without any express explanation of what constitutes an impediment.[64] In other cases, courts and arbitral tribunals addressed the question of whether a specific event qualified for an exemption, but did not provide a general definition of what constitutes an impediment.[65] In one arbitral award, the attempt was made to provide a general definition of the impediment under Article 79 CISG, and led to the definition according to which the exemption applies in the event of "an unmanageable risk or a totally exceptional event, such as a *force majeure*, economic impossibility or excessive

---

[64]   *See, e.g.*, Tribunal of International Commercial Arbitration at the Russian Federation Chamber of Commerce (Russian Federation), Arbitral Award n. 155/1996 of 22 January 1997, available in English at http://cisgw3.law.pace.edu/cases/970122r1.html.

[65]   *See, e.g.*, Bulgarian Chamber of Commerce and Industry (Bulgaria), Arbitral Award of 12 February 1998, available in English at http://cisgw3.law.pace.edu/cases/980212bu.html.

onerousness".[66] This definition, however, leaves several issues still open, to the extent that it refers to notions that cannot be interpreted on the basis of domestic laws and must be defined autonomously from within the context of the CISG. Therefore, the reported definition can only be taken as a starting point for a case–by–case analysis, which, in these authors' view, must be conducted on the basis of the premise that an impediment is relevant under the CISG insofar as it caused a "failure to perform", which in turn suggests that any event that makes performance of a contractual obligation impossible in the form that was envisaged at the time of conclusion of the contract may be treated as an impediment.

One could reasonably argue that the definition of impediment that has been proposed is a rather loose one; however, it is suggested here that it is not the notion of impediment that should operate so as to restrict the availability of the exemption, but rather the restriction should result from the application of the additional requirements that the impediment must be beyond the obligor's control, unforeseeable and unavoidable. In particular, it is relevant to notice that no exemption can be claimed with respect to the occurrence of impediments that were within the obligor's sphere of control, which may include both what the obligor could in practice control and avoid, and what he contractually

---

[66] Schiedsgericht der Handelskammer Hamburg (Germany), Partial Award of 21 March 1996, available in English at http://cisgw3.law.pace.edu/cases/960321g1.html.

assumed as a risk falling within his sphere of control. Furthermore, when trying to determine whether an impediment is beyond the obligor's control, the time when the impediment occurs is generally of no consequences. The CISG does not appear to distinguish between initial and subsequent impediments; as a result, even an impediment beyond control already existent at contract formation and unknown to the obligor can lead to the obligor's exemption.[67]

It is not sufficient for an impediment to exempt the obligor from liability that the impediment occurs outside the obligor's sphere of control. The external impediment must not have been foreseen or foreseeable (by the obligor, as well as by a reasonable person in the same circumstances as the obligor)[68] at the time of contract conclusion. This means, among others, that the risk pertaining to the event claimed to amount to an impediment under Article 79 cannot have been the object of any contractual agreement between the parties, since such agreement would make it impossible to consider the event unforeseeable. Strictly speaking, however, one could argue that any impediment (including wars, earthquakes, or other natural disasters) is, in itself, foreseeable. Indeed, the notion of foreseeability relevant for the purpose of

---

[67]   *Contra*, however, AG Willisau (Switzerland), 12 March 2004, available in English at http://cisgw3.law.pace.edu/cases/040312s1.html.

[68]   For a similar statement, *see*, *e.g.*, RB Koophandel Tongeren (Belgium), 25 January 2005, available in English at http://cisgw3.law.pace.edu/cases/050125b1.html.

exempting a failure to perform must be integrated by a requirement of likelihood, so that the impediment cannot be invoked as an exemption to the extent that it was foreseeable as reasonably likely to occur.

Furthermore, in order to exempt the obligor's failure to perform, in addition to the impeding event not being foreseeable, its consequences must not be avoidable, nor surmountable.[69] If, for instance, an event occurs (e.g. a flood) that was not foreseeable at the time of conclusion of the contract, but was announced the day before its occurrence, the obligor is expected to take any precautions reasonably necessary to prevent the exceptional event from affecting his performance. Similarly, if the impediment prevents the obligor from performing his obligation as originally planned, he is under a duty to seek alternative means to render to the obligee the very same performance, or what arbitral tribunals and courts have identified as a "commercially reasonable substitute".[70]

An issue often discussed in relation to Article 79 CISG is whether economic hardship (which has been defined in scholarly writing as "the occurrence of events fundamentally alter[ing] the equilibrium of

---

[69]   *See, e.g.,* OLG Zweibrücken (Germany), 2 February 2004, available in English at http://cisgw3.law.pace.edu/cases/040202 g1.html.

[70]   *See* ICDR (United States), Arbitral Award of 23 October 2007 (*Macromex Srl v. Globex International Inc.*), available at http://cisgw3.law.pace.edu/cases/071023a5.html, affirmed by U.S. District Court [S.D.N.Y.], 16 April 2008, 2008 WL 1752530 (S.D.N.Y.)

the contract, either because the cost of a party's performance has increased or because the value of the performance a party receives diminished") is among the grounds of exemption covered under Article 79, or, to put it differently, whether there is space under the CISG for a *rebus sic stantibus* excuse, in spite of the general obligation that *pacta sunt servanda*. First of all, it should be noted that the prevailing view of commentators today is that hardship is (somehow) governed by the CISG, mainly on the grounds that the CISG does not equate the term "impediment" only with an event that makes performance absolutely impossible. With specific regard to price fluctuations, however, (which are among the circumstances that are most frequently referred to by obligors claiming an exemption) the prevailing view is that fluctuations are a normal risk of commercial transactions which are foreseeable by a reasonable party, so that "a contract that is not lucrative or that is even a losing proposition, is part of the risks that belong to commercial activities".[71]

In a landmark decision rendered in 2009, the Supreme Court of Belgium stated (in a case where the seller gave notice to the buyer that it was forced to recalculate the agreed price because of an unforeseeable 70% increase in the price of steel) that while Article 79(1) CISG covers *force majeure* cases exempting from liability, it does not implicitly

---

[71]   *See* RB Koophandel Hasselt (Belgium), 2 May 1995, available in English at http://cisgw3.law.pace.edu/cases/950502 b1.html.

exclude the relevance of less than *force majeure* situations such as hardship. The Court stated that "[c]hanged circumstances that were not reasonably foreseeable at the time of the conclusion of the contract and that are unequivocally of a nature to increase the burden of performance of the contract in a disproportionate manner, can, under circumstances, form an impediment in the sense of this provision of the Convention".[72] Although the premises about the notion of impediment, restated by the Belgian Supreme Court and cited above, can be agreed upon, the conclusions drawn from those premises cannot be shared. On the one hand, the statement positing that changed circumstances consisting of price fluctuation can amount to an impediment that the obligor "could not reasonably be expected to have taken [. . .] into account"[73] seems untenable in light of the arguments set forth above. On the other hand, one cannot agree with the position maintained by the Belgian Supreme Court that "the party who invokes changed circumstances that fundamentally disturb the contractual balance [. . .] is also entitled to claim the renegotiation of the contract". As already pointed out, the only claim provided for as a result of the availability of an exemption under Article 79 CISG is that the party who failed to perform cannot be held liable for damages resulting from his non–performance. In fact, the Supreme Court of Belgium reached the

---

[72]   Supreme Court of Belgium, 19 June 2009, available in English at http://cisgw3.law.pace.edu/cases/090619b1.html.

[73]   Cf. the language of Article 79(1) CISG.

aforementioned conclusion on the basis of the UNIDROIT Principles of International Commercial Contracts, on the assumption that those Principles can be resorted to in order to fill a gap left by the CISG. However, this conclusion rests on the untenable premise that the UNIDROIT Principles can be considered "general principles upon which [the CISG] is based" under the gap–filling rule set forth in Article 7(2) CISG, whereas in these authors' view the general principles referred to in that provision must be derived from within the text of the CISG.

The foregoing leads us to consider in further details the consequences of the occurrence of an impediment exempting the obligor from performance. It has already been said that the only consequence under Article 79(1) CISG is that the obligor who failed to perform due to an exempting impediment cannot be held liable for damages. On the other hand, either party may exercise any other remedy available under the contract or the CISG. These alternative remedies, including contract avoidance, will be available primarily to the obligee, to the extent that the obligor's failure to perform (although not leading to liability in damages) amounts to a fundamental breach of contract under Article 25 CISG. Conversely, the occurrence of an event qualifying as an exempting impediment under Article 79(1) CISG, in itself, does not grant to the obligor, whose performance is prevented, a right to avoid the contract. This conclusion can be safely argued on the grounds that the reciprocal non–

performance by the obligee appears to be justified in the light of the obligee's right to suspend performance under Article 71 CISG. Furthermore, among the remedies that remain available to the obligee, notwithstanding the occurrence of an impediment, is also the claim for specific performance. This leads to a somewhat puzzling situation when the obligor does not perform his obligation because of an event qualifying as an exempting impediment. In these circumstances, the obligee cannot claim damages from the obligor, but he can claim specific performance, thus compelling the obligor to render the performance that was impeded by the supervening event. Of course, if performance became impossible as a result of the impediment, it is a globally accepted rule that *ad impossibilia nemo tenetur*. It has been pointed out, however, that the impediment under Article 79(1) can also consist of an event that significantly changes the circumstances under which performance is to be rendered so as to make it more burdensome. Now, as the concrete availability of a judgment for specific performance depends on whether or not specific performance would be granted by the competent national court in a purely domestic transaction,[74] it seems correct to conclude that where the obligor does not perform due to an impediment which made performance extremely more burdensome than originally envisaged, the obligee may not have a claim for damages under Article 79(1) CISG. However, the obligee may still

---

[74]   *See supra* this Chapter, Section 2.

have a claim for specific performance, unless under the domestic laws of the forum a claim for specific performance is unavailable when its enforcement would be unreasonably burdensome.

Under Article 79(4) CISG the obligor, whose non–performance is exempted as a result of an unforeseeable impediment, must "give notice to the other party of the impediment and its effect on his ability to perform [. . .] within a reasonable time after the party who fails to perform knew or ought to have known of the impediment". The consequences of the failure to timely and fully inform the obligee are rather harsh, in that the obligor "is liable for damages resulting from such non–receipt" of information. It should be noted that the liability for damages resulting from the failure to inform does not correspond to the liability for failure to perform that the obligor would have been subject to, had he not been exempted under Article 79. Instead, the failure to inform makes the obligor liable to compensate the obligee to the extent necessary to place him in the same position he would have been, had the obligor given the information timely.

It is worth mentioning in conclusion, in accordance with Article 6 CISG, that the parties can derogate from any part or the whole of Article 79. In fact, in practice parties to international contracts for the sale of goods more often than not include in their agreements clauses that preempt, in whole or in part, the application of Article 79 CISG. Clauses of the kind just mentioned include, first of all, *force majeure* clauses and hardship clauses, which the parties can draft autonomously, or merely incorporate in their agreement by reference to existing model clauses;[75] however, other types of clauses address part of the matters covered by Article 79, including price–fluctuation and price–adjustment clauses. Moreover, contract clauses providing representations and warranties may preempt the application of Article 79 CISG to the extent that they can be interpreted as containing a risk–taking commitment excluding any possible exemption.

Completely different grounds for exemption of the obligor for his failure to perform are set forth under Article 80 CISG, which is included, along with Article 79, in the specific Section (namely Section IV) of Chapter V of Part III, devoted to *Exemption.* Under Article 80 CISG the obligor is exempted if his failure to perform is caused by an act or omission of the obligee, as in the case of a buyer failing to prepare suitable business premises for the goods.[76] It should be noted, however, that the act or omission of the obligee must be the direct and physical (not merely "legal", as in an *inadimplenti* defense) cause of the non–performance of the obligor, as in the case of a buyer's failure to perform his obligation to

---

[75]   Such as, for instance, the 2003 ICC Force majeure clause and Hardship clause.

[76]   *See* OLG Hamburg (Germany), 25 January 2008, available in English at http://cisgw3.law.pace.edu/cases/080125 g1.html.

notify the seller and the carrier in charge of the transportation of the time and place of delivery.[77]

Unlike Article 79, which only blocks the claim for damages against the obligor, Article 80 CISG prevents the obligee from exercising any remedy for non–performance of the obligor, including claiming performance or avoiding the contract.

---

[77] *See* Chinese International Economic and Trade Arbitration Commission (CIETAC), Arbitral Award of 9 January 2008, available in English at http://cisgw3.law.pace.edu/cases/080109c1.html.

CHAPTER 9
REMEDIES FOR FUNDAMENTAL BREACH

1.   FUNDAMENTAL BREACH

As pointed out earlier, while there are remedies that are available to any aggrieved party, irrespective of the gravity of the breach of contract, there are certain remedies that are available to an aggrieved party only where the breach is a fundamental one. Pursuant to Article 46(2), for instance, for the buyer to be entitled to require delivery of substitute goods if the goods delivered do not conform with the contract, the lack of conformity has to constitute a fundamental breach of contract, even though specific performance is a remedy otherwise generally available to both the aggrieved seller and the aggrieved buyer (Articles 46(1) and 62). To give another example, both the aggrieved seller and the aggrieved buyer may avoid the contract only where opposing party's failure to perform any of his obligations under the contract or the CISG amounts to a fundamental breach of contract (Articles 49(1) and 64(1)).

Whether a breach amounts to a fundamental one, capable of triggering the particularly far–reaching legal consequences just hinted at, to be elaborated on later, is to be determined on the basis of Article 25 CISG. But while Article 25 defines what breach amounts to a fundamental one and, thus, constitutes a tool for distinguishing between a simple breach of contract and a fundamental one, it does not identify the various instances in which a fundamental breach is relevant. As for the legal consequences of a fundamental breach, these must be derived from other provisions in the CISG or from the contract. This is why it is correct to emphasize, as some commentators have done, that Article 25 cannot be applied by itself, but only in conjunction with those provisions that require a fundamental breach to trigger the consequences they provide for.

The reason for limiting particularly drastic legal consequences (such as the avoidance of the contract) to cases in which the breach of contract is fundamental lies, on the one hand, in ensuring the performance of the contract despite a (non–fundamental) breach so as to avoid unnecessary and unproductive costs, such as those associated with the return or storage of the goods. On the other hand, this limitation helps to contain the number of cases in which the damaged party may take advantage of the defaulting party's breach in order to revise an agreement based on a specific economic situation or to shift the risk of a change in the market conditions to the other party.

Pursuant to Article 25, "[a] breach of contract committed by one of the parties is fundamental if it results in such detriment to the other party as substantially to deprive him of what he is entitled to expect under the contract, unless the party in breach did not foresee and a reasonable person of the same kind in the same circumstances would not have foreseen such a result." Although some commentators believe the definition contained in Article 25 to be rather vague,[1] in these authors' opinion this does not preclude the definition from proving useful in the CISG's practical application.

The most important prerequisite for a "fundamental breach" is the breach of an obligation deriving from either the contract, the practice established between the parties, the usages referred to in Article 9(2), or the CISG. Where no such breach has occurred, Article 25 cannot apply. Thus, there can be no fundamental breach where a party, whose behavior is incompatible with its obligations, is entitled not to comply with those obligations. This can occur where the debtor exercises the right to refuse performance or where the creditor fails to collaborate with the debtor, thus making it impossible for the latter to perform.

The CISG does not distinguish between the breach of principal and ancillary obligations.[2] "[E]ven the violation of an obligation which is not a principal obligation under the contract, but an

---

[1]   *See, e.g.*, Trib. Padova (Italy), 25 February 2004, available in English at http://cisgw3.law.pace.edu/cisg/wais/db/cases2/040225i3.html.

[2]   *See* Supreme Court of Germany, 3 April 1996, available in English at http://cisgw3.law.pace.edu/cisg/wais/db/cases2/960403g1.html; *contra see* Supreme Court of Switzerland, 15 September 2000, available at http://cisgw3.law.pace.edu/cisg/text/000915s1french.html.

ancillary one can [thus] be fundamental",[3] as long as the obligation is closely connected to the exchange of goods or the parties have subjected it to the rules of the CISG. It is therefore not surprising that a French court has applied Article 25 to the breach of a contractually agreed upon re–import prohibition.[4] Nor is it surprising that a German court has held that "the buyer may, in accordance with Article 49(1)(a) CISG, request the avoidance of the contract if the non–performance constitutes a fundamental breach of the contract, which may also be the case where an ancillary obligation arising for instance from an exclusivity agreement is breached."[5]

It is worth pointing out that Article 25 CISG does not distinguish between the various types of breaches either,[6] but rather creates a unitary concept of the breach of contract.

A "fundamental breach" further requires that the damaged party suffers a detriment such that that party is substantially deprived of what it could have expected under the contract. The term "detriment", which is not being used in any other provision of the

---

[3]   *See* OLG Frankfurt (Germany), 17 September 1991, available in English at http://cisgw3.law.pace.edu/cisg/wais/db/cases2/910917g1.html.

[4]   *See* CA Grenoble (France), 22 February 1995, available in English at http://cisgw3.law.pace.edu/cisg/wais/db/cases2/950222f1.html.

[5]   OLG Koblenz (Germany), 31 January 1997, available in English at http://cisgw3.law.pace.edu/cases/970131g1.html.

[6]   *See* Supreme Court of Germany, 3 April 1996, available in English at http://cisgw3.law.pace.edu/cisg/wais/db/cases2/960403g1.html.

CISG, must be interpreted extensively and is not to be analogized to the concept of "damages" referred to in Article 74. The concept of "detriment" comprises all (actual and future) negative consequences of any possible breach of contract, not only actual and future monetary loss, but any kind of negative consequences.

A breach of contract is fundamental when the detriment suffered by the damaged party is such that it is "substantially deprived of what [the party] is entitled to expect under the contract". From the wording of Article 25 CISG it can be derived that the fundamental nature of the breach does not depend on the extent of the detriment,[7] but rather on the impairment of the justified contractual expectations of the damaged party.[8] This impairment must be so serious that it leads to the injured party losing interest in the performance of the contract, or that the injured party can no longer be expected to be satisfied with less drastic remedies such as damages, price reduction or repair.[9] This is in line with the general principle underlying the CISG according to which the avoidance of the contract in cases of fundamental

---

[7] *See* Supreme Court of Switzerland, 15 September 2000, available in English at http://cisgw3.law.pace.edu/cisg/wais/db/cases2/000915s1.html.

[8] *See* HG Kanton Aargau (Switzerland), 5 November 2002, available in English at http://cisgw3.law.pace.edu/cisg/wais/db/cases2/021105s1.html.

[9] *See* Supreme Court of Germany, 28 October 1998, available in English at http://cisgw3.law.pace.edu/cases/981028s1.html.

breach should constitute an *ultima ratio* remedy.[10] Whether the impairment is, in fact, of such seriousness must be decided on a case–by–case basis. However, it is possible to identify certain lines of cases that strongly suggest the existence of a fundamental breach of contract. These lines of cases will be examined *infra*.

It can be derived from the wording of Article 25 that the extent of the detrimental consequences of a breach of contract must be assessed by reference to what the damaged party "could have expected under the contract". This assessment must be based on the objective contractual expectations of the aggrieved party as they result from the specific contract. This is a matter of contract interpretation, which requires one to turn not only to the contractual language, but also to the practice established between the parties, as well as other circumstances preceding the conclusion of the contract (such as the contractual negotiations).

The interpretation is unproblematic when the parties have (without the use of standard contract terms) expressly or tacitly agreed that a particular obligation or a specific kind of detriment must be regarded as fundamental. The situation is more difficult when the parties use standard terms. In this respect, it must be observed that the validity of such standard terms must be determined in

---

[10]   *See, e.g.*, Supreme Court of Austria, 7 September 2000, available in English at http://cisgw3.law.pace.edu/cases/000907 a3.html.

accordance with the applicable domestic law, since the CISG itself does not deal with this issue.

Where the parties have not themselves specified the importance of the various contractual obligations, that importance must be determined on the basis of the rules of contract interpretation set forth by the CISG itself, namely Article 8 CISG.

A breach of contract is not fundamental when the defaulting party did not foresee the detrimental consequences and when a reasonable person of the same kind in the same circumstances would not have foreseen those consequences. From this, it can be derived that one must not only take into account the actual subjective knowledge of the party in breach; but rather, one also has to inquire into whether an average party to the same kind of contract involved and in the same circumstances would have foreseen the result. This objective evaluation is mandated by Article 8(2).

Unlike the ULIS, the CISG does not specify which moment in time is relevant for the determination of the foreseeability. The majority opinion considers that the relevant moment is the time of the conclusion of the contract, while some commentators suggest also taking into consideration information communicated after the conclusion of the contract. In these authors' view, the majority opinion is preferable. This is due to the fact that the fundamental nature of the breach relates to the legitimate expectations "under the contract", *i.e.*, the expectations set forth in the contract and, thus, at the time of the contract conclusion. Allowing for communications made after the conclusion of the contract to become relevant would mean to allow for a unilateral modification of the balance of the parties' interests as laid down in the contract.

Although the existence of a fundamental breach has to be evaluated on a case–by–case basis, as mentioned earlier, it is possible to establish different lines of situations which more easily allow for such an evaluation.

In the case of definite non–performance, the aggrieved party is essentially deprived of what it could have expected under the contract. A definite non–performance must thus be considered as a fundamental breach of contract in the sense of Article 25 CISG,[11] and this must be considered independently from whether the definite non–performance is due to objective or subjective impossibility.

An unjustified and definite refusal to perform must be assimilated to the definite non–performance, at least as long as the refusal is not limited to a secondary obligation. Whether a specific declaration or a particular behavior amounts at all to a definite refusal to perform (rather than to a mere inquiry into whether there is a willingness to terminate the contract) is an issue of interpretation to be solved on the grounds of Article 8 CISG.

---

[11] *See* Pretura Parma–Fidenza (Italy), 24 November 1989, available in English at http://cisgw3.law.pace.edu/cisg/wais/db/cases2/891124i3.html.

As for the delivery of defective goods, it only amounts to a fundamental breach of contract when the defect is such that the aggrieved party cannot be expected to be satisfied with damages or a price reduction.[12] This is in line with the general principle underlying the CISG pursuant to which the upholding of the contract is to be preferred over its termination.[13] Thus, the delivery of defective goods, the defect of which can only be cured within an unreasonable period of time or with excessive efforts on the part of the party in breach, must generally be considered a fundamental breach of contract.[14] Consequently, an easy and expeditious possibility and willingness by the party in breach to repair the defect excludes the breach from being fundamental, "[s]ince, as long and insofar as (even) a serious defect may be cured through repair or substitute delivery, performance by the seller remains possible and the buyer's interest in performance is intact. According to legal writers and case law under the CISG, a serious defect does therefore not constitute a fundamental breach of contract if the defect can be cured and the seller is willing to do so, as long as

---

[12]   *See* Supreme Court of Germany, 3 April 1996, available in English at http://cisgw3.law.pace.edu/cisg/wais/db/cases2/960403g1.html; OLG Köln (Germany), 14 October 2002, available in English at http://cisgw3.law.pace.edu/cisg/wais/db/cases2/021014g1.html.

[13]   *See* HG Kanton Aargau (Switzerland), 5 November 2002, available in English at http://cisgw3.law.pace.edu/cisg/wais/db/cases2/021105s1.html.

[14]   *See* OLG Köln (Germany), 14 October 2002, available in English at http://cisgw3.law.pace.edu/cisg/wais/db/cases2/021014g1.html.

the buyer does not suffer undue delay or any other burden."[15] This reasoning also applies where the defective goods can, without disproportionate additional efforts or in the context of the ordinary business activity, be used or sold[16] (albeit only to knockdown prices). This is also true with respect to the delivery of an *aliud*, unless the buyer has a particular interest in a specific good.

Like the late delivery of conforming documents, the delivery of non–conforming documents can also constitute a fundamental breach. In respect of this line of cases as well, in determining whether a breach is fundamental, one must also take into account the possibility of curing the defect by means of reasonable efforts as well as the possibility of using the goods despite the defect. The same is true in respect of packaging defects: as long as they do not considerably affect the interests of the buyer as laid down in the contract, they do not constitute a fundamental breach.[17]

It should be noted that a mere delay in delivery of the goods does not amount *per se* to a fundamental

---

[15]   HG Kanton Aargau (Switzerland), 5 November 2002, available in English at http://cisgw3.law.pace.edu/cisg/wais/db/cases2/021105s1.html.

[16]   *See* OLG Köln (Germany), 14 October 2002, available in English at http://cisgw3.law.pace.edu/cisg/wais/db/cases2/021014g1.html.

[17]   *See* Supreme Court of Germany, 8 March 1995, available in English at http://cisgw3.law.pace.edu/cisg/wais/db/cases2/950308g3.html.

breach.[18] Late delivery can only be considered a fundamental breach of contract where compliance with a particular deadline is essential for the buyer. This can be derived from either the agreement of the parties, the practice established between them, or the usages that bind the parties pursuant to Article 9 CISG.[19]

As far as the principal obligation of the buyer is concerned, it must be observed that a mere delay in payment does not generally constitute a fundamental breach under the CISG. Typically, the buyer's failure to take delivery of the goods does not constitute a fundamental breach of contract either. The breach of the obligation to take delivery constitutes a fundamental breach only when the seller has a particular interest in the timely taking of delivery on the part of the buyer or when the failure to take delivery is due to a definite refusal to do so.

As far as the breach of additional obligations is concerned, it only amounts to a fundamental breach when it leads to a serious impairment of the legitimate interests of the aggrieved party in the sense discussed above.[20] This may be the case, for

---

[18]   *See* OLG München (Germany), 1 July 2002, available in English at http://cisgw3.law.pace.edu/cisg/wais/db/cases2/020701 g1.html.

[19]   *See* OLG Düsseldorf (Germany), 24 April 1997, available in English at http://cisgw3.law.pace.edu/cisg/wais/db/cases2/ 970424g1.html.

[20]   *See supra* Chapter 2, Section 2.

instance, where an exclusivity agreement or a prohibition to re–import the goods is breached.

It must also be observed that the breach of an obligation is not necessarily "fundamental" only because that breach is malicious. This is due to the fact, mentioned earlier already, that the fundamental nature of the breach is not linked to the importance of the breach, but rather to the impairment of an (important) interest of the creditor. Only where the malicious behavior negatively impacts on the trust between the parties that is essential to the contractual relationship (as in those cases, where the defaulting party has to still perform some other obligations) can the maliciousness itself turn an ordinary breach into a fundamental one.

2. CLAIM FOR SUBSTITUTE GOODS

The distinction between a fundamental and non–fundamental breach is of utmost relevance to the remedial system provided for under the CISG. Under the Convention, the minimum requirement that the debtor has to comply with in order to substantially perform (and thus in order not to commit a fundamental breach) is the fulfilment of the creditor's substantial reasonable expectations under the contract. Substantial performance thus prevents the consequences of a fundamental breach from being invoked, although it still does not fully discharge the obligor, as other less drastic remedies to react against minor non–compliances are made available to the aggrieved party. If it is determined that substantial performance has not been rendered by the obligor, then the aggrieved party is granted more drastic remedies, which under the CISG are made conditional upon the non–performance amounting to a fundamental breach. These remedies for fundamental breach include, in particular, avoidance of the contract and the right to claim substitute goods.

The basic approach to remedies under the CISG makes it generally possible for the aggrieved party to claim from the obligor performance of his contractual obligations, either as originally arranged by the parties, or in an adapted form reflecting the fact that at least one of the parties has not perfectly complied with his obligations. This rule is explicitly set forth as regards both the remedies available to the buyer in the event of a breach committed by the seller, and the remedies available to the seller in the event of breach by the buyer. In light of the possible different types of non–performances, however, the rule may be read in slightly different manners. If the obligor fails to perform his obligation entirely, the aggrieved obligee has the right to require the entire performance of the obligation. If the obligor's performance does not comply with the requirements agreed upon (*i.e.*, if the breach takes the form of a non–conformity of the goods, or that of an incomplete performance, or if the goods are delivered to a place other than that agreed upon by the parties), the aggrieved party has the right to require that performance be adjusted to make it comply with the contractual arrangements. In both cases, the remedy accessible to the aggrieved party aims toward the perfect completion of the contractual bargain as originally agreed upon by the parties.

Given the foregoing general principles, with regard to the remedies available to the buyer, Article 46 CISG provides the buyer with a general right to require performance from the seller. This right may take different forms, depending on the type of breach committed by the seller. In particular, if the seller delivers goods that do not conform with the contractual arrangements, the buyer has the right to require substitute goods, but only to the extent that three separate pre–requisites are met. First, the aggrieved buyer has a right to require substitute goods only if the seller has delivered non–conforming goods; secondly, the non–conformity of the goods must amount to a fundamental breach of contract; thirdly, the request for substitute goods must be made by the buyer in conjunction with, or shortly after, the notice of non–conformity required under Article 39 CISG. If these pre–requisites are met, then the buyer is entitled to require substitute goods.[21]

The first pre–requisite mentioned above merely restates that the obligee's right to claim a remedy arises only to the extent that the obligor failed to

---

[21]   *See*, *e.g.*, China International Economic and Trade Arbitration Commission (CIETAC), Arbitral Award of 24 July 2007, available in English at http://cisgw3.law.pace.edu/cases/070724c1.html.

duly perform his obligations. The criteria for evaluating the conformity of performance are to be drawn from the contract or the Convention, in accordance with Article 35 CISG.

The second pre–requisite is a substantive one and relates to the severity of the non–conformity. It constitutes a significant limitation to the buyer's right to require substitute goods, since the remedy is not available unless the non–conformity results— pursuant to Article 25 CISG—in a detriment that substantially deprives the buyer of the benefits that he legitimately expected under the contract, and such detriment was objectively foreseeable.[22] In particular, on the basis of this limitation, several court decisions maintained that the buyer cannot claim substitute goods if he can reasonably use the goods or resell them, even with a rebate.[23] Similarly, other courts held that, even if the goods are seriously defective, the remedy of their substitution is precluded if they can easily be repaired,[24] taking into due consideration the proportionality of the costs and efforts that a substitution would require.[25]

---

[22] Supreme Court of Poland, 11 May 2007, available in English at http://cisgw3.law.pace.edu/cases/070511p1.html.

[23] *See, e.g.,* Supreme Court of Germany, 3 April 1996, available in English at http://cisgw3.law.pace.edu/cases/960403 g1.html.

[24] *See* HG Kanton Zürich (Switzerland), 26 April 1995, available in English at http://cisgw3.law.pace.edu/cases/950426 s1.html.

[25] *See* China International Economic and Trade Arbitration Commission (CIETAC), Arbitral Award of 11 November 2002, available in English at http://cisgw3.law.pace.edu/cases/021111 c1.html.

Finally, the CISG also provides for a temporal requirement in order for the remedy of substitution of goods to be available. The remedy will therefore not be available unless the buyer acts promptly after the goods are delivered to him. He must first examine the goods in as short a period as is practicable in the circumstances; then, he must give notice of the non–conformity to the seller within a reasonable time; finally, he must claim substitution of the goods in conjunction with, or shortly after, the notice of non–conformity.[26]

Should the non–conformity of the goods not amount to a fundamental breach, or should the buyer fail to make a timely request for substitute goods, the remedy of substitution of the goods will not be available to the buyer. Moreover, Article 82(1) CISG sets forth another limitation to the buyer's right to require the seller to deliver substitute goods. In fact, the buyer loses the right to substitution "if it is impossible for him to make restitution of the goods substantially in the condition in which he received them". If the buyer is, in practice, barred from requiring substitute goods, he can only require performance of the contractual obligation as originally agreed upon in the form of the repair of the goods by the seller, to the extent that it is reasonable to claim repair of the goods. Otherwise, the only option to compel

---

[26] *See* Foreign Trade Court attached to the Serbian Chamber of Commerce (Serbia), Arbitral Award of 5 January 2007, available in English at http://cisgw3.law.pace.edu/cases/070105sb.html.

performance of the contract (in an adjusted form) is to claim reduction of the purchase price. However, relevant exceptions to the limitation set out in Article 82(1) CISG are provided for in the subsequent paragraph. Accordingly, the buyer may claim substitute goods, even if he cannot make restitution of the goods substantially in the condition in which he received them, if either one of three circumstances occurs. First, if the impossibility of making restitution "is not due to [the buyer's] act or omission." Second, if the goods or part of the goods have perished or deteriorated "as a result of the examination" provided for under Article 38 CISG. Third, if the goods or part thereof have been sold, or have been consumed or transformed in the normal course of business or use before the buyer "discovered or ought to have discovered the lack of conformity."

As pointed out above,[27] the substantive right to claim substitute goods under Article 46 CISG is of limited benefit in cases where the seller is not willing to cooperate, if that right is not accompanied by legal tools making the enforcement of that right possible. Therefore, in a situation where the buyer intends to claim substitution and the seller does not spontaneously satisfy the buyer's claim, it is necessary to verify the availability to the buyer of a judgment for specific performance compelling the delivery of substitute goods. This evaluation must be made on the basis of Article 28 CISG, according to which a national court "is not bound to enter a

---

[27]   *See* Chapter 8, Section 2.

judgment for specific performance unless the court would do so under its own law in respect of similar contracts of sale not governed by" the CISG. Domestic courts are thus urged to proceed in the very same manner they would with respect to a domestic contract, a solution which has already been commented on by saying that Article 28 CISG operates so as to restrict the availability of a claim for substitution of the goods on the basis of the domestic law of the forum.[28]

3.   AVOIDANCE AND ITS EFFECTS

As pointed out before, the CISG largely favors remedies leading to the performance of the contractual obligations over remedies that bring the contract to an end. Accordingly, avoidance of the contract is treated in the CISG as an *extrema ratio* remedy, available only with respect to failures to duly perform that meet the standard of a "fundamental breach" of contract in the sense of Article 25 CISG. Moreover, the aggrieved party loses his right to declare the contract avoided if he does not do so by means of a reasonably clear notice given to the other party in due course.

The CISG's preference for the performance of the contract and thus the completion of the contractual bargain is also substantially enhanced by the broad opportunity granted to the party in breach to "cure" its non–complying performance and therefore to

---

[28]   *See* HG Bern (Switzerland), 22 December 2004, available in English at http://cisgw3.law.pace.edu/cases/041222s1.html.

prevent the avoidance of the contract. Consistently, the CISG grants to the party in breach not a mere possibility to cure, but rather a full–fledged right to remedy whenever the circumstances make the cure possible without unreasonably burdening the aggrieved party. In particular, this conclusion can be drawn in light of the provision set out in Article 48 CISG: subject only to the condition that the contract has not already been declared avoided because of the fundamental nature of the breach, the seller may, "even after the date for delivery, remedy [. . .] any failure to perform his obligations." This rule, however, should not be misunderstood, as it does not imply, as wrongly affirmed by some court decisions,[29] that the buyer is not entitled to declare the contract avoided in the event of a fundamental breach, as long as the seller has offered remediation, or as long as remediation is possible. Of course, the need to grant to the seller the opportunity to remedy any kind of defect may be stipulated by the parties in their contract;[30] however, failing such stipulation, it cannot be disputed that in the event of a fundamental breach the aggrieved party may declare the contract avoided, without the need to grant to the party in breach a prior opportunity to cure his performance.

---

[29]   *See* HG Kanton Aargau (Switzerland), 5 November 2002, available in English at http://cisgw3.law.pace.edu/cases/021105 s1.html.

[30]   *See* Federal Court of Australia, 20 May 2009 (*Olivaylle Pty. Ltd. v. Flottweg GmbH & Co KGAA*), available at http://cisg w3.law.pace.edu/cases/090520a2.html.

In any event, as expressly specified by Article 26 CISG, a notice from the aggrieved party to the party in breach is necessary in order to avoid the contract. The Convention does not provide for an *ipso facto* avoidance of contract, but, in order to ensure that the party in breach knows about the coming–to–an–end of the contractual relationship, it requires that a notice of avoidance be given.[31] The only exceptions to this rule apply either if the parties stipulate in their agreement a mechanism for automatic termination of the contract upon the occurrence of certain circumstances, or—given the informative purpose of the notice under Article 26 CISG that has just been highlighted—if the obligor "unambiguously" declares that he will not perform.[32]

In accordance with the general principle of informality laid down in Article 11 CISG, no particular forms or formalisms are required for the notice of avoidance and even a statement that "the glass if full" has been regarded as an effective declaration of avoidance.[33] The solution adopted in this bizarre case seems too extreme and cannot be shared; nonetheless it is correct to affirm that the

---

[31] *See* Audiencia Provincial de Navarra (Spain), 27 December 2007, available in English at http://cisgw3.law.pace.edu/cases/071227s4.html.

[32] *Accord*, OLG München (Germany), 15 September 2004, available in English at http://cisgw3.law.pace.edu/cases/040915g2.html.

[33] *See* RB Koophandel Kortrijk (Belgium), 4 June 2004, available in English at http://cisgw3.law.pace.edu/cases/040604b1.html.

sole requirement for an effective declaration of avoidance is that in the notice be expressed with sufficient clarity that the party making the declaration intends to bring the contract to an end. Accordingly, a declaration subject to conditions and further declarations that the contract will be avoided in the future, after a certain period of time, or to the extent that the party in breach does not take action to cure, cannot be regarded as effective notices of avoidance and a subsequent notice to that effect must be given by the aggrieved party intending to bring the contract to an end.

From a substantive point of view, under Article 49(1)(*a*) CISG, only in the event of a fundamental breach committed by the seller (as defined under Article 25 CISG) can the buyer declare the contract avoided. On the other hand, under Article 64(1)(*a*) CISG, the seller is entitled to declare the contract avoided only when the buyer's non–performance (that is, his refusal to take delivery or, more commonly, his failure to pay the price) amounts to a fundamental breach of the contract. Overall, the CISG aims at preserving the parties' commitments and encouraging the performance of their obligations, thus relying on a general principle of *favor contractus*. The Convention does this by granting to the breaching party a right to cure the breach. Moreover, the Convention favors the completion of the contractual project also by limiting the availability of claims for the avoidance of the contract, which are relegated to the role of *extrema ratio* remedies.

A superficial reading of the provisions of the CISG might suggest a different conclusion about the possibility to declare the contract avoided. Such a conclusion, in fact, might be inferred from the fact that both Article 49(1)(*b*) and Article 64(1)(*b*) CISG refer to alternative grounds for avoidance, in that they both provide that avoidance of the contract may be declared as a consequence of the persistent lack of cure of the breach, notwithstanding an additional period of time of reasonable length granted to that effect by the aggrieved party to the party in breach.

However, a closer look at the language of the rules providing for this mechanism—often referred to as *Nachfrist* after the German model to this rule—suggests that the availability of these alternative grounds for avoiding the contract is rather limited. Indeed, Article 49(1)(*b*) CISG expressly limits the availability to the buyer of the *Nachfrist* mechanism to the "case of non–delivery."[34] Similarly, Article 64(1)(*b*) limits the availability to the seller of the same mechanism to the case of buyer's failure to "perform his obligation to pay the price or take delivery of the goods."[35] Hence, not every kind of breach makes it possible to avoid the contract in the event of persistent non–performance after the expiration of the additional time granted

---

[34]   *See* KG Schaffhausen (Switzerland), 27 January 2004, available in available at http://cisgw3.law.pace.edu/cases/040127 s1.html.

[35]   *See* ICC Court of Arbitration, Arbitral Award n. 8574 of September 1996, available in English at http://cisgw3.law.pace. edu/cases/968574i1.html.

by the aggrieved party. To the contrary, the *Nachfrist* mechanism is available only in the event that one of the fundamental obligations expressly referred to by the aforementioned provisions has not been performed at all. Accordingly, the buyer has the right to avoid the contract after an additional period of time only if "delivery" of the goods has not taken place at all; the seller has the right to avoid the contract after an additional period of time only if "payment" has not taken place at all, or if the buyer persists in not "taking delivery" of the goods. Therefore, partial performances and non-conforming performances preclude the possibility to trigger the *Nachfrist* mechanism, although they do not preclude avoidance of contract (irrespective of the *Nachfrist* mechanism) whenever such partial or defective performance amounts in itself to a fundamental breach. The mechanism in question allows, as a final result, the avoidance of the contract in situations where the original non-performance might not have qualified as a fundamental breach, provided that the debtor fails to perform within the additional period of time granted to him.[36] This suggests that the rationale behind the mechanism is primarily to prevent disputes as to the fundamental nature of the obligor's delay in performance.

---

[36]   *Accord*, *e.g.*, China International Economic and Trade Arbitration Commission (CIETAC), Arbitral Award of 19 December 1997, available in English at http://cisgw3.law.pace.edu/cases/971219c1.html.

Not only does the CISG require a fundamental breach of contract and an express notice to the effect of avoiding the contract, but in cases where one of the basic obligations of the sale has been performed, it also requires that the notice be given within a "reasonable time." It is of particular significance to point out that the consequences of this temporal requirement are provided by both Article 49(2) and Article 64(2) CISG. Indeed, the acknowledgment of the existence of a "duty to avoid the contract within a reasonable time" implies that a late declaration to that effect is to be regarded as ineffective, notwithstanding the fundamental nature of the breach committed by the non–performing party.

Under Article 49(2) CISG the requirement that the notice of avoidance be given within a "reasonable time" applies in the event that "the seller has delivered the goods". Similarly, under Article 64(2) CISG the same temporal requirement applies if "the buyer has paid the price". On the contrary, the buyer's right to declare the contract avoided is not subject to any time limitation as long as the seller has not delivered the goods, and the seller's right to declare the contract avoided is not restricted as long as the buyer has not paid the price.

If the temporal requirement applies, the time as of which the reasonable time period begins to run varies depending on the circumstances of the case. In respect of "late deliveries" by the seller, under Article 49(2)(*a*) the buyer must declare the contract avoided within a reasonable time "after he has become aware that delivery has been made". A more articulated rule applies, on the other hand, in respect of "any breach [of the seller] other than late delivery." In fact, three alternatives are set out in Article 49(2)(*b*) in order to determine the moment from which the reasonable time for notice of avoidance runs. First, as a general rule, the buyer must give notice of avoidance of the contract within reasonable time "[a]fter he knew or ought to have known of the breach."[37] However, if the buyer fixed an additional period of time for performance by the seller, the buyer can declare the contract avoided only after the expiration of that additional time, or after the seller's express declaration that he will not perform within that additional time. Finally, if in accordance with Article 48(2) CISG, the seller requested whether the buyer would accept performance within a certain additional time and the buyer did not object to this possibility, then the buyer can declare the contract avoided only after the expiration of that additional time indicated in the seller's request, or after the seller's express declaration that he will not perform within the additional time indicated in his request.

Similarly, under Article 64(2)(*a*) CISG (which only applies "in cases where the buyer has paid the price"), the seller must give notice of avoidance in respect of late performances by the buyer "before [he] has become aware that performance has been

---

[37]   *See* Supreme Court of Switzerland, 18 May 2009, available in English at http://cisgw3.law.pace.edu/cases/090518s1 .html.

rendered". A more differentiated rule, on the other hand, applies in respect of any breach other than late performance by the buyer. In fact, under Article 64(2)(*b*), the seller must give notice of avoidance within a reasonable time after he "knew or ought to have known of the breach";[38] however, if additional time was granted to the buyer to cure his performance, the seller can give notice of avoidance only after the expiration of the additional period of time fixed by the seller, or after the buyer's declaration that he will not perform his obligations within the additional period of time.

The aforementioned articulated rules serve the purpose of identifying the moment as of which the reasonable time begins to run. Once that moment has been determined, the issue must be addressed of what constitutes "reasonable time" within which the notice of avoidance must be given by the aggrieved party. However, this issue cannot be solved by providing an abstract general rule; instead, a case–by–case analysis must be conducted on the basis of the specific circumstances of the case and in view of the fair balancing of the interests involved. Just to provide some examples, a notice of avoidance delivered about forty days after the buyer ought to have known of the seller's breach was regarded as given within a reasonable time, thus bringing the

---

[38]   *See* ICC Court of Arbitration, Arbitral Award n. 11849, available in English at http://cisgw3.law.pace.edu/cases/031849i1.html.

contract to an end;[39] whereas, a notice given five months after the buyer was informed of the breach was regarded as unreasonably late and therefore ineffective.[40]

The notion of fundamental breach is the most relevant tool serving the purpose of limiting the possibility for a declaration of avoidance. However, avoidance of the contract on the part of the buyer is also significantly limited in light of the possible effects of that remedy with respect to the subsequent need for restitution. Indeed, avoidance of the contract has the effect of releasing the parties from their obligations. However, it may often be the case that the parties (either one of them, or both) have already performed their obligations at the time when the contract is avoided; avoidance thus gives rise to a claim for restitution of whatever the parties have supplied and/or paid. Under Article 82 CISG, however, the buyer's possibility to declare the contract avoided is limited in that he can only do so if it is possible to make restitution of the goods "substantially in the condition in which [the buyer] received them." Although relevant exceptions to that rule apply under Article 82(2) CISG, it is apparent that the provision at hand further justifies the conclusion that contract avoidance is largely disfavored by the CISG, which conversely aims at

---

[39]   *See* Supreme Court of Switzerland, 18 May 2009, available in English at http://cisgw3.law.pace.edu/cases/090518s1.html.

[40]   *See* Supreme Court of Germany, 15 February 1995, available in English at http://cisgw3.law.pace.edu/cases/950215g1.html.

favoring the completion of the contractual bargain whenever possible.

As mentioned above, avoidance of the contract has the effect of releasing the parties from their obligations. Article 81(1) CISG expressly acknowledges this effect of a declaration of avoidance, although "subject to any damages which may be due". It should be noted that the rule at hand, and the ones set forth in the following Articles contained in Section V on "Effects of avoidance" (*i.e.*, Articles 81 to 84 CISG), operate only with respect to unilateral avoidance declared on the grounds of Article 49, or Article 64 CISG. Conversely, the rules on "Effects of avoidance" laid out in the Convention do not apply in the event of termination of the contract by mutual consent, which is entirely governed by the parties' termination agreement.[41] Moreover, avoidance of the contract does not have the effects of a complete annulment of the contract in that, under Article 81(1), "[a]voidance does not affect any provision of the contract for the settlement of disputes or any other provision of the contract governing the rights and obligations of the parties consequent upon the avoidance of the contract". More generally, it has been held that contract avoidance changes the nature of the

---

[41]   *Accord*, *e.g.*, Tribunal of International Commercial Arbitration at the Russian Federation Chamber of Commerce and Industry (Russian Federation), Arbitral Award n. 82/1996 of 3 March 1997, available in English at http://cisgw3.law.pace.edu /cases/970303r1.html.

contractual relationship "into a winding–up relationship."[42]

If the prerequisites for avoidance of the contract are met and a proper notice of avoidance is given, the declaration of avoidance made by either party releases both parties from their obligations. On the other hand, failure to effectively avoid the contract (*e.g.*, because of the lack of a proper notice, or because of the non–fundamental nature of the breach) causes the parties to remain bound to the original terms of the agreement.[43] As mentioned above, avoidance does not completely annul the contract, but rather changes the scope and goals of the relationship between the parties, thus leaving some contractual obligations intact. In particular, avoidance does not affect the right of the party who suffered damage to claim compensation from the party in breach under Article 74 ff. CISG. Moreover, under Article 81(2) if a party has performed the contract either wholly or in part, he "may claim restitution from the other party of whatever the [performing] party supplied or paid under the contract." If both parties have performed the contract, both of them are bound to the restitutionary obligation and the mutual restitutions must be performed concurrently.

---

[42]   *See* Supreme Court of Austria, 29 June 1999, available in English at http://cisgw3.law.pace.edu/cases/990629a3.html.

[43]   *See* Supreme Court of Germany, 4 December 1996, available in English at http://cisgw3.law.pace.edu/cases/961204 g1.html.

The buyer's right to declare the contract avoided may be precluded, under Article 82(1) CISG, in the event that the buyer cannot return the goods "substantially in the condition in which he received them". The limitation to the buyer's right clearly does not apply whenever the buyer is in the position to return the goods exactly in the condition in which he received them. The puzzling question stemming from the provision under consideration, however, is up to what degree of alteration the goods can still be regarded as being "substantially" in the condition in which the buyer received them. Called upon to deal with this issue, the Supreme Court held that the buyer loses the right to declare the contract avoided under Article 82(1) CISG only in cases where "the condition of the goods has changed in such a way that it would be unreasonable to expect the seller to redeem the goods."[44] In these authors' view, it is not necessary to interpret Article 82(1) in a way that favors restitution in cases of relevant alteration of the goods, where this causes detriment to the seller receiving restitution. This conclusion is, in fact, supported by the consideration that the resulting harshness of the rule of Article 82(1) is significantly alleviated by the exceptions provided for under Article 82(2) CISG. The presence of relevant exceptions in paragraph (2) of the provision at hand thus makes the need to introduce some flexibility in the construction of the rule in paragraph (1) less urgent.

---

[44] *See* Supreme Court of Switzerland, 18 May 2009, available in English at http://cisgw3.law.pace.edu/cases/090518 s1.html.

Indeed, Article 82(2) CISG sets forth three extremely relevant and broad exceptions to the limitation provided under Article 82(1) to the buyer's right to declare the contract avoided. Accordingly, if any one of the three situations described in the sub–paragraphs of Article 82(2) occurs, then the buyer can declare the contract avoided, and he can do so even if it is impossible for him to make restitution of the goods substantially in the condition in which he received the goods. If this happens, Article 84(2)(*b*) provides that the buyer must account to the seller for all benefits that the buyer has derived from the goods or part of them.

The first exception to the rule limiting the availability of the right to declare the contract avoided is laid down in sub–paragraph (*a*) of Article 82(2): even if the buyer is unable to give restitution of goods substantially in the condition in which he received them, he can nonetheless declare the contract avoided if such impossibility "is not due to his act or omission". The rule at hand is based on an objective criterion of causal link between the buyer's act or omission and the impossibility of restitution of goods in the pre–existing condition;[45] no relevance, to the contrary, should be attributed to a subjective element of negligence in the buyer's act or omission. Article 82(2)(*b*) provides the second exception to the rule limiting the right to declare the contract avoided. In particular, it preserves the

---

[45]   *Accord* Supreme Court of Austria, 29 June 1999, available in English at http://cisgw3.law.pace.edu/cases/990629 a3.html.

buyer's right to avoidance where his inability to make restitution of the goods in the pre–existing condition is due to the fact that "the goods or part of the goods have perished or deteriorated as a result of the examination provided for in Article 38."[46] Finally, the third exception applies under Article 82(2)(*c*) CISG if the goods have been "sold in the normal course of business", or have been "consumed or transformed by the buyer in the course of normal use", provided that the act of disposition or transformation took place before the buyer "discovered or ought to have discovered the lack of conformity". Therefore, under the provision at hand a buyer operating in the usual course of business, whether by reselling products or transforming them, is in most cases in the position to react to a fundamental breach by declaring the contract avoided. The buyer can do so even if he is unable to make restitution of the goods substantially in the condition in which he received them.

The broad spectrum of exceptions to the rule limiting the availability of the right to avoid the contract under Article 82(1) leads to the conclusion that, in practice, the rule applies to a much smaller number of cases than the exceptions do. However, if the rule applies and the buyer is precluded from declaring the contract avoided, under Article 83 the buyer retains all other remedies under the contract

---

[46]   *See, e.g.*, Supreme Court of Germany, 25 June 1997, available in English at http://cisgw3.law.pace.edu/cases/970625g2 .html.

and the CISG, including repair of the goods, price reduction and damages.

As a consequence of avoidance of the contract, not only is the buyer bound to make restitution of the goods, but also the seller is bound to refund the price. According to Article 84(1) CISG the duty to refund the price is accompanied by the obligation to pay interest at a rate to be determined according to the same criteria examined with respect to Article 78 CISG.[47] Moreover, the buyer must account to the seller for all benefits which he has derived from the goods, not only in the event of restitution of the goods, but also if it is impossible for him to make restitution substantially in the condition in which he received the goods.

A relevant issue, which is highly controversial in case law addressing the matter of the effects of avoidance, relates to the place where the restitutionary obligation must be performed. Some court decisions held that the issue at hand is not expressly settled in the CISG and that no general principle can be identified, in conformity of which the issue could be settled under Article 7(2) CISG. Accordingly, these courts have come to the conclusion that the issue is governed by the domestic law applicable by virtue of the conflict–of–law rules of the forum.[48] Other courts have taken

---

[47]   *See supra* Chapter 8, Section 4.

[48]   This approach was adopted, *e.g.*, by LG Landshut (Germany), 5 April 1995, available in English at http://cisgw3 .law.pace.edu/cases/950405g1.html; *see* also CA Paris (France), 14

the different view that the CISG's rules on the place of delivery (Article 31 CISG) and on the place of payment (Article 57 CISG) may be applied by analogy also to the restitutionary obligations consequent to the avoidance of the contract.[49] In these authors' view, however, neither one of the foregoing solutions is correct. Instead, as affirmed also by the Supreme Court of Austria,[50] the issue must be resolved pursuant to Article 7(2) CISG, on the basis of the general principles on which the Convention is based. Relevant principles, in particular, may be drawn from the consideration of the close connection between the rules on the place of performance of the obligations of the parties and the rules on the passing of risk. For, it should be recalled that in sales of goods involving carriage, the place of performance of the delivery obligation of the seller is determined, as a general rule, on the basis of where delivery to the first carrier takes place, which in turn coincides with the place where the risk passes from the seller to the buyer. The place of performance of the buyer's restitutionary obligation should thus serve the same purpose of allocating risks efficiently between the parties. Therefore, the restitutionary obligation must take place in the location where the buyer hands the goods over to

---

January 1998, English abstract available at http://cisgw3.law.pace.edu/cases/980114f1.html.

[49]   *See* OLG Hamm (Germany), 5 November 1997, available in English at http://cisgw3.law.pace.edu/cases/971105g1.html.

[50]   *See* Supreme Court of Austria, 29 June 1999, available in English at http://cisgw3.law.pace.edu/cases/990629a3.html.

the first carrier and by means of such handing–over. On the other hand, if no transportation is required, the restitutionary obligation must be performed by placing the goods at the seller's disposal in accordance with rules mirroring (but opposite to) those set forth in Article 31 CISG. In particular, in sales not involving carriage, the buyer may make restitution of the goods by placing them at the disposal of the seller at the particular place where the goods were located (to the extent that this rule may be applied to the specific circumstances of the case), or at the buyer's premises.

As for the seller's obligation to refund the buyer the purchase price paid, a general principle applicable to this matter may be drawn from Article 57(1)(*b*) CISG. According to this general principle, any payment obligation that has to be made against the handing over of the goods or of documents must be performed where the handing over takes place. With respect to the price refund resulting from the avoidance of the contract, this rule is of particular relevance in the event that the restitutionary obligations of the parties are to be performed concurrently under Article 81(2) CISG. In fact, under these circumstances the refund of the price must take place where the restitution of the goods occurs. Otherwise, if the refund of the price does not need to be performed at the same time of the restitution of the goods, the rule applicable may be drawn from the general principle expressed by Article 57(1)(*a*) CISG, which mandates that payment obligations are to be performed at the place of business of the payee.

4.   SUSPENSION OF PERFORMANCE AND ANTICIPATORY BREACH

As pointed out in the previous paragraphs, the CISG contains provisions granting specific remedies in the event of a breach of contract so severe as to amount to a fundamental breach. These provisions are paralleled by others, which grant to the aggrieved party self–defenses and anticipatory remedies in the event of a prospective non–performance. These types of remedies are largely available under the CISG, although only on the ground that specific requirements are met, which indicate that the situation is worsening to the possible detriment of the obligee. In fact, the main purpose of the self–defenses and remedies under consideration here seems to be to induce the party in breach to spontaneously cure. Under Article 71 CISG a party to the sales contract can "suspend" his performance, thus stimulating the party in breach to cure, only if it becomes "apparent" that the other party will not perform. Moreover, Article 72 CISG grants the possibility to the aggrieved party to immediately avoid the contract, only to the extent that it "is clear" that the other party will commit a fundamental breach. The CISG thus appears to be based on the general principle that, in the event of contracts that do not provide for simultaneous performance by both parties, the party bound to perform first deserves protection if it is likely that the other party will commit a breach of contract. [51]

According to Article 71(1) CISG, "a party may suspend the performance of his obligations if, after the conclusion of the contract, it becomes apparent that the other party will not perform a substantial part of his obligations as a result of: (*a*) a serious deficiency in his ability to perform or in his creditworthiness; or (*b*) his conduct in preparing to perform or in performing the contract." If the suspension is rightful under Article 71, the party suspending performance cannot be held to be in breach for his failure to render performance. Otherwise, suspension of performance amounts itself to a breach of contract.[52] Moreover, suspension is possible only in the period of time between the conclusion of the contract and the time when performance is due; after that time the aggrieved party may only resort to the standard remedies for breach of contract.

The first requirement set out by the CISG in order to allow a party to suspend performance is that the prospective non–performance of the other party "becomes apparent". The obligor's inability to perform must thus be objectively recognizable on the basis of the standard of a neutral objective

---

[51]   For a similar statement, *see* Supreme Court of Austria, 8 November 2005, available in English at http://cisgw3.law.pace.edu/cases/051108a3.html.

[52]   *See* Supreme Court of Switzerland, 17 July 2007, available at English at http://cisgw3.law.pace.edu/cases/070717s1.html.

observer. The CISG does not provide specific criteria for determining the degree of certainty required as to the prospective breach; however, the prevailing view requires that the likelihood of a breach amount to a virtual certainty by normal business standards. In addition to the prospective breach becoming apparent, the CISG further requires that it consists of the failure to perform "a substantial part of the [obligor's] obligations," and that it be the result of either one of the two causes set out in subparagraphs (*a*) and (*b*). It is not necessary that the failure to perform amount to a fundamental breach.[53] Nevertheless, as a general rule, the performance of ancillary obligations may not be forced by suspending performance.[54]

As to the various indicia that a breach will be committed, Article 71(1)(*a*) CISG indicates, in the first place, a "serious deficiency in [the] ability to perform." The cause of such deficiency is irrelevant; what is relevant is its effect, consisting of the prospective non–performance. The said deficiency may be either subjective (e.g., insolvency,[55] non–

---

[53]   *See* U.S. District Court [W.D. Mich.], 17 December 2001 (*Shuttle Packaging Systems v. Tsonakis*), available at http://cisg w3.law.pace.edu/cases/011217u1.html.

[54]   OLG Dresden (Germany), 27 December 1999, available at English   at   http://cisgw3.law.pace.edu/cases/991227g1.html; Zurich Chamber of Commerce (Switzerland), Arbitral Award n. 273/95 of 31 May 1996, available at English at http://cisgw3.law. pace.edu/cases/960531s1.html.

[55]   *See* Supreme Court of Austria, 12 February 1998, available in English at http://cisgw3.law.pace.edu/cases/980212a3 .html.

performance of other parallel contracts,[56] expiration of a license, etc.) or objective (e.g., forthcoming strike, fire in the manufacturer's factory, embargo measures, etc.). A deficiency in the seller's ability to perform may be made apparent, for example, by recurrent delays in deliveries in violation of mandatory contractual deadlines, or by the delivery of damaged goods to the buyer or even to third parties if the existence of the defects causes serious doubts regarding the performance of the contract.[57] Another indication that a breach will be committed may consist of the "serious deficiency in [the obligor's] creditworthiness." In order to be relevant under Article 71(1)(a), a serious deficiency in creditworthiness must not have existed at the time of the conclusion of the contract.[58] It occurs, just to give one example, in the event of delays in payments.[59]

Other indicia that a breach of contract will be committed may be drawn under Article 71(1)(b) CISG, which refers to the defaulting party's "conduct in preparing to perform or in performing the contract." Common examples of preliminary

---

[56]   *See* U.S. District Court [S.D.N.Y.], 29 May 2009 (*Doolim Corp. v. R Doll, LLC*), available at http://cisgw3.law.pace.edu/cases/090529u1.html.

[57]   *See* Supreme Court of Austria, 6 February 1996, available in English at http://cisgw3.law.pace.edu/cases/960206a3.html.

[58]   *See* Supreme Court of Switzerland, 17 July 2007, available in English at http://cisgw3.law.pace.edu/cases/070717 ss1.html.

[59]   *See* RB Koophandel Hasselt (Belgium), 1 March 1995, English abstract available at http://cisgw3.law.pace.edu/cases /950301b1.html.

activities which may be relevant under the provision at hand include the making of shipment arrangements (cf. Article 32 CISG), the handing over of documents (cf. Article 34 CISG), the opening of a letter of credit (cf. Article 64 CISG), or the supplying of specifications (cf. Article 65 CISG).

If the conditions of Article 71 CISG are met, any type of performance may be suspended,[60] provided only that a relationship of reciprocity exists between the obligation suspended and the one whose prospective breach is foreseen. Thus, the seller is entitled not only to delay the delivery, but also to interrupt the manufacture of the goods or their procurement if he becomes aware of the buyer's impending insolvency. Similarly, the buyer may not only delay the payment of the price, but also suspend the establishment of a letter of credit, or the organization of the taking over of the goods, if, for example, it becomes apparent that the seller will not deliver the goods. Furthermore, also the seller's remedy obligations to deliver substitute goods, or to repair defective goods, can be suspended on the grounds of Article 71 CISG.

Unlike Article 71(1), which can be invoked by either party to the sales contract, Article 71(2) CISG grants a special right available only to the seller. The provision at hand deals with cases in which, after the goods have been dispatched, it becomes apparent (or, as the provision states, "evident") that

---

[60]   *See, e.g.,* ICC Court of Arbitration, Arbitral Award n. 8786, available at http://cisgw3.law.pace.edu/cases/978786i1 .html.

the buyer will not perform his obligation to pay the price. The seller is thus authorized to exercise a right of "stoppage in transit" by preventing the carrier from handing the goods over to the buyer, even if the buyer holds a document, such as a bill of lading, which entitles him to obtain the goods. It should be noted that the last sentence of Article 71(2) CISG indicates that this paragraph "relates only to the rights in the goods as between the buyer and the seller." In other words, the seller's right to prevent delivery of the goods to the buyer neither impairs the rights of third persons to whom the buyer may have resold the goods, or who may have obtained title in the goods, nor does it affect the relationship between the carrier and the buyer. First, under the CISG, the seller loses the right of stoppage in transit if the buyer has transferred the document to a third party who has taken it for value and in good faith. Second, the CISG does not set forth obligations binding the carrier to comply with the seller's request for stoppage. The carrier may be precluded, under the law applicable, from withholding the goods.

Under Article 71(3) CISG, the party suspending performance "must immediately give notice of the suspension to the other party and must continue with performance if the other party provides adequate assurance of his performance." The notice of suspension must be given immediately.[61] It is

---

[61]   *See* Netherlands Arbitration Institute (The Netherlands), Arbitral Award n. 2319 of 15 October 2002, available at http:// cisgw3.law.pace.edu/cases/021015n1.html.

subject to Article 27 CISG and it is therefore effective upon dispatch, without the need for it being received by the addressee. However, given that the purpose of the notice is to allow the addressee to provide adequate assurance of performance, it is arguably in the interest of the party suspending performance to ensure that the notice of suspension is received by the addressee. Moreover, although the provision at hand does not make an explicit reference to this effect, in these authors' view the notice of suspension must indicate the reasons alleged for suspension, so as to put the other party in the position to provide adequate assurance. Indeed, pursuant to Article 71(3) CISG, the party who has suspended performance "must continue with performance if the other party provides adequate assurance of his performance." In practice, what constitutes "adequate assurance of performance" must be established on a case–by–case basis, although the issue seems to have received little attention, as made apparent by the fact that there are no reported cases dealing with this issue.

Article 71 CISG addresses the issue of a prospective breach of contract in order to grant the right to suspend performance; in particular, it requires the prospective breach to consist of the non–performance of a "substantial part" of the debtor's obligation. Also Article 72 CISG addresses the issue of a prospective breach; however, it does so in order to grant to the party who would suffer from the prospective breach the more trenchant right to declare the contract avoided before the time set for performance. This, however, can only be done to the extent that the prospective breach is a "fundamental" one in the sense of Article 25 CISG, and provided that it is "clear" that a fundamental breach will occur. The wording of Article 72 thus suggests that a very high probability of occurrence of a fundamental breach is necessary.[62] The burden of proving the aforementioned prerequisites rests on the party claiming contract avoidance; however, it has been held that if the obligor expressly declares that he will not perform, the prerequisites for anticipatory repudiation may be deemed to have been met.[63] Similarly, it has been held that if the seller informs that he intends to "sell the materials elsewhere", his conduct amounts to an anticipatory repudiation, thus making avoidance possible under Article 72 CISG.[64]

As regards the first pre–requisite mentioned above, Article 72(1) CISG requires that it be "clear" that the obligor will commit a fundamental breach of contract. Mere suspicion, even if well–founded, is therefore not enough. It is apparent that the degree of certainty required for the application of Article 72

---

[62]   *See* Schiedsgericht der Börse für landwirtschaftliche Produkte in Wien (Austria), Arbitral Award n. S 2/97 of 10 December 1997, available at http://cisgw3.law.pace.edu/cases /971210a3.html.

[63]   *See, e.g.*, China International Economic and Trade Arbitration Commission (CIETAC), Arbitral Award of October 2007, available in English at http://cisgw3.law.pace.edu/cases/ 071000c1.html.

[64]   *See* U.S. District Court [N.D. Ill.], 7 December 1999 (*Magellan International v. Salzgitter Handel*), available at http:// cisgw3.law.pace.edu/cases/991207u1.html.

CISG is higher than that required under Article 71 CISG. However, scholars and courts agree that Article 72 CISG does not require absolute certainty that a breach will be committed, although a very high degree of probability is necessary.[65] The circumstances that caused the probable fundamental breach are irrelevant, unlike under Article 71 CISG, which lists the possible relevant causes of non–performance. According to the Secretariat's Commentary on the predecessor of Article 72 CISG (*i.e.*, Article 63), "the future fundamental breach may be clear either because of the words or actions of the party which constitute a repudiation of the contract or because of an objective fact, such as the destruction of the seller's plant by fire or the imposition of an embargo or monetary controls which will render impossible future performance."[66]

The second requirement set out in Article 72(1) CISG for the innocent party to be entitled to declare the contract avoided is that the suspected breach be a fundamental one, in the sense of Article 25 CISG. This requirement applies to any kind of prospective non–performances likely to occur, irrespective of whether the prospective breach consists of a delayed performance, a partial performance or a defective performance. What matters is only that the

---

[65]   *See, e.g.*, Supreme Court of Queensland (Australia), 17 November 2000 (*Downs Investments Pty Ltd. v. Perwaja Steel SDN BHD*), available at http://cisgw3.law.pace.edu/cases/001117 a2.html.

[66]   *See* SECRETARIAT COMMENTARY OF THE 1978 DRAFT, Art. 63.

impending non–performance would amount to a fundamental breach.

Not unlike Article 71, Article 72(2) CISG sets out the obligor's possibility to provide "adequate assurance of his performance".[67] However, this possibility may be limited in specific cases on the basis of time concerns. In fact, the provision at hand imposes on the party willing to avoid the contract the obligation to give notice of his intent to the other party; however, this duty is limited only to circumstances where "time allows". It is therefore possible to infer that, if time does not allow, the obligee may avoid the contract without a previous notice of his intent, thus depriving the obligor of the possibility of offering "adequate assurance of performance". What is of the essence, in any event, is that the party willing to avoid the contract on the basis of Article 72 CISG gives notice of his intention to avoid the contract due to anticipatory breach. Moreover, such notice must be given to the party in breach prior to the date set for performance. If the party willing to avoid the contract fails to give notice of avoidance prior to the date set for performance, he loses the right to exercise the rights arising from the provision under consideration, although he retains the right to resort to any other (non–anticipatory) remedy available under the contract or the Convention, including the right to

---

[67] *See, e.g.*, U.S. District Court [S.D.N.Y.], 29 May 2009 (*Doolim Corp. v. R Doll, LLC*), available at http://cisgw3.law.pace .edu/cases/090529u1.html.

declare the contract avoided under Article 49(1), or under Article 64(1) CISG.[68]

If a party declares the contract avoided on the basis of an alleged non–performance by the other party, which does not amount to a fundamental breach, it is the party declaring avoidance who may be deemed to have committed a fundamental breach. The other party, whose performance has been rejected, may thus resort to all remedies made available to him for the event of a fundamental breach.

5.   FUNDAMENTAL BREACH IN INSTALLMENT CONTRACTS

According to the definition provided by the Official Commentary to the draft text of the CISG, "[t]he contract calls for the delivery by installments if it requires or authorizes the delivery of goods in separate lots."[69] The issue of installment contracts is dealt with under Article 73 CISG, whose text to a large extent corresponds to that of its predecessor, *i.e.*, Article 75 ULIS. Although the CISG does not expressly state, neither in Article 73 nor elsewhere, that installment contracts are within the scope of application of the Convention, this conclusion can safely be drawn from the very fact that Article 73 CISG provides substantive rules specifically devoted to the kind of contracts under consideration. As a

---

[68]   *See* China International Economic and Trade Arbitration Commission (CIETAC), Arbitral Award of 1989, available in English at http://cisgw3.law.pace.edu/cases/890000c1.html.

[69]   SECRETARIAT COMMENTARY OF THE 1978 DRAFT, Art. 64.

consequence, it is correct to affirm that sales transactions under the CISG are not only discrete ones, but can also be long–term transactions, as confirmed by the fact that Article 73 CISG is not the only provision dealing with partial avoidance. In fact, an effect similar to that provided by Article 73 may occur also under Article 51 CISG, according to which the buyer may trigger all remedies for non–performance available to him in the event of partial or partially defective performance, with respect to the missing or defective part of the performance. However, unlike Article 73, Article 51 CISG is applicable in the event that the contract is supposed to be performed in its entirety. Conversely, Article 73 deals with an on–going relationship between the parties, which suggests that installment contracts need not determine the quantity of individual installments;[70] nor do they need to be characterized by a unitary function of the several installments[71]— as confirmed by the different prerequisites of application of paragraph (3) as opposed to the preceding paragraphs. In light of the foregoing, it is correct to conclude that the long–term installment contracts falling within the sphere of application of the CISG may include several contractual schemes of relational contracts for the supply of goods. These

---

[70] For a court decision stating the same, *see* Schiedsgericht der Handelskammer Hamburg (Germany), Arbitral Award of 21 March 1996, available in English at http://cisgw3.law.pace.edu/cases/960321g1.html.

[71] *See* HG Zürich (Switzerland), 30 November 1998, available in English at http://cisgw3.law.pace.edu/cases/981130s1.html.

are to be treated as a single contract on the basis of a mere subjective element and the parties' intent (the same parties are pursuing a common commercial goal in an on–going relationship), rather than on the basis of an objective element, based on the teleological connection of the single supplies in view of the pursuance of an overall unitary commercial venture.

Article 73 CISG deals with installment contracts only to a limited extent, in that it only sets forth rules about the entitlement of the buyer to avoid the contract as a result of a breach regarding a single installment. Three different cases are considered. Under Article 73(1), the aggrieved party is granted the possibility of avoiding the contract with respect to one single installment when the breaching party fails to perform that specific installment obligation.[72] Under Article 73(2), the aggrieved party is entitled to avoid the contract as to future installments if the party has good grounds to conclude that the other party will commit a fundamental breach of contract with respect to future installments. Finally, Article 73(3) stands somewhat on its own: first, unlike the preceding paragraphs—which grant identical rights to both parties—paragraph (3) grants the right to avoid the contract only to the buyer; moreover, it can only be invoked when a special functional connection exists

---

[72] For an arbitral award upholding the buyer's right to avoidance with respect to one installment, *see* Schiedsgericht Hamburger Freundschaftliche Arbitrage (Germany), 29 December 1998, available in English at http://cisgw3.law.pace.edu/cases/981229g1.html.

between separate installments, so that the failure to perform a single installment entirely frustrates the purpose contemplated by the parties at the time the contract was concluded.

Under Article 73(1) CISG, "in the case of a contract for delivery of goods by installments, if the failure of one party to perform any of his obligations in respect of any installment constitutes a fundamental breach of contract with respect to that installment, the other party may declare the contract avoided with respect to that installment." The provision at hand thus emphasizes the independence of each individual installment within the framework of larger contracts. Accordingly, the party aggrieved by the obligor's fundamental breach with respect to an individual installment may avoid the contract with respect to that installment. The standards to be adopted to determine whether the breach with respect to a single installment amounts to a fundamental breach are those provided by Article 25 CISG. Therefore, the remedy under Article 73(1) has been held to apply in cases of failure to deliver goods pertaining to a certain installment,[73] as well as in cases where the goods of a specific installment were defective.[74] Under these or similar circumstances the buyer may, for

---

[73] *See* HG Kanton Zürich (Switzerland), 5 February 1997, available in English at http://cisgw3.law.pace.edu/cases970205 s1.html.

[74] *See, e.g.,* China International Economic and Trade Arbitration Commission (CIETAC), Arbitral Award of 5 April 1999, available in English at http://cisgw3.law.pace.edu/cases 990405c1.html.

instance, cancel an individual order of goods, without prejudice to previous and future orders. Moreover, under Article 73(1) CISG not only "can" the aggrieved party avoid the contract with respect to the single installment, but he also arguably "must" limit the effects of avoidance to that single installment. In other words, Article 73(1) operates not only so as to grant to the aggrieved party the remedy of avoidance of a single installment, but also so as to limit the effects of avoidance to that single installment, unless the requirements set forth in Article 73(2) or (3) CISG are met.

Under Article 73(2) CISG, if the obligor's failure to perform any of his obligations in respect of any installment gives the aggrieved party good grounds to conclude that a breach in respect of installments not yet due will occur, that party may declare the contract avoided with regard to future installments, provided that he does so within a reasonable time. Thus, Article 73(2) CISG provides for three concurring pre-requisites of the right to avoid the contract with respect to future installments. First, a breach of contract with respect to any of the installments must have occurred, although the Convention does not necessarily require that the actual non-performance amounts to a fundamental breach, nor does the Convention require that the obligee rejects the goods received with the current installment.[75]

---

[75]   *See* for this statement Supreme Court of Austria, 17 December 2003, available in English at http://cisgw3.law.pace .edu/cases/031217a3.html, stating that where the buyer accepts

In addition to the foregoing, although under Article 73(2) the failure itself need not constitute a fundamental breach, it must nonetheless give the aggrieved party "good grounds to conclude that a fundamental breach of contract will occur with respect to future installments." In other words, there must be an anticipatory fundamental breach with respect to future installments. Whilst Article 25 sets out the standards that may be used to determine if there has been a fundamental breach, it is apparent that the pre–requisite set out in Article 73(2) CISG largely mirrors that of Article 72 CISG. However, the requirement that there be "good grounds to conclude" that a fundamental breach will be committed sets a less rigid and more subjective standard for avoidance than the objective standard of certainty that must be reached under Article 72 CISG, according to which it must be "clear" that a fundamental breach of contract will be committed.[76] Accordingly, an arbitral decision correctly held that avoidance with respect to future installments on the part of the buyer was possible as a result of delivery by seller of a first installment of goods that were severely defective.[77] Similarly, another decision held

---

defective installments, he does not lose the right to avoid the contract as a whole if the seller again delivers defective goods.

[76] For a court decision holding that the seller had "good grounds" to avoid the contract *see*, *e.g.*, CA Grenoble (France), 22 February 1995, available in English at http://cisgw3.law.pace.edu/cases/950222f1.html.

[77] *See* China International Economic and Trade Arbitration Commission (CIETAC), Arbitral Award of August 2006, available in English at http://cisgw3.law.pace.edu/cases/060800c1.html.

that the seller had good grounds to avoid the contract as a whole upon failure by the buyer to open a letter of credit due for payment of the first installment.[78]

As an additional requirement for Article 72(2) CISG to apply, notice of avoidance with respect to future installments must be given "within a reasonable time". The CISG, however, does not specify when the reasonable period of time starts, nor does it define parameters according to which the "reasonable" time must be measured. In these authors' view the reasonable period of time starts to run when the party affected by the prospective breach acquires knowledge, not only of the breach committed by the obligor,[79] but also of the risk that a breach will be committed with respect to future installments. In line with this conclusion, it has been held that, although a party may be precluded from avoiding the contract with respect to a specific installment if he fails to give timely notice, he may still be entitled to avoid the contract with respect to future installments to the extent that the breach gives the aggrieved party "good grounds" to conclude that a fundamental breach will take place in respect

---

[78] *See, e.g.*, Chamber of Commerce and Industry of Budapest (Hungary), Arbitral Award of 17 November 1995, English abstract available at http://www.unilex.info/case.cfm?id= 217.

[79] As requested by OLG Brandenburg (Germany), 18 November 2008, available in English at http://cisgw3.law.pace. edu/cases/081118g1.html.

to future installments.[80] Finally, with respect to the "reasonableness" of the time for giving notice, it should be assessed on a case–by–case basis, taking the specific circumstances of the case into account, including, in particular, the length of the interval between the last and the next installment.[81]

Under Article 73(3) CISG "[a] buyer who declares the contract avoided in respect of any delivery may, at the same time, declare it avoided in respect of deliveries already made or of future deliveries if, by reason of their interdependence, those deliveries could not be used for the purpose contemplated by the parties at the time of the conclusion of the contract". As mentioned above, paragraph (3) of Article 73 stands somewhat on its own. First, unlike the preceding paragraphs, which grant identical rights to both parties, paragraph (3) grants the right to avoid the contract only to the buyer; moreover, it can only be invoked when a special functional connection exists between separate installments, so that the failure to perform a single installment entirely frustrates the purpose contemplated by the parties at the time the contract was concluded. Article 73(3), however, does not create an independent remedy, but it provides for an extension to the entire contract of the remedy available to the buyer under Article 73(1). In fact,

---

[80]   _See_ Netherlands Arbitration Institute (The Netherlands), Arbitral Award n. 2319 of 15 October 2002, available at http://cisgw3.law.pace.edu/cases/021015n1.html.

[81]   _See, e.g._, Audiencia Provincial de Barcelona (Spain), 3 November 1997, English abstract available at http://cisgw3.law.pace.edu/cases/971103s4.html.

the provision under consideration presupposes that a failure on the part of the seller occurred, in respect of one single installment, which qualifies as a fundamental breach justifying avoidance with respect to that installment. Given this precondition, Article 73(3) authorizes extension of avoidance as to past or future installments on the grounds that there is "interdependence" between the installment fundamentally breached and the other installments, with respect to which the aggrieved party intends to declare avoidance. To this effect, the aggrieved party must notify the other party at the same time that it declares avoidance with respect to both the installment already fundamentally breached, and the other interdependent installments.

As to the notion of "interdependence" relevant under Article 73(3), it has been held that, unlike under Article 75 ULIS, which adopted a criterion of "worthlessness to the buyer", both parties must be aware of the interdependence of the different installments.[82] Moreover, such common awareness must be evaluated with regard to the time of conclusion of the contract. What exactly must be regarded as interdependent can only be assessed on a case–by–case basis, taking into account the economic function of the different installments. However, in these authors' view it must be affirmed that the interdependence cannot be assessed on the sole ground of objective criteria, but subjective

---

[82]   *See* Trib. Cantonal de Vaud (Switzerland), 11 April 2002, English abstract available at http://cisgw3.law.pace.edu/cases/020411s1.html.

elements must also be taken into account. This conclusion, in fact, is supported by the fact that Article 73(3) refers to the "purpose contemplated by the parties" at the time of contract conclusion. Finally, it is relevant to point out that, to the extent that the requirements for its application are met, Article 73(3) CISG authorizes extension of the remedy of avoidance to both past installments and future installments. Accordingly, one could argue that two different rules are merged into the provision of Article 73(3). On the one hand, there is the general rule on contract avoidance with a special focus on retrospective effects of avoidance in the event of interdependence between the fundamentally breached installment and the past interdependent installments. On the other hand, there is the anticipatory breach rule, as applied to the situation where a fundamental breach of a single installment is invoked as justification for avoidance of future interdependent installments, as well as past interdependent installments.

6. DAMAGES IN CASE OF AVOIDANCE

Avoidance of the contract is declared by the aggrieved party as a consequence of a fundamental breach of contract committed by the other party. As a result, both parties are released from their respective contractual obligations. The effects of avoidance are expressly indicated in Article 81 CISG, which further clarifies that the release of the parties is "subject to any damages which may be due." In fact, as already pointed out in the previous

Chapter,[83] the right to claim damages can, as a general rule, concur with any other remedy, including the right to declare the contract avoided. This statement is confirmed by the wording of Articles 45(2) and 61(2) CISG, both of which state that the aggrieved party "is not deprived of any right he may have to claim damages by exercising his right to other remedies." Accordingly, in the event that one of the parties commits a fundamental breach of contract, the aggrieved party may concurrently declare the contract avoided and claim damages resulting from the breach. The provision of Article 74 CISG thus applies to damages for breach of contract irrespective of the severity of the breach, and everything that has been said about the claim for damages as a general remedy for breach of contract can safely be referred to here without the need for repetition. In particular, it is beyond dispute that the general principle of full compensation, embedded in Article 74 CISG, applies to all claims for damages, including claims arising from a non–fundamental breach, claims for damages coupled with other remedies aiming at compelling performance of the contract, and claims for damages resulting from the avoidance of the contract.

Furthermore, Article 74 CISG is also the basic rule that one has to refer to in order to determine what losses are compensable under the Convention. However, as Article 74 sets forth the general formula for calculation of losses, in the event of a

---

[83]   See supra Chapter 8, Section 5.

declaration of contract avoidance Article 74 is supplemented by other provisions, contained in Articles 75 and 76 CISG, which are worth considering here. The scope of these two provisions is narrower than that of Article 74, as the former provisions only come into relevance in the event of avoidance of the contract.

Article 75 CISG deals with the case where, shortly after avoidance and in a reasonable manner, the buyer has made a cover purchase or the seller has resold the goods. Under these circumstances, the provision at hand provides a readily available mechanism to calculate the amount of damages recoverable: "the difference between the contract price and the price in the substitute transaction." Furthermore, Article 75 also allows for the possibility to claim further compensation in the event that the mechanism fails to take into account part of the damages suffered by the aggrieved party. Article 75 thus provides the aggrieved party with a concrete criterion to calculate damages, by reference to a substitute transaction. A buyer entitled to damages, for instance, may claim the difference between the contract price and the higher price paid for the same kind of goods under the cover transaction; a seller entitled to damages may claim the difference between the contract price and the lower price obtained from the cover transaction.

The rule provided in Article 75 CISG may be applied only to the extent that four pre–conditions are met concurrently. First, as already pointed out, the rule only applies in the event of contract avoidance.[84] Cover transactions concluded before avoidance have been held not to fall within the scope of the rule under consideration.[85] Secondly, the party claiming damages must have entered into a cover transaction. The mere fact that the party could have entered a cover transaction is of no avail if such transaction is not concretely entered into. Similarly, the aggrieved party cannot rely on Article 75 CISG if he fails to establish a clear connection between the cover transaction and the original sale; in particular, the aggrieved seller cannot rely on the provision at hand if he fails to prove that the goods sold under the cover transaction are the same goods that were identified to the avoided contract.[86] The third pre–condition for the application of Article 75 CISG is that the party claiming damages entered into the covered transaction "in a reasonable manner". Although the text does not expressly refer the requirement of reasonableness to the price of the cover transaction, it is apparent that in most cases the reasonableness of the cover transaction

---

[84]   See, e.g., Supreme Court of Poland, 27 January 2006, available in English at http://cisgw3.law.pace.edu/cases/060127 p1.html.

[85]   See U.S. Court of Appeals [2nd Cir.], 6 December 1995 (*Delchi v. Rotorex*), available at http://cisgw3.law.pace.edu/cases/ 951206u1.html; *contra* OLG Graz (Austria), 29 July 2004, available in English at http://cisgw3.law.pace.edu/cases/040729 a3.html, stating that the need to promote the observance of good faith in international trade can justify the application of Article 75 CISG prior to contract avoidance if the promisor has declared expressly that he will not perform.

[86]   See Supreme Court of Queensland (Australia), 17 November 2000 (*Downs Investments v. Perwaja Steel*), available at http://cisgw3.law.pace.edu/cases/001117a2.html.

must be evaluated primarily on the basis of the reasonableness of the price of such transaction. This clearly leads to the application of a comparative criterion of evaluation based on the contract goods' market price.[87] This is the case, in particular, where the contract goods are readily available on the market, although even with respect to goods available on the market, temporary shortages, difficulties in supply, time constraints and other similar circumstances may justify departures from the market price, to be evaluated on a case–by–case basis. Moreover, the overall reasonableness of the cover transaction must be assessed by keeping in mind the general principle expressed in Article 77 CISG, which imposes on the party entering the cover transaction the duty to mitigate the damages resulting from the avoidance of the contract. The last pre–condition for the application of Article 75 CISG is that the cover transaction be entered into "within a reasonable time after avoidance". What constitutes a reasonable time depends on the nature of the goods and the circumstances.[88] Also in this regard, the mitigation principle in Article 77 CISG has a role to play, in that a longer period of time can be justified, to the extent that the later date of the cover transaction is likely to result in better

---

[87]   *See, e.g.,* China International Economic and Trade Arbitration Commission (CIETAC), Arbitral Award of 25 July 2006, available in English at http://cisgw3.law.pace.edu/cases/060725c1.html.

[88]   *See, e.g.,* Supreme Court of Denmark, 17 October 2007, English abstract available at http://cisgw3.law.pace.edu/cases/071017d1.html.

conditions due, for instance, to the seasonal character of the specific goods.[89]

If the pre–conditions for the application of Article 75 CISG are met, then the aggrieved party may claim compensation for the less favorable price terms of the cover transaction. Moreover, if the amount calculated, on the basis of the difference between the price of the avoided contract and the price of the cover transaction is not sufficient to assure full compensation to the aggrieved party, the amount may be adjusted by adding further damages recoverable under Article 74, including loss of profit.[90]

Article 76 CISG sets forth a rule that is subsidiary to the rule provided in Article 75 CISG. Under Article 76, as an alternative to or in the absence of reference to a cover purchase, the aggrieved party may refer to the current market price at the time of avoidance. If the market price varies in different locations, Article 76(2) specifies that the price to be taken into account is "the price prevailing at the place where delivery of the goods should have been made or, if there is no current price at that place, the price at such other place as serves as a reasonable substitute, making due allowance for differences in the cost of transporting the goods".

---

[89] *See, e.g.,* OLG Düsseldorf (Germany), 14 January 1994, available in English at http://cisgw3.law.pace.edu/cases/940114 g1.html, dealing with the cover sale of winter shoes.

[90] *See, e.g.,* OLG Graz (Austria), 31 May 2002, available in English at http://cisgw3.law.pace.edu/cases/020531a3.html.

There are four pre–conditions for the application of Article 76 CISG. First, not unlike Article 75, the provision at hand only applies as a means of calculation of damages in claims resulting from contract avoidance.[91] Secondly, the aggrieved party must not have entered a cover transaction under Article 75. Third, the contract goods must have a current market price, although this does not mean that they need to have a price officially quoted. What is required, instead, is that the goods have a price generally charged in the market for goods of the same kind under comparable circumstances.[92] Finally, there must be a "price fixed by the contract" that needs to be compared to the current market price. The wording used by the drafters of the CISG makes it clear that a "contract price" determinable as per Article 55 CISG is not sufficient to satisfy the pre–condition of application of Article 76 CISG. Instead, it is necessary that the parties "fixed" the price in the contract, that is, they explicitly made a quotation, which can be referred to as relevant to determine the agreed value of the contract goods.

If the pre–requisites for the application of Article 76 are met, then the party entitled to compensation can claim the difference between the contract price and the current market price, as well as any further damages recoverable under Article 74 CISG. The

---

[91]   *See* Tallinna Ringkonnakohus (Estonia), 19 February 2004, available in English at http://www.globalsaleslaw.org/content/api/cisg/urteile/826.pdf.

[92]   *See*, *e.g.*, OLG Celle (Germany), 2 September 1998, available in English at http://cisgw3.law.pace.edu/cases/980902g1.html.

current price to be taken into account is to be assessed as of the time of avoidance. However, a partly different rule applies in the event that the party claiming damages has avoided the contract after taking over the goods. Under these circumstances, the current price must be evaluated as of the time of the taking over of the goods.

INDEX

References are to Pages

DELIVERY
Obligation to take delivery, 237–241
Of declarations, 160–163
Of goods, 171–180
Of non–conforming documents, 344
Partial delivery of goods, 309

DEROGATION OF THE CISG, 31, 32, 35, 38–41

DDP, 183, 184, 261

DISPATCH
Of a declaration, 22, 158
Of goods, 177, 178, 242, 256

DISPOSITIVE NATURE OF THE CISG, IV, V, 20, 30, 133

DISTRIBUTION AGREEMENTS, 94–95

DOCUMENTS
And notice of non-conformity, 199
Controlling the delivery of goods, 107, 233, 234, 296
Delivery of non-conforming documents, 344
Handing over of the documents, 185–188, 233, 235, 373

DOMESTIC REMEDIES, 113–123

DURESS, 110, 113, 114, 115, 116, 118, 131, 138

DUTY
To act in good faith, 164
To avoid the contract within reasonable time, 358
To cooperate, 238
To disclose information, 169
To mitigate damages, 314, 315, 393
To preserve the goods
    See Preservation of the Goods
To refund the price, 367
To sell the goods, 266

ECONOMIC HARDSHIP, 326–328, 332

ECONOMIC IMPOSSIBILITY, 323